TEACHING HACKS

FIXING EVERYDAY CLASSROOM ISSUES

WITH METACOGNITION

TEACHING HACKS

FIXING EVERYDAY CLASSROOM ISSUES

WITH METACOGNITION

EDITED BY

NATHAN BURNS

1 Oliver's Yard
55 City Road
London EC1Y 1SP

CORWIN
A Sage company
2455 Teller Road
Thousand Oaks, California 91320
(800)233-9936
www.corwin.com

Unit No 323-333, Third Floor, F-Block
International Trade Tower Nehru Place
New Delhi 110 019

8 Marina View Suite 43-053
Asia Square Tower 1
Singapore 018960

Editor: James Clark
Editorial Assistant: Esosa Otabor
Production Editor: Tanya Kapoor
Copyeditor: Sarah Bury
Indexer: KnowledgeWorks Global Ltd
Marketing Manager: Dilhara Attygalle
Cover Design: Wendy Scott
Typeset by KnowledgeWorks Global Ltd

Library of Congress Control Number: 2023950162

British Library Cataloguing in Publication data

A catalogue record for this book is available from the British Library

ISBN 978-1-5296-2792-3
ISBN 978-1-5296-2791-6 (pbk)

Contents

About the Editor and Contributors

Editor

Nathan Burns is currently the Head of Maths in a Derbyshire school. He has previously worked as an Assistant Progress and Achievement Leader for Key Stage 3, More Able and Talented Co-ordinator and as a Second in Maths. Aside from these roles, Nathan is a metacognitive researcher, who has dedicated his teaching career to researching and understanding the theory and its applications to the classroom. He is the author of *Inspiring Deep Learning with Metacognition: A Guide for Secondary Teaching* (Sage/Corwin, 2023), and has previously written for Oxford University Press, *TES* and *HMRK* Magazine.

Contributors

Kate Allen is a mum, a fiancée, a doctoral student, and a Head of English. While undertaking her MA in Education, Kate realised her passion for educational research – a passion which has now become a complete obsession. Kate is particularly interested in metacognition and the enormous benefits of oracy for learning.

Patrice Bain is a veteran K–12 educator, speaker and author of *Powerful Teaching* and *A Parent's Guide to Powerful Teaching*. As a finalist for Illinois Teacher of the Year and a Fulbright Scholar in Europe, she has been featured in national and international podcasts, webinars, presentations and popular press, including NOVA and Scientific American.

Genevieve Bent is an Associate Vice Principal leading Sixth Form, Assessment & Data, and Initial Teacher Training. A former Head of Science, she is passionate about equity in STEM and diversity and inclusion. Her MA in Science Education focused on the experiences of Black children in the (science) British educational system.

Paul Carney is a nationally recognised art & design consultant, having delivered specialist art CPD in schools, colleges, galleries and universities across the UK and for the UK's leading art education providers, including the National College, Kapow Education,

Access Art, NSEAD, BBC Bitesize, Mary Myatt and Osiris Education. Paul is the author of two books: *Drawing for Science, Invention and Discovery* and his latest book *Drawing to Learn Anything*. He has over 20 years' teaching experience at primary, secondary and post-16 levels of education, is an Advanced Skills Teacher, ex-Subject Leader for Art and was a member of the DfE Expert Advisory Group for Art and Design.

Sarah Dowey is an experienced English teacher and leader, now working as Principal Development Lead for English Mastery Secondary. Sarah is passionate about bridging the gap between research theory and pedagogical practice and has completed a PhD in Education at the University of York. Her research interests are centred around cognitive science, particularly metacognitive practice, and how it can be successfully applied in the classroom.

Charlotte Findlay is the Head of Psychology in a Rutland school and has previously worked in the mental health sector. She has previously created resources on memory, metacognition and learning for the British Psychological Society, and revision materials for Seneca. In her free time, she researches decision making in A-level students for her PhD. She can be found on Twitter (@Findlotte).

Jonathan Firth is a senior teaching fellow at the University of Strathclyde, having previously worked as a secondary school teacher. His research interests include metacognition, study skills, learning theories and creativity. He has written several education books, including *What Teachers Need to Know About Memory* (with Nasima Riazat), and *How to Learn.*

Katie Holmes is a teacher of PE and Assistant Faculty Leader in a secondary school in Bradford. Over the past three years, Katie has also undertaken a role as Faculty Research Lead, working with colleagues to embed evidence-informed practice at a subject-specific level. Katie has more recently centred her reading and research around how students learn and how to support students in understanding this process. As part of this school improvement project, Katie has developed a Year 7–13 tutor time curriculum about learning and how to revise. Katie can be found on twitter at: @MissHolmes_PE

Elizabeth Mountstevens is a chemistry teacher in Hertfordshire. She is passionate about evidence-informed teaching and in 2019 was one of the first teachers to be awarded Chartered Teacher status through the Chartered College of Teaching. Elizabeth has carried out her own research into using metacognition to support KS5 students.

Daniel Muijs is Head of the School of Social Sciences, Education and Social Work and Professor of Education at Queen's University Belfast. Previously he has held professorial and management positions at a range of UK and international universities and led the Research and Evaluation team at Ofsted. Daniel is an expert on school and teacher effectiveness and has published widely in this field. He is editor of the journal *School*

Effectiveness and School Improvement and authored the review of self-regulated learning and metacognition for the Education Endowment Foundation (EEF).

Marco Narajos graduated with degrees in neuroscience and medicine before training in secondary science education. Based in Oxford, he is a biology teacher at an independent senior school, where he completed practitioner research for his Master's on whole-class feedback for self-regulated learning at the University of Oxford.

Debbie Tremble has over 20 years' experience in education, enjoying a variety of roles. She currently leads on teaching and learning at an East Staffordshire school. Debbie is an SLE for English, an ELE for Staffordshire Research, writes for *SecEd* and is a certified life coach.

Dave Tushingham is currently a secondary maths lead practitioner working in Bristol for the Greenshaw Learning Trust. Co-author of the book *The Edu-Book Club: Making CPD Resources Work in the Classroom* and accredited National Centre for Excellence in the Teaching of Mathematics (NCETM) Professional Development (PD) lead, Dave is passionate about staff development and is always learning.

Michael Walsh is Lead Let's Think English (LTE) Tutor for primary and secondary. Michael co-developed and created the LTE programme at King's College London University. Michael also leads a voluntary collaboration of 22 schools in Islington called Futurezone. He was a secondary English teacher before being seconded to an Education Action Zone. He was a senior consultant for the school improvement team and has worked, advised and collaborated with the Arsenal Study Support, British Film Institute, English Heritage, Open University as well as leading LTE internationally.

Acknowledgements

To Catherine,

For your never-ending support and belief in me.

The best cheerleader anyone could have!

Introduction

Have you ever wondered how that teacher just down the corridor always manages to get students to write pages and pages when they set essay-style questions? Or how that teacher on the other side of the school always has students answering in full sentences whenever they ask students verbal questions? Or perhaps you have visited schools where students just seem to 'know' how to revise or act on the feedback they have been given?

These issues are perennial. Every single year we seem to return with slightly new ideas or pedagogies, yet the same problems persist. Students are still unable to take on board the viewpoints of others, are still reluctant to read, lack motivation, resilience and the ability to complete coursework on time and to a high standard.

Yet there are teachers out there who have cracked these problems. And often, it is done with the power of metacognition! Building on my first book, *Inspiring Deeper Learning with Metacognition* (Burns, 2023), this book will harness the knowledge and expertise of some of the best practitioners in the world, who will share how they tackle these perennial issues so successfully in their classrooms.

This chapter will begin by exploring the purpose of this book, outlining the issues it will help you to solve and detailing the format of each chapter. It will then go on to remind you of the positive impact that metacognition and metacognitive theory can have on the educational progress of students in all age groups. For those who have read my work before, you will know how much emphasis I place on understanding the theory *before* trying to implement the strategies.

The Purpose and Problems

Although I have researched and written about metacognition extensively over the last half a dozen years, I have only ever taught secondary mathematics. While I can see the usefulness of metacognition in other subjects and age groups, and can guide and support its implementation, I have never been at the coalface of any other subjects (i.e. other than maths), tackling the issues that arise day in, day out. So, rather than trying to provide my best insights on some of the subject-specific issues, I have turned to the experts. That means that, having provided the introduction, I will hand you over to the insights of some of the most remarkable teachers currently working in and around our profession. Their years of experience, know-how and innovation shine through, and will in turn provide you with the inspiration, knowledge and strategies required to finally end some, or all, of these perennial issues in your classroom, faculty and schools.

As with *Inspiring Deeper Learning with Metacognition*, this book is underpinned by high-quality research and practice, but is written in an easy-to-understand and digestible manner. The aim of the book is to provide you with explicit strategies and approaches, and sufficient theory, so that you can instantly apply them in your classrooms. And if you are concerned that this book isn't for you, then you would be mistaken. The ideas provided, and the issues tackled, in this book will provide food for thought for all, from teaching assistants (TAs) to senior leaders, from Early Career Teacher (ECTs) to the most experienced classroom teachers. These issues beset us all, and all of us are looking for solutions.

So, what will you find as you delve further into this book?

Here is a headline summary, in no particular order or relative importance, of the issues tackled in this book:

- Students who struggle to develop alternative viewpoints, identify with the opinions of others and place themselves in the shoes of another individual.
- How to develop your curriculum, with metacognition in mind, without shoehorning in certain strategies 'for the sake of it'.
- Students who lack the motivation and resilience to complete independent work, even when they have the knowledge and capacity to do so.
- Students who are unable to revise, or do not know the most effective ways to revise, believing that re-reading notes will ensure they ace a test.
- Students who are reluctant readers, both inside and outside school, where we know how significant an impact reading has on the attainment of students.
- Post-16 students who struggle to balance their free time and independent study, and who struggle to understand the information it is key to know and what is less important, and who have a poor understanding of their own abilities and knowledge.
- Students who have poor independent learning skills that coincide with poorly planned and utilised tutor time within schools.
- Students who struggle to stay on track with their coursework, and who find it difficult to break down the success criteria of given tasks.
- Students who struggle with extended writing, in part due to poor planning strategies and an inability to reflect sufficiently and effectively on their work, either independently or following teacher feedback.
- Students who struggle with their monitoring skills – who obviously go quite wrong during a task but do nothing about it until it is too late.
- Students who do not effectively learn from or utilise online learning opportunities.
- Students who are unable to take ownership of their learning and develop a learner identity.
- Students who struggle to engage with feedback and do not utilise it to improve the quality of their own work.
- Students who struggle to turn their superb ideas, which perhaps they can explain verbally, into writing tasks on paper.

There we have it! A selection of the most frequently raised issues in schools across the UK – and even the world! Issues that you will have heard raised. Issues that you will have no doubt raised yourself at some point. Possibly even today, earlier this week or since the term began. Whenever it may have been, these are real and live issues in our schools that are screaming out for the suggestions and solutions presented in the pages that follow.

To make things even easier, the layout of each chapter follows a common template, with emphasis being placed on readability and take-aways. To begin, each author goes into a little more depth on the perennial issue that they are tackling (at which point you're likely to get a sore neck from all the nodding along that you are doing). From there, the chapter author will challenge you with some questions as to your current practice, which will really help to get you thinking about what it is you are currently doing, before you delve into the solutions that the chapter author then presents to you. Finally, the author will provide you with some key take-aways – nuggets of crucial information to help you get started on addressing the issue – and some further readings to allow you to delve even deeper into the topic. Hopefully, this chapter structure will give you all food for thought and ideas to carry forward to tackle these issues head on!

The Rationale and Theory Behind Metacognition

So, why do you need to bother with metacognition in the first instance? There is a half-century – arguably a full century – of evidence showing just how powerful metacognition can be. However, the two most helpful and supportive summaries are those provided by the Education Endowment Foundation (EEF) and Ofsted. As you will likely be aware, the EEF is the font of educational knowledge, regularly synthesising its research on education into digestible reports.

The EEF (2018) also reports a 'months boost' figure, which provides a broad guide to the additional benefits that any given intervention should bring to an individual's academic progress. At the time of this book going to press, there is not a single intervention which the EEF deems more beneficial for students than metacognition. That's right. Not a single one! So, while you are hearing about questioning, feedback, revision, and a whole host of other things during your school training, the most beneficial area for improvement – metacognition – is just sitting there ready to be exploited! Can you see how it may be the solution to a lot of these perennial issues now? The EEF summarises practising metacognition in the classroom can advance a child's progress by seven months, and whether however confident we are in the measure, the only thing that matters is that this is one area of pedagogy that can bring more benefit than any other (EEF, 2018). Moreover, the EEF espouses the benefits of metacognition in its report, *Putting Evidence to Work* (EEF, 2021).

Ofsted also provides useful backing for metacognition. In recent years, Ofsted has moved towards a more evidence- and research-based approach to its school inspections (Ofsted, 2019). Within this, it has defined what it sees as high-quality professional development for staff within in-school training to develop the professional skills of teachers. As part of that, Ofsted identifies that metacognition is a core component of teacher development, due to the benefits that it can bring to students. So once again, here is some very strong evidence for introducing metacognition into your classrooms and schools!

Hopefully, this research has convinced you of the benefits of metacognition, and so you are now ready to read on in order to understand the theory a little better. The greater your understanding of metacognition, the more you will be able to implement metacognition into your classroom. This is because metacognitive theory is intricate! It can be complicated, but, importantly, it is subtle. Very subtle changes can have many positive impacts.

Therefore, the more you understand the inner mechanics of metacognitive theory, the more you will understand the key parts of each strategy that you are introducing, the better you will do it, and the more impactful you will be in the classroom! Hopefully, the theory will seem incredibly simple once you have read the next few paragraphs...

Whenever I define metacognition, I always like to begin with what it is not (thus, tackling those misconceptions!). Metacognition is NOT self-regulation. I often think of 'self-regulation' as an umbrella term, which contains metacognition, but also contains emotional and behavioural self-control, motivation, resilience and other key self-learning characteristics. So, although metacognition is a part of this, it is certainly not all of this.

What actually is metacognition, then? There are two key definitions that need to be considered here – my own and one by Flavell. Flavell (1976: 232) wrote:

> I am being metacognitive if I notice that I am having more trouble learning A than B; if it strikes me that I should double check C before accepting it as fact.

And I wrote:

> [Metacognition is] the little voice inside your head that constantly evaluates and informs your actions.

The emphasis here, then, is being placed on noticing – monitoring and evaluating – your own thought processes and cognitive actions in order to improve their efficiency, effectiveness and utility. Metacognitive thinking is the process of constantly reviewing what you are doing and seeking a better way of doing it, perhaps by changing your approach, addressing your weaknesses, building on your strengths, learning new cognitive approaches, improving your planning and recognising when something you are doing is not working and changing tack, for example. The point of all of this, of course, is that it is invisible! Fortunately, metacognition can be broken down a little further, helping to shine a light on its inner workings.

Metacognition itself comprises two strands (which can themselves be further subdivided). These two strands are knowledge of cognition and regulation of cognition.

Knowledge of cognition

This area of metacognitive thought focuses on what you, as an individual, know about your own cognition. What strategies do you have in your locker? What knowledge do you have? It can be subdivided into:

Knowledge of self – this refers to the core knowledge – facts, figures, dates, etc. – that you directly know in order to complete a given task.

Knowledge of strategies – this refers to the range of approaches that you have in your locker to complete a given task. It also includes an ability to carry out these strategies correctly and to know when to apply different strategies to a range of different situations.

Knowledge of task – here, emphasis is placed on your understanding of the task in front of you. A strong knowledge of the task will mean that you have a clear understanding of the nature and requirements of the task, and the format in which a solution or answer should be provided.

Regulation of cognition

This area of metacognition focuses on how you control your own cognition. How do you evaluate your thinking? How effectively do you plan for tasks and monitor the progress of the tasks as you proceed? If difficulties arise, how do you go about changing your approach in future tasks?

The regulation of cognition can be broken down into:

Planning – this is how you plan for the task that you need to complete. It may include consideration of the best approach to take and your comprehension of task requirements.

Monitoring – this is an in-task consideration of whether the currently produced work is heading in the correct direction – that is, will the task criteria still be met if progress continues in the current direction.

Evaluation – evaluation occurs at the task completion stage, where a full considera-tion of the efficiency and effectiveness of the approaches taken is made, as well as a full consideration of the task solution as compared to the task requirements.

Hopefully this analysis improves your understanding of the subtle nature of meta-cognitive. Before we move on, though, let us consider a caveat to putting it into practice. It must be noted that metacognitive abilities do not translate well from one area to another. The reason for this is that the 'meta' and the 'cognitive' parts are inextricably linked. If the elements of 'cognition' vary, then the 'meta' elements also vary. Thus, subject-specific thinking will have its own type of metacognition. It means that students can have a good grasp of metacognitive approaches in one subject or area or topic, but may not be very strong in other areas or topics or subjects, where the metacognitive approaches are different.

Thus, metacognitive abilities do not just vary across subjects, but also within subjects, when you move from one topic area to another. Nevertheless, there are still generalisable strategies that strong metacognitive practitioners will be able to carry across from one area of cognition to another, meaning that they do not need to start their 'meta' development from scratch each time they come across a different cognitive requirement.

There we have it, metacognitive theory in a nutshell! Over the coming chapters, you will see how the authors have homed in on specific parts of this theory, drawing on the key subtleties that make metacognition so powerful. Should you want to know more about the theory, then do not forget to check out my first book, *Inspiring Deeper Learning with Metacognition!*

So, now on to solving those perennial problems!

References

Burns, N. (2023). *Inspiring deeper learning with metacognition.* London: Sage/Corwin.

Education Endowment Foundation (EEF) (2018). *Metacognition and self-regulated learning: Guidance report.* Available at: https://educationendowmentfoundation.org.uk/education-evidence/guidance-reports/metacognition (accessed 25 October 2023).

Education Endowment Foundation (EEF) (2021). *Putting evidence to work: A school's guide to implementation.* Available at: https://educationendowmentfoundation.org.uk/education-evidence/guidance-reports/implementation (accessed 25 October 2023).

Flavell, J. H. (1976). Metacognitive aspects of problem solving. In L. B. Resnick (Ed.), *The nature of intelligence* (pp. 231–235). Hillsdale, NJ: Lawrence Erlbaum.

Ofsted (2019). *Education inspection framework – overview of research.* Available at: www.gov.uk/government/publications/education-inspection-framework-overview-of-research (accessed 25 October 2023).

1

Metacognitive Tools for Writing

Jonathan Firth

An Educational Issue

Extended writing is important for students to communicate their ideas, and it is often necessary for assessed coursework or exams at school level, too. Whether such tasks consist of essays, scientific reports or creative writing, many students underperform. The focus of this chapter is to explore the metacognitive processes at work when students write, and to establish strategies for tackling underperformance.

Writing is a highly complex skill, especially for more extended written tasks. It is cognitively demanding, because students need to gather together many thoughts and ideas before forming these into a persuasive and accurate piece of text. It is also metacognitively demanding, because they must assess and evaluate their knowledge, considering its relevance to the task at hand, and select strategies to help them communicate their ideas successfully (Hacker et al., 2009; Wischgoll, 2017). None of this is straightforward, and more could be done to develop the requisite skills among school students.

As with other aspects of metacognition, it is productive to consider what is happening before, during and after the process of student writing. Prior to the student beginning the task, flawed planning and strategy can impact on later outcomes, as can failing to understand the task. During the process, students may fail to recognise where they are going wrong, due to the demands of monitoring their own writing as they work on it. They may also fail to recognise major gaps in their own knowledge, or lack an awareness of the norms of the genre. Then, after a piece has been written, a further task comes into play – reading and redrafting what they have written.

Throughout this extended process, any failure to reflect and/or to understand where difficulties and errors come from will make it harder for students to self-correct. Some students may wrongly believe that they have completed the task to the best possible standard, underestimating what a reader or marker will be expecting, such as specific details or higher-order skills. Others may fail to realise when some of the knowledge that they have tried to apply is irrelevant to the task. Even when they do recognise that some aspects of their writing are weak, students may be unsure about what to do about it.

In short, their metacognition about writing might be flawed.

Your Approach

Take a moment to consider your current strategies for supporting students' writing. Where and how do they do it, and what preparation goes into the process? Is any coaching or scaffolding involved?

Consider, too, where and when writing is done. Is extended writing generally done outside class and, if so, what guidance is given to help with the process?

When it comes to preparation, what currently happens to support learners to construct an argument and to use evidence or examples effectively? Are there other, specific areas of weakness in students' responses that you aim to tackle? In terms of feedback, does this focus on style and structure issues that will allow them to redraft or is the feedback more about spelling, grammar or grades?

All of these issues affect how students are set up for extended writing. As with any complex skill, learners will benefit from preparation, practice and specific feedback (Ericsson, 2017). And as with any area of teaching, it can be effective to break things down into smaller elements, allowing practice of each part before the learner is expected to put them together (Rosenshine, 2012). This can point the way to a productive metacognitive approach to improving extended writing.

The Metacognitive Approach

The mysteries of writing

Writing may seem mysterious to students at the outset. Students may underestimate two things in particular:

- The extent to which good writing makes a difference to readers, and therefore to their grades.
- The extent to which they can improve via strategy and practice.

Part of the process of taking a metacognitive approach to teaching writing is beginning to illuminate these mysteries for your classes. A key idea at the outset is that this is a learnable skill, not something that people are good or bad at by nature. After communicating that to a class, you can focus on *how* to do it.

Another common misconception about writing is the idea that writers come up with ideas in their head before writing them down. However, it is flawed to view writing as purely an output process. Writing and thinking are tied together much more closely than that. The process of constructing an argument is something that happens *as you write*, not before you write (Murray, 1990), and writing and thinking therefore affect each other. Many learners will be entirely unaware of how writing can play a role in thinking.

Raising awareness of the above issues might help learners to address their misconceptions, but won't always not be enough to motivate a passion for writing. In part, this is because much of the writing that is done in schools is not strongly focused on student interests. It is worth exploring with a group of students what circumstances lead them to find writing fun and enjoyable to do, and perhaps to try to engage them in extracurricular writing, such as for a school newsletter. Some schools have run projects where students are encouraged to engage in self-directed independent research outside their school subjects (e.g., see Firth, 2016).

Having said that, motivation also depends on competence (Ryan & Deci, 2017), so developing writing skills will make the process more enjoyable. The next two sections explore how these skills can be improved via a metacognitive approach.

Better reading

A starting point that my colleagues and I take when tackling our students' writing is to help them *read* more effectively. Can they understand and analyse what other effective authors are doing? Without this capacity, it will be much harder for them to write good pieces of their own.

It is well known that the best student writers typically read a lot, and many teachers rightly encourage their students to read more. But it is also important for them to read analytically, with purpose. If this can feed into their own writing, both reading and writing skills can develop recursively.

For this reason, the next step after telling students to 'read more' is to engage in activities where they read short passages critically to better understand what the authors achieved, and how. For scientific writing, this can focus on common sections or subsections of a research report, such as a method section, or the section where aims and hypotheses are set out. For essays, a single short paragraph can be a good focus.

Reading should of course focus on entire pieces too. Good writing typically builds up an argument – the whole is greater than the sum of its parts. But these whole pieces will be easier for readers to follow when supported by periodic study of shorter texts.

Overall, the author's skill won't always be obvious, but teachers can work to bring these elements to their students' attention in small steps. Questions that are used to bring skills and strategies to learners' attention are called metacognitive mediations (Colognesi et al., 2020). This is a broader strategy used to activate metacognition and can be applied to the issues raised in the following subsections, too.

Nuts and bolts

As mentioned earlier, writing (just like discussions or debates) forms an important way of developing your thinking. However, the skill of writing longer pieces also requires certain basic elements. The more a learner masters these fundamentals (and the more automatic each one becomes), the easier it will be for them to write at a more advanced level.

Among these elements is knowledge. This forms a barrier for many learners as they tackle a writing task, but they will have more success if they have had time to take in and consolidate the relevant knowledge. For this reason, an extended piece of writing may not be the most appropriate task for day one of a topic! You might instead consider a long lead-in to a piece of writing, mindful of the time needed for students to consolidate new knowledge and come to use it flexibly.

Encourage learners to self-test or to engage in a group discussion prior to writing, in order to better judge their own knowledge level. Such tasks also serve to make prior knowledge more accessible (Anderson, 2018) and less prone to forgetting (Agarwal et al., 2021). It may also be necessary to guide students away from topics where their enthusiasm outstrips their expertise.

At the other end of the scale, the 'curse of knowledge' is where something appears so obvious to those who have mastered it that it doesn't seem worth mentioning. This metacognitive bias can impact the work of high-attaining students. They may fail to introduce a topic properly, for example.

Other 'nuts and bolts' of writing include:

- **Grammar**. A metacognitive tool here is to encourage learners that a first draft doesn't need to be perfect. They can also be encouraged to sound out sentences in their head, to see if things sound right.
- **Vocabulary**. Learners may stumble over terminology or get stuck on a word. This is demotivating and occupies working memory. A metacognitive tool here is to encourage learners to use a filler word or phrase that they can search for afterwards, so that they can move on and come back to specific terms when editing.
- **Spelling**. As with vocabulary, stopping to check or look words up can distract the student writer. Work on spelling is best separated from the writing process.

The processes above are underpinned by a student's working memory and long-term memory. Working memory is where we retain and think about something in the here-and-now. It is closely connected to their ability to focus their attention. As learners are composing a sentence in their mind, their attention and working memory will be fully occupied, making it hard for them to pay attention to other tasks. They will also have to focus hard to retrieve both knowledge and linguistic elements (such as spellings) from long-term memory.

However, as some of the nuts and bolts of writing become more automatic, some of this limited capacity is able to focus on higher-level skills, such as thinking about linguistic style and about the broader argument in a piece. Teachers can discuss the composition process with students, helping them to better understand their own limitations. The strategies suggested above (such as consolidating key knowledge or skipping over difficult terminology) make more sense when learners better understand their cognitive limitations.

Structure and style

As time goes on, it will often prove necessary to instruct learners in the style of good written pieces in a way that goes beyond basic spelling and grammar. Many might not know how best to divide their work into paragraphs, for example. This and other skills of writing structure can become part of their metacognitive knowledge.

Some tips to highlight include:

- Pinker (2015) explains how the first part of a sentence or paragraph typically focuses on 'knowns', which leads on to new and more complex ideas towards the end.
- There is no 'right' length for a sentence, but shorter ones improve overall readability. It's also considered good style to vary the length of your sentences.

If students re-read their own work with the above points in mind, they may notice that they tend to stick to simple sentence structures or write overly long, rambling sentences.

Linking words are a good way of building an argument, and exam markers will notice these. For example, how well does the writer use words such as 'because' and 'however' to connect a claim with grounds (evidence) or to contrast two viewpoints? Skill in doing so is part of mature writing.

One way to scaffold this is to encourage learners to first practise using linking words in a very clear and concrete context that is well-known to them. For example, they can practise these structures when explaining how a caterpillar transforms into a butterfly, or why they think one sports team is better than another. The familiarity helps to reduce cognitive load, freeing attention to focus on the language used. Practise with several such examples, and gradually move away from the concrete to a more abstract focus of the language forms and how they work in more abstract terms – a technique known as concreteness fading (Fyfe et al., 2015).

More broadly, these types of writing skills are best supported via deliberate practice (Kellogg, 2008). This means practice which is focused, purposeful and self-aware, and which receives rapid and specific feedback from a teacher or coach (Ericsson, 2017). The more that specific elements of writing in the target genre can be broken down and made explicit, the more successful this is likely to be. In addition, teachers should not underestimate the benefits of returning to practise skills after a delay.

Planning writing

A lot of metacognition happens before a classroom task begins, as learners anticipate the requirements of the task and begin to plan (Nelson & Narens, 1990). Planning writing may seem like a given, but some learners may fail to realise that good writers typically plan their work. Plans aren't obvious when reading a piece!

As part of planning, learners need to have a clear goal. For students, this means engaging with task instructions and expectations. It will be more effective if this is done actively, rather than via a teacher explanation. Consider, therefore, giving students the chance to discuss task instructions or exam board documents, and having them engage together in metacognitive talk about what a marker will be looking for.

As time goes on, students' approach to planning their writing will probably develop. An initial planning concept consists of the paragraphs of a discursive essay, or the main sections (Introduction, Methodology, Findings, Discussion) used in scientific writing. Many teachers encourage essay writers to use an introduction, three body paragraphs and a conclusion, but over time, this scaffold may become limiting (to the extent that Warner (2016) encourages us to 'kill' the 5-paragraph essay altogether). As they develop, encourage learners to see plans as fluid and able to be adapted to the needs of the task.

To develop students' understanding of how to construct an argument, start small. Have them plan short pieces, and gradually extend the length and demands. It can also be good to give feedback on plans, rather than just on fully written pieces. These can be submitted as homework, for example, prior to the main writing process. This strategy reinforces the importance of planning.

Metacognitive monitoring

It is challenging for students to reflect on their own writing as they are doing it, partly because (as noted earlier) it occupies working memory so fully. Students also have limited insight into the processes at work while they are completing a task (Nelson & Narens, 1990). However, we can help them to develop metacognitive knowledge of relevant skills and difficulties, working on these step by step.

In any skill, tasks that are appropriately demanding (neither too simple nor too challenging) help students to get into a focused 'flow' state, a positive psychological state associated with better self-confidence and performance (Nakamura & Csikszentmihalyi, 2009). For productivity, it is desirable for students to spend periods of time in the flow state when writing (we might also say 'in the zone').

At the same time, this presents a challenge to metacognition. How are learners to monitor and evaluate their own progress if they are entirely absorbed by the task? At times, it may be necessary for the teacher to interrupt them, asking students to pause for a moment and look back at their last few paragraphs. Are they sticking to the task and maintaining relevance? How technically accurate is it?

Pausing for reflection like this can become a habit. Of course, we have to rely on students to do this for themselves during self-directed writing, for example, when completing homework or essays in exams. As they become more experienced, it needn't interrupt flow – it just becomes part of their writing skillset.

Another issue that can cause problems is when the learners think that they are fulfilling the task successfully, but they are not. I used to see this as an exam marker. Many candidates had written fairly accurate descriptive essays; the problem was that the marking scheme didn't reward *description*, but rather higher-order skills such as *evaluation* and *analysis*. Similarly, students may fail to stick to their aim, but rather go off on tangents. Remember – it is very challenging for beginners to maintain their goal in working memory while composing the text itself.

To address the problems above, it may help to use a 'target diagram' (see Figure 1.1) as part of the planning process, and refer to it during composition. The most important information goes in the centre circle. The other concentric circles are like ripples, with key information near the middle and less important details further out. This can easily be sketched freehand in a notebook.

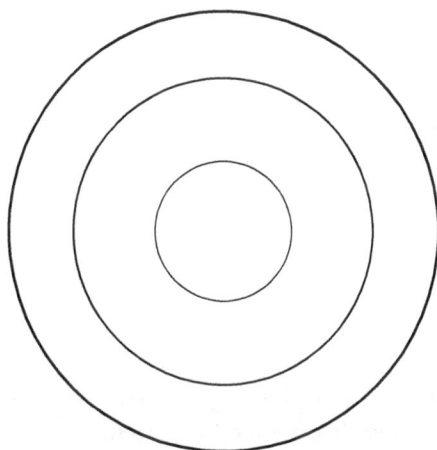

Figure 1.1 A target diagram

As well as guiding students while writing, a target diagram can be used during editing – if a text is too long, word count cutting should focus on the outer circles. Some teachers encourage the use of mind-map plans. These are similar, but the circles of the target diagram do make the levels of relevance more precise and force learners to make choices.

Another strategy to support metacognitive monitoring is to use modelling and peer learning in the classroom. A teacher can project what they are writing onto a screen, showing how they construct a relevant point, elaborate on the point, add examples and evidence, and so on. Students can then have a try, swapping their practice paragraphs

with a classmate for feedback. As time goes on, these strategies will help learners to identify flaws in their writing for themselves.

Expertise and audience

A further challenge for writers when monitoring their own work is to consider their
audience and the genre in which they are writing. Expert writers take account of the
readers' viewpoint (Kellogg, 2008). And even in school settings, good writing is not just
the output of text, but involves composing for a specific purpose. Students are beginning
to think about a notional audience. For example, in a persuasive essay, who is the writer
trying to persuade? Giving some thought to this is a metacognitive task in itself, and it
is worth asking students to discuss this at the outset.

At the same time, teachers should be aware that writing with the reader in mind is
a skill associated with accomplished adult writers and takes years to develop (Hayes &
Flower, 1980; Kellogg, 2008). It is fine for newer writers to focus mainly on expressing
things clearly. However, teachers can at least raise awareness of audience, and nudge
more confident students to think about how readers may react to particular arguments.

As part of their metacognitive knowledge, skilled writers possess an understanding
of genre. They can write for an audience, appreciating what a reader will be expecting,
and at times subverting those expectations. A very obvious genre distinction mentioned
earlier is writing an essay versus a scientific paper, but each of these categories contain
multiple versions, and vary across subjects. To start building competence in genre, make
learners aware of the unique features in your own subject by showing them contrasting
short texts, and by discussing what skilful examples achieved successfully.

Revising a written piece

Sommers (1980: 379) argues that the capacity for pieces to be revised 'distinguishes the
written text from speech', and that it is a mistake to neglect this aspect of writing. It is
also a misconception to see it as something that only happens *after* a full first draft is
complete. Instead, most authors pause to reword and revise sections of their work at
frequent intervals (Bereiter & Scardamalia, 1987).

Later, as a full draft is worked on, the skilled writer attempts to develop the strength
of their argument and the clarity of their prose. Newer writers may underestimate how
much redrafting is involved in writing a successful piece. They may have simplistic
notions based on their previous education; perhaps they became used to the idea that
they should make only a single set of changes. Some may also believe that revising their
writing is only about correcting spelling and grammar mistakes (Sommers, 1980).

These misconceptions are best tackled directly. It can be useful to share examples of
how some authors rework their pieces (ideally not just fiction authors). Encourage students to assume that several revisions will be necessary.

Pinker (2015) suggests other strategies to apply when editing, including:

- Tackling a piece with fresh eyes. That is, building in delays to help learners see their piece afresh, as a reader would do.
- Read the text aloud. This makes it much easier to perceive how it will be understood by others, and to notice errors.
- Be wary of the temptation to replace words with fancier alternatives. Good writing doesn't sound like it's been put through a thesaurus.

Students may also underestimate the extent to which experienced writers cut text. They may feel that once written, material should ideally stay in the final version. Due to this misconception, accomplished authors cut much more than inexperienced ones do (Sommers, 1980).

Connected to this idea, learners may see reaching the word count as their main target. They should instead be encouraged to aim to write a strong argument, whether this does or does not match the target word count. If a draft ends up too short, aspects can later be elaborated on; if too long, the least relevant points and examples can be cut.

Naturally, teacher feedback can play a key part in improving a writer's skill. To facilitate the deliberate practice mentioned earlier, this should be as specific as possible. Also, try to focus on the most representative and important problems, and consider providing students with a 'top three' of issues to tackle. Often, students may have forgotten your suggestions by the time they next start to write, so encourage them to note down and retain feedback.

This process brings learners back to the issue of planning, and it will be worthwhile to discuss and raise awareness of their planning and composition process towards the end of a writing task. What aspects of their planning went well and what could be changed? Reflecting on these things helps them to develop a strategic, metacognitive writing process.

Ideas for the Classroom

Building on what has been said, the following are next steps for teaching writing:

- Begin to tackle misconceptions about writing, raising awareness that it is a learnable skill. Identify experienced writers who can explain all aspects of their process, and share your own experiences, too.
- Motivate learners to engage with writing by finding topics of interest.
- To better understand skilled writing, engage in focused reading and discussion of short passages within everyday lessons.
- Devote more time and attention to planning writing, giving students opportunities to discuss task instructions and collaborate on essay plans.

- Develop composition skills via well-known topics, helping to make the cognitive load more manageable, and avoid setting writing just for consolidation.
- Show learners how to use a 'target diagram' for planning and during composition and editing, helping them decide what to prioritise.
- Gradually build their metacognitive tools for drafting and redrafting. These include using filler words to stay in flow, pausing to reflect on the last few sentences/paragraphs, and considering their audience.
- Ensure that learners are starting to become aware of the unique linguistic features in your own subject.

Further Reading

Pinker, S. (2015). *The sense of style: The thinking person's guide to writing in the 21st Century*. Harmondsworth: Penguin Books.

Aimed at the writer rather than the teacher, this is a comprehensive and accessible guide written by a leading researcher.

Colognesia, S., Piret, C., Demorsy, S., & Barbier, E. (2020). Teaching writing – with or without metacognition? An exploratory study of 11- to 12-year-old students writing a book review. *International Electronic Journal of Elementary Education, 12*(5), 459–470.

This is a useful research study on students writing a book review, and provides more detail on the stages of metacognition and the use of questioning.

Kellogg, R. T. (2008). Training writing skills: A cognitive developmental perspective. *Journal of Writing Research, 1*(1), 1–26.

This is a longer academic text, but an important one. Well worth diving into.

References

Agarwal, P. K., Nunes, L. D., & Blunt, J. R. (2021). Retrieval practice consistently benefits student learning: A systematic review of applied research in schools and classrooms. *Educational Psychology Review, 33*(4), 1409–1453.

Anderson, R. C. (2018). Role of the reader's schema in comprehension, learning, and memory. In D. E. Alvermann, N. J. Unrau, M. Sailors, & R. B. Ruddell (Eds.), *Theoretical models and processes of literacy* (7th ed., pp. 136–145). Abingdon, UK: Routledge.

Bereiter, C., & Scardamalia, M. (1987). *The psychology of written composition*. Hillsdale, NJ: Lawrence Erlbaum Associates.

Colognesia, S., Piret, C., Demorsy, S., & Barbier, E. (2020). Teaching writing – with or without metacognition? An exploratory study of 11- to 12-year-old students writing a book review. *IEJEE*, *12*(5), 459–470.

Ericsson, K. A. (2017). Expertise and individual differences: The search for the structure and acquisition of experts' superior performance. *WIREs Cognitive Science*, *8*(1–2), e1382.

Firth, J. (2016). Research engagement for the school teacher and its role in the education community. *Education in the North*, *23*(2), 161–166.

Fyfe, E. R., McNeil, N. M., & Borjas, S. (2015). Benefits of 'concreteness fading' for children's mathematics understanding. *Learning and Instruction*, *35*, 104–120.

Hacker, D. J., Keener, M. C., & Kircher, J. C. (2009). Writing is applied metacognition. In D. J. Hacker, J. Dunlosky, & A. Graesser (Eds.), *Handbook of metacognition in education* (pp. 154–172). Routledge.

Hayes, J. R., & Flower, L. (1980). Identifying the organization of writing processes. In L. W. Gregg & E. R. Steinberg (Eds.), *Cognitive processes in writing* (pp. 3–30). Hilldale, NJ: Erlbaum.

Kellogg, R. T. (2008). Training writing skills: A cognitive developmental perspective. *Journal of Writing Research*, *1*(1), 1–26.

Murray, D. M. (1990). *Learn to write* (3rd ed.). New York: Holt, Rinehart & Winston.

Nakamura, J., & Csikszentmihalyi, M. (2009). Flow theory and research. In C. R. Snyder & S. J. Lopez (Eds.), *Handbook of positive psychology* (pp. 195–206). Oxford: Oxford University Press.

Nelson, T. O., & Narens, L. (1990). Metamemory: A theoretical framework and new findings. *The Psychology of Learning and Motivation*, *26*, 125–141.

Pinker, S. (2015). *The sense of style: The thinking person's guide to writing in the 21st Century*. Harmondsworth: Penguin Books.

Rosenshine, B. (2012). Principles of instruction: Research-based strategies that all teachers should know. *American Educator*, *36*(1), 12–39.

Ryan, R. M., & Deci, E. L. (2017). *Self-determination theory: Basic psychological needs in motivation, development, and wellness*. Guilford Publications.

Sommers, N. (1980). Revision strategies of student writers and experienced adult writers. *College Composition & Communication*, *31*(4), 378–388.

Warner, J. (2016). *Kill the 5-Paragraph essay*. Available at: www.insidehighe red.com/blogs/just-visiting/kill-5-paragraph-essay

Wischgoll, A. (2017). Improving undergraduates' and postgraduates' academic writing skills with strategy training and feedback. *Frontiers in Education, Sec. Educational Psychology*, *2*, 00033.

2

Metacognition and Reading Comprehension

Debbie Tremble

An Educational Issue

In his book, *Reading Reconsidered* (Lemov et al., 2016), Doug Lemov claims: 'Of the subjects taught in school, reading is first among equals – the most singular in importance because all others rely on it.' As Lemov states, all subjects rely on reading comprehension and that includes maths. This notion is further supported in GL Assessment's publication *Read All About It: Why Reading is Key to GCSE Success* (2020), which outlines its findings from research into the relationship between reading and academic success: 'The correlation between good literacy and good student outcomes at GCSE was higher in maths (0.63) than in some arts subjects like history (0.61) and English literature (0.60).' Reading comprehension is described by Kintsch (1998) as the process and product of ideas represented in the text linked to the reader's prior knowledge and experiences and the mental representation in memory of the text. A problem faced by students in schools is if reading comprehension is tested, but not specifically taught. The Education Endowment Foundation (EEF)'s *Improving Literacy in Key Stage 2 Guidance Report* (2021) recommends especially teaching reading strategies (to activate prior knowledge, predict, question, clarify and summarise), and are explicit about supporting readers to become strategic readers. Doing so will contribute to developing reading and literacy, and therefore must be a priority in schools if we are to improve outcomes for all learners, but especially in closing the gap between the genders and between the advantaged and disadvantaged. Indeed, as the Director of Education for GL Assessments, Crispin Chatterton, states in his article for *TES* magazine, 'It is often said that there are no magic bullets in education – but literacy comes pretty close' (Chatterton, 2020).

In-school challenges

A key issue for teachers is that we are expert readers, especially in our own disciplines, and therefore we can fall into the trap of expert blindness when it comes to reading comprehension. Perhaps even more significantly for educators are those students who have weaknesses in their reading. Too often, struggling students can go undetected or become expert at disguising their reading comprehension difficulties. It is noteworthy that numerous studies have shown that weak readers and those who struggle to comprehend also lack metacognitive skills whereas stronger readers apply metacognition to reading comprehension in order to monitor their own understanding. However, the problem remains for schools and teachers of providing training and the perennial issue of time to implement, as Alex Quigley notes in the foreword to *Read All About It* (GL Assessment, 2020), 'too many secondary school teachers and leaders prove under-trained and simply too busy to support their students to best access the demands of the academic curriculum'.

Other challenges

As educators, we are competing with an array of other challenges when it comes to supporting the development of reading, namely competing with digital distractions. Johann Hari, in his book *Stolen Focus* (2022), examines the impact of digital distractions and explores the acceleration of information and the impact this is having on focus, attention, reading and comprehension. The 'infinite scroll' function on social media encourages skim reading, and therefore faster reading. Hari claims that faster reading means taking in less information, comprehending less and overwhelming the working memory. Furthermore, limited exposure to reading materials and lack of motivation to read further exacerbate promoting reading and comprehension in students. Only 35% of 10-year-olds purport to enjoy reading 'very much' and 46% of young people (aged 16–24) do not read in their free time (Reading Agency, n.d.). Combining reading instruction with metacognition may well assist students in their enjoyment of reading, as it is often the case that for those who lack reading engagement, it is because they struggle to understand and comprehend. While schools face challenges in competing with digital distractions, teachers can play a crucial role in addressing reading habits. By instructing students in metacognitive approaches to reading comprehension, educators can help them avoid developing the detrimental reading habits often acquired through online reading.

Your Approach

James Murphy's blog *Seven Steps to Improving Reading Comprehension* claims that reading comprehension 'is not developed merely by administering comprehension tests, although repeated testing does tend to have a slight positive effect on learning' (Murphy, 2016). So how do you currently support reading comprehension in your class, and in your subject? It is worth reflecting on the following questions:

1 How do you currently prioritise reading comprehension instruction in your classroom across the subjects you teach?
2 Are there any topics or units of work where you feel reading comprehension might be given less emphasis?
3 Reflect on your experiences with struggling readers. How do you identify and support students who may be expertly disguising their reading comprehension difficulties? Are there any specific strategies that you have found effective in providing targeted assistance to these students?
4 Reflecting on your teaching experiences, can you identify specific instances where you have observed both effective and ineffective approaches to supporting students' reading comprehension? What key factors do you think contributed to the success or limitations of these approaches?
5 In the face of digital distractions and the impact of faster, superficial reading habits, how do you engage students in deeper reading and comprehension?

The Metacognitive Approach

When designing my approach to reading comprehension in my own classroom, and as teaching and learning lead across my school, I initially considered how reading comprehension ties in with:

1 Metacognitive knowledge (knowledge of the task, strategies and ourselves).
2 Metacognitive regulation (how we apply this knowledge to a task through planning, monitoring and evaluating).

Ofsted's 'Now the Whole School is Reading' research report states: 'As the secondary curriculum places increasing demands on reading comprehension, older pupils who struggle with reading comprehension do not catch up' (Ofsted, 2022). And Alex Quigley argues that the purpose of metacognition is 'to equip students with the skills and strategies they need to be effective learners throughout their educational journey and beyond' (Quigley, 2020). I then considered the fact that the Education Endowment Foundation's (EEF) Teaching and Learning Toolkit | EEF (educationendowmentfoundation.org.uk) states that both metacognition and reading comprehension strategies have the highest impact for the lowest cost, and with the strongest evidence base (an uplift of 7+ months each). It made sense to consult both metacognitive and reading comprehension strategies suggested by the EEF in improving student outcomes at my school. I concluded that metacognition is fundamental in developing students' self-awareness, which is often critical in reading comprehension, allowing them to build knowledge and understanding of their strengths, weaknesses and the strategies they can select to assist them.

Metacognition is crucial in guiding and improving reading comprehension. The Scarborough Reading Rope (a model that illustrates the complex and interconnected processes involved in skilled reading) shows that in order to read skilfully there is an array of processes necessary, including both word recognition and language comprehension (Seidenberg, 2005). This first begins with word recognition (phonological awareness, decoding and sight recognition), which supports automaticity. Increasingly, strategic readers need background knowledge, access to vocabulary, verbal reasoning and literary knowledge to become skilful readers who can comprehend successfully. When beginning secondary school in Year 7, students are faced with a significant increase in the range of texts they need to be able to understand, from a variety of different disciplines, which can contribute to a 'dip or plateau' (Ofsted, 2015). This is a trend I have seen in all the schools where I have worked, but it will be evident now more than ever as the 2023/24 Year 7 cohort have had unprecedented disruption while learning to read due to the Covid-19 lockdowns. This in turn will have a had a knock-on effect with developing fluency and comprehension. While my school has a clear intervention programme for the weakest readers, I was aware that we needed to do more at the 'chalkface' to support reading comprehension for all learners to enable them to read, to learn and to keep up with the demands of the curriculum at Key Stage 3.

What does a metacognitive reader do?

The research paper 'The role of metacognition in reading comprehension' by Christina E. van Kraayenoord (2010) states that reading is an active, strategic process, involving metacognition before, during and after reading. She observed that self-regulated readers engage in 'constructively responsive reading' to actively construct meanings and that metacognition is essential in reading comprehension, including metacognitive knowledge and monitoring/control. Essentially, she argues that:

- Younger readers (side note: and perhaps older, struggling readers) initially lack awareness of reading as comprehension, not just decoding.
- Metacognitive awareness increases with age and experience.
- Good comprehenders understand reading purpose and text features better than poor comprehenders.
- Younger readers struggle with accurate comprehension monitoring.

When profiling metacognitive readers, van Kraayenoord states that they will:

- Evaluate the text consistency with prior knowledge and language expectations.
- Employ 'error detection paradigm' to assess monitoring.

Significantly, van Kraayenoordshe explores British researchers Cain and Oakhill, who wrote *Understanding and Teaching Reading Comprehension: A handbook* (Oakhill, 2014).

While good readers are more aware of the text's meaning, structure, and context when they comprehend a text and use strategies before, during, and after reading, poor comprehenders often focus on decoding and lack the ability to use both metacognitive and reading comprehension strategies suggested by the EEF. van Kraayenoord also draws on Cornoldi's research (1996), which explores the cognitive and metacognitive profiles of good and poor comprehenders and concludes that there is a noticeable diversity or variation in how those who struggle with comprehension approach reading. In other words, poor comprehenders do not all share the same characteristics or methods; there is a range of differences among them. Cornoldi therefore suggests that explicitly teaching reading comprehension techniques will benefit weaker readers.

Özgür Babayiğit's (2019) 'Examination the Metacognitive Reading Strategies of Secondary School Sixth Grade Students' highlights what metacognitive readers do. Identified in their research are three stages of metacognitive reading:

1   Planning: In this stage, readers set goals for their reading and make predictions about how they will approach the text. They identify what skills and resources they need for successful reading.
2   Monitoring: During reading, students monitor the validity of their estimates and predictions. They pay attention to the structure of the text and intensify their focus on important points. Good readers control their understanding process and analyse complex expressions.
3   Evaluation: After reading, readers evaluate their reading activity. They determine the strategies and approaches used during the reading and identify areas of improvement for future readings.

Understanding these strategies will help teachers to model them to students in order to enhance students' metacognitive approach, develop their reading comprehension and lead to them becoming more independent readers. In Babayiğit's (2019) study, metacognitive strategies improved reading comprehension, increased awareness (evidenced by active involvement in class discussion) and engagement (evidenced by increased motivation), and created a positive learning atmosphere. The strategies used with the experimental group included:

1   Planning: Learners engaged in activities that prepared them for effective reading, involving setting goals, making predictions and activating prior knowledge.
2   Monitoring: Learners engaged with self-questioning, clarification and summarising what they had read.
3   Evaluating: Learners were able to judge the importance and relevance of the information they had read (i.e., its significance in relation to the main purpose of reading), could check understanding and reflect on learning.

However, Dunlosky and Lipko's (2007) research on metacomprehension over two decades consistently found that the accuracy of people's judgement is quite poor. Comprehension monitoring is a specific aspect of metacognition that involves evaluating and adjusting understanding during reading. In the research paper 'Reading comprehension and metacognition: The importance of inferential skills', Christian Soto and colleagues (2019) found that '[h]aving strong inferential skills and metacognitive knowledge enables readers to better understand the text as they read and enhances their ability to regulate their learning efforts in the future'. Metacomprehension is the process of readers assessing their understanding of the text as they read, identifying areas of confusion or difficulty, and making adjustments to improve comprehension. Soto et al. concluded that metacognitive students are able to monitor their understanding of a text and adjust their strategies accordingly. They also found that their research highlights the significance of both understanding implied meanings and having awareness of reading strategies, especially those related to the process of evaluating and regulating one's own thinking, in improving reading comprehension. Crucially, metacognitive readers are able to select from a range of strategies to assist their comprehension and choose the most appropriate one. However, metacognition is not innate and must be taught, especially where reading comprehension is concerned. Soto et al. suggested that their findings have implications for educators, in that inferential reasoning plays a crucial role in deepening levels of understanding, especially for complex materials. Teachers can emphasise the importance of inferential reasoning in instruction to improve both comprehension and metacomprehension. However, it may be beneficial to give direct instruction on global inference (going beyond grasping individual details and making connections, identify patterns, and interpret the text in a holistic manner. It involved the ability to draw overarching conclusions or understand the broader meaning of a text) in particular, which can prove more challenging to all readers, but especially weaker readers.

Using metacognition to support comprehension

The research paper 'Applying Metacognition into Reading Comprehension', by Theerapong Kongduang (2020) suggests that weaker readers may benefit from training in reading strategies similar to inferential and metacognitive learners, and metacognitive strategy training can be applied effectively in the classroom. Kongduang recommends that teachers guide students in using metacognition to comprehend reading materials effectively. The research paper, which was based on findings from students with English as an additional language (EAL), offers the following suggestions (Kongduang, 2020):

1   Explicit Teaching: Begin by explicitly teaching students what metacognition is and how it can be applied to improve reading comprehension. Provide clear explanations and examples to help students understand the concept.
2   Goal Setting: Encourage students to set reading comprehension goals. Discuss the importance of having clear objectives while reading and how it can help them monitor their understanding.
3   Monitoring and Self-Reflection: Teach students how to monitor their own comprehension while reading. Encourage them to ask themselves questions

like, 'Do I understand what I just read?' and 'Does this make sense?' Encourage self-reflection after reading to assess their level of understanding.

4   Metacognitive Strategies: Introduce students to specific metacognitive strategies, such as previewing the text, summarizing key points, making connections, and asking questions. Demonstrate how these strategies can be applied during reading.

5   Think Alouds: Model metacognitive thinking for students by doing think-alouds. Show them how you think through a text, use strategies, and monitor comprehension.

6   Metacognitive Reading Journals: Have students keep reading journals where they record their thoughts, reflections, and the strategies they used while reading. This will help them become more aware of their thinking process.

7   Group Discussions: Encourage students to discuss their reading experiences and share the strategies that worked best for them. Group discussions can foster a supportive learning environment and provide opportunities for peer learning.

8   Differentiation: Consider the varying abilities of students in the classroom and adapt the metacognitive strategy training to meet individual needs. Some students may require more guidance and support, while others may be ready for more advanced strategies.

9   Feedback and Assessment: Provide regular feedback to students on their metacognitive approach to reading comprehension. Use formative assessments to gauge their progress and make adjustments as needed.

10 Integration into the Curriculum: Integrate metacognitive strategy training into the overall curriculum, not just in reading lessons. Students can apply these strategies in other subject areas and real-life situations.

11 Encourage Autonomy: Foster a sense of autonomy in students by encouraging them to take ownership of their learning and apply metacognitive strategies independently.

12 Teacher Training: Provide professional development for teachers to understand the importance of metacognitive strategy training and how to effectively implement it.

Kongduang concludes that the application of metacognitive approaches is 'crucial' in comprehending texts and in wider literacy, and that these approaches led to improved academic performance in EAL students. Further supporting this research is a paper *Instruction of Metacognitive Strategies Enhances Reading Comprehension and Vocabulary Achievement of Third-Grade Students* (by Boulware-Gooden and colleagues (2007) that examines the outcome of an intervention involving 30 minutes of daily reading comprehension instruction over a five-week period. Boulware-Gooden et al. determined that the intervention group showed a statistically significant improvement in vocabulary (40% difference in gains) and reading comprehension (20% difference in gains) compared to the comparison group. Teachers observed that students in the intervention group actively engaged in the lessons and demonstrated a deeper understanding of the content. They connected new vocabulary words to their prior knowledge and made more meaningful connections. The intervention proved beneficial for students with comprehension and language difficulties, as it provided them with tools to better understand what they read and to make connections to their background knowledge. The metacognitive reading comprehension instruction was found to be particularly effective in improving students' ability to understand written text.

Ideas for the Classroom

1   Reciprocal reading: Incorporating reading strategies like activating prior knowledge, predicting, questioning, clarifying and summarising into your teaching is a useful starting point. These prompt questions from the Education Endowment Foundation's *Improving Key Stage 2 Literacy* (2021) are a helpful guide:

Predict

- What do the title and front cover tell me about the book and what to expect?
- Is the author leaving me hints about what might happen next?
- Can I find and use the hints and clues to make my predictions?
- Oh no, I didn't expect that to happen... Can I 'squeeze' more evidence from what I've read to make a new prediction?

Question

- Keep a note of any questions you would like to ask while reading. I'm recording mine on a mini whiteboard.
- Where is the story set? What do I know about the countryside?
- Why did the author choose this word? What does this word tell me about the character?
- I wonder if...?

Activating Prior Knowledge

- What do you know about the setting of this story?
- What have we learned about this in our science/topic lesson?
- Can you make a link to other texts we have read?
- That's right in Year 3. What do you remember?

Clarify

- Keep an eye on what's happening. If you get lost, look for words and phrases you are unsure of.
- It helps to go back and re-read if we're not quite sure what's happened or why.
- Next, are there any words or phrases that we are not sure of in the text?

Summarise

- To really enjoy this text, it's important to take a summary after every chapter.
- Your summary could be 5 words.
- A summary could be a quick picture with annotations.
- A post-it note summary can help you take our story home so you can share it with a grown up in your house.

Alongside this, provide clear instructions on how to apply these strategies to enhance comprehension. As educators, we can utilise reciprocal teaching approaches to foster students' independence as well as supporting struggling readers. This can be achieved by applying these strategies through 'I, we, you' – moving from modelling the strategy to collaborative and peer-assisted application of strategies.

2 Identify struggling readers: It is crucial, of course, to identify struggling readers. These readers may need support with decoding, vocabulary knowledge and reading comprehension. However, comprehension is not merely a reading-age issue. Lest we forget, it is the 'process and product of ideas represented in the text linked to the reader's prior knowledge and experiences and the mental representation in memory of the text' (Kintsch, 1998: 4). Comprehension is context-based. For example, I would have difficulty comprehending a manual on building a car engine simply because I lack prior knowledge and vocabulary awareness. Even as a proficient reader, I would have difficulty in understanding the text and would need explicit instruction. Therefore, be vigilant in identifying students who might be disguising their reading comprehension difficulties and do not assume stronger readers are always sufficiently comprehending complex texts. Regularly assess their comprehension and monitor their progress to offer timely support.

3 Model metacognitive approaches to reading comprehension: Integrate metacognitive approaches to enhance students' self-awareness of their reading process. Teach them to set goals, monitor their understanding and reflect on their strategies. Again, EEF's *Improving Key Stage 2 Literacy* (2021: 24) offers metacognitive prompts which can be modelled to readers:

Explicitly teaching children these strategies supports them to become strategic readers. What does a strategic reader do before, during, and after reading?

Before reading...

- Asks questions about the text
- Activates prior knowledge
- Makes predictions

During reading...

- Monitors understanding
- Makes connections within and beyond the text
- Makes mental models of the text
- Updates and makes new predictions

After reading...

- Clarifies understanding of the text
- Revisits and revises predictions
- Asks further questions
- Reflects on their own reading
- Summarises key points from the text

This can be further supported through demonstrating metacognitive thinking through think-alouds. Show students how you apply strategies while reading, fostering a culture of active engagement and critical thinking.

Further Reading

The following research papers are fantastic sources of information about the role meta-cognition plays in reading comprehension:

van Kraayenoord, C. E. (2010). 'The role of metacognition in reading comprehension', *ResearchGate*. Available at: www.researchgate.net/publication/46401318_The_role_of_metacognition_in_reading_comprehension

Soto, C., Gutiérrez de Blume, A. P., Jacovina, M., McNamara, D., Benson, N., & Riffo, B. (2019). 'Reading comprehension and metacognition: The importance of inferential skills', *Cogent Education*, 6(1).

Kongduang, T. (2020). 'Applying metacognition into reading comprehension', *International Journal of Arts Humanities and Social Sciences Studies*, 5(6).

Dunlosky, J., & Lipko, A. R. (2007). 'Metacomprehension: A brief history and how to improve its accuracy', *Current Directions in Psychological Science, 16*(4), 228–232.

On reading and comprehension, these are my go-to books:

Murphy, D., & Murphy, J. (2018). *Thinking Reading.* London: Hodder Education.
Quigley, A. (2020). *Closing the Reading Gap.* Abingdon, UK: Routledge.

References

Babayiğit, Ö (2019). 'Examination the metacognitive reading strategies of secondary school sixth grade students', *International Journal of Progressive Education, 15*(3), 1–12, Available at: https://ijpe.inased.org/makale/891 (accessed 19 October 2023).

Boulware-Gooden, R., Carreker, S., Thornhill, A., & Joshi, R. M. (2007). 'Instruction of metacognitive strategies enhances reading comprehension and vocabulary achievement of third-grade students', *The Reading Teacher, 61*(1), 70–77.

Chatterton, C. (2020). 'There is a magic bullet in education, after all', *TES*, 5 March [online]. Available at: www.tes.com/magazine/archive/there-magic-bullet-education-after-all (accessed 19 October 2023).

Cornoldi, C., De Beni, R., & Pazzaglia, F. (1996). Reading comprehension profiles. In C. Cornoldi & J. Oakhill (Eds.), *Reading Comprehension Difficulties: Processes and Intervention* (pp. 113–136). Mahwah, NJ: Erlbaum.

Dunlosky, J., & Lipko, A. R. (2007). 'Metacomprehension: A brief history and how to improve its accuracy', *Current Directions in Psychological Science, 16*(4), 228–232.

Education Endowment Foundation (EEF) (2021). *Improving Literacy in Key Stage 2.* Available at: https://educationendowmentfoundation.org.uk/education-evidence/guidance-reports/literacy-ks2 (accessed 19 October 2023).

GL Assessment (2020). *Read All About It: Why Reading is Key to GCSE Success.* Brentford: GL Assessment.

Hari, J. (2022). *Stolen Focus: Why You Can't Pay Attention.* London: Bloomsbury.

Kintsch, W. (1998). *Comprehension: A Paradigm for Cognition.* New York: Cambridge University Press.

Kongduang, T. (2020). 'Applying metacognition into reading comprehension', *International Journal of Arts Humanities and Social Sciences Studies, 5*(6).

Lemov, D., Driggs, C., & Woolway, E. (2016). *Reading Reconsidered: A Practical Guide to Rigorous Literacy Instruction.* San Francisco, CA: Jossey-Bass.

Murphy, J. (2016). 'Seven steps to improving reading comprehension', *Thinking Reading* [blog], 27 October. Available at: https://thinkingreadingwritings.wpcomstaging.com/2016/10/27/seven-steps-to-improving-reading-comprehension/ (accessed 19 October 2023).

Ofsted (2015). *Key Stage 3: The Wasted Years?* Available at: www.gov.uk/government/publications/key-stage-3-the-wasted-years (accessed 19 October 2023).

Ofsted (2022, October). *'Now the Whole School is Reading': Supporting Struggling Readers in Secondary School*. Available at: www.gov.uk/government/publications/now-the-whole-school-is-reading-supporting-struggling-readers-in-secondary-school (accessed 19 October 2023).

Oakhill, J. (2014). *Understanding and Teaching Reading Comprehension: A Handbook*. New York, NY: Routledge.

Quigley, A. (2020). *Closing the Reading Gap*. Abingdon, UK: Routledge.

Reading Agency (n.d.). *Reading Facts*. Available at: https://readingagency.org.uk/about/impact/002-reading-facts-1 (accessed 19 October 2023).

Seidenberg, M. S. (2005). 'The Scarborough Reading Rope: A framework for reading comprehension', *Reading Research Quarterly*, 40(3), 374–378.

Soto, C., Gutiérrez de Blume, A. P., Jacovina, M., McNamara, D., Benson, N., & Riffo, B. (2019). 'Reading comprehension and metacognition: The importance of inferential skills', *Cogent Education*, 6(1).

van Kraayenoord, C. E. (2010). 'The role of metacognition in reading comprehension', *ResearchGate*. Available at: www.researchgate.net/publication/46401318_The_role_of_metacognition_in_reading_comprehension (accessed 19 October 2023).

3

Dealing with Students' Lack of Motivation and Resilience

Charlotte Findlay

An Educational Issue

Talk to any teacher in your school, and you will hear the same issues – the specification is too content-heavy; exam dates have moved earlier in the season, which then has a knock-on effect for teaching time and study leave periods; exams are getting harder and students struggle with higher-order questions; there are disruptions that lead to lost learning time (strikes, extra Bank Holidays, illness) or the pressure of the Progress 8 benchmark or maintaining your subject's exam results for data-driven league tables. Whatever your reason, you may be guilty of spoon-feeding at one point or another to overcome the issue of lost learning time. As educators, it's our responsibility to ensure our learners are prepared for society once they leave us, but spoon-feeding can hinder their progress and opportunities, and we need to be mindful of this, even when it feels like the easiest and only solution.

Spoon-feeding was once a traditional method of teaching (Boyer, 1987), where teachers would 'feed' their students knowledge so they could regurgitate it in an exam. This approach didn't encourage students to engage with content or ask questions, but simply transmitted information to passive learners, and reinforced the notion that some-one else will think for them. Modern education promotes a 'student-centred' approach, whereby students are encouraged to be active learners in the classroom by questioning, researching and engaging through digital literacy, creativity and problem solving (Kim et al., 2019).

This teaching approach can have various impacts on student learning. For example, providing students with information is surface-level learning, which prioritises memoris-ing facts rather than understanding them and thus requires no engagement, questioning or justification. Alternatively, deep-level learning encourages students to think critically about information, develop arguments, make connections to prior learning and to create new ideas (Entwistle & Waterson, 1988). This is the difference between asking a student what colour the grass is and asking students why the grass is green. Surface-level teaching limits students' ability to develop critical thinking skills or the ability to problem-solve, ultimately creating learners who are intellectually dependent on teachers to provide answers. This alone can lead to learned helplessness, where students start to believe they can't succeed without explicit guidance. As students' progress through education, this expectation can prevent students from potential academic achievement, as they memorise information instead of critically assessing it, meaning the transition from post-16 to higher education and beyond is steep. To demonstrate this, Jones et al. (2014) found that 600 students from five UK universities had forgotten around 60% of their A-level syllabus, which universities expect high-performing students to retain and is the basis of their universities offers. They suggest that this is due to secondary schools teaching content explicitly for an exam and for league-tables placement; it doesn't support long-term retention of knowledge (Jones et al., 2014). Therefore, it's not surprising that intellectual dependency can inhibit creativity, innovation and prevent desirable modern skills from developing. This is also a larger problem. The World Economic Forum (2023) revealed that analytical and creative thinking, as well as curiosity, motivation and a drive for lifelong learning, are a few of the top-10 skills that employers in 2023 deem desirable, and each requires a level of cognitive awareness. By limiting students' potential to learn how to think in secondary school, we are hindering their future opportunities in society.

Your Approach

- Think about your own professional practice. How often do you spoon-feed information? Are you aware that you're doing it? How often do you encourage discussion and opportunities for students to develop and practise thinking?
- How much of the lesson is focused on you talking and delivering content?
- If you're guilty of spoon-feeding (we all have at some point), is it because you lack time? Do you lack the knowledge or confidence to support a critical discussion? Were you a recipient of spoon-fed teaching as a student?
- Do you have opportunities to develop critical thinking skills written into your scheme of work?
- Is spoon-feeding something that individual teachers can tackle? Or does it require a whole-school cultural shift? Or societal change?
- Think about a time you have posed questions to students and have been greeted with silence and blank stares. Did you continue to question? And how long did you question until you succumbed to 'feeding' them clues or sharing the answer?

The Metacognitive Approach

The curse of knowledge

It is easy to forget that, as adult learners with degrees and life experience, we are the experts of our subject, and that students are novices. This 'curse of knowledge' (Camerer et al., 1989) suggests that as we become experts, we find it increasingly difficult to remember what it was like to be a novice, which can result in challenges in explaining concepts. Tullis and Feder (2023) found that increasing our knowledge of a topic impairs the accuracy of judgements of other's knowledge, and that our estimations of other's knowledge is based on our personal perspective. Ultimately, this means that the more we know about a topic (our subject area) the more difficult it becomes to simplify concepts for those who lack a schema in the area.

This is an unfortunate cognitive flaw as teachers who can successfully predict students' knowledge are able to effectively support their learning in the classroom (Sadler et al., 2013). This 'curse' can lead teachers to overestimate student understanding and can lead to poor attainment in the long run (Camerer et al., 1989). It is a pitfall that is also present in students too. Research has revealed that students often overestimate their own knowledge when asked to predict their likely score before sitting a test (Casselman & Atwood, 2017). This highlights an issue in both teachers and students that we are not necessarily aware of. If teachers (experts) forget how much knowledge they possess, and students struggle to correctly judge their own ability, it is no wonder that spoon-feeding becomes a quick fix.

Cognitive biases, like this 'curse', are somewhat inevitable unless we are consciously aware of our thinking (this alone is a metacognitive strategy), but our thinking should be challenged frequently to ensure we are fostering an environment that is suitable for intellectual curiosity and growth. This means we are regularly allowing our thoughts and processes to be modified and questioned by students to ensure that we are thinking and processing in the best way for us and our learners.

A fantastic example of this curse was demonstrated by Newton (1990), who assigned research participants to two groups, the Tappers and the Listeners. The tappers were given a song (Happy Birthday) and the Listeners had to listen to the taps they made and guess the name of the song. Only 2.5% of the tapped tunes were identified, despite the Tappers believing that 50% of the songs would be recognised. If we apply this to teaching, we pose questions and teach content, knowing what we know as experts and expecting specific answers. At times, we are greeted with silence and blank stares, which can be demoralising for us as the answer is obvious (to us) and which results in spoon-feeding the answer to remove the uncomfortable silence. We must be aware that our way of thinking is natural to us because of our experiences and ability to practise our thinking. To support our students, we need to share our expert way of thinking.

Sharing our inner monologue

Students who understand how they learn and think are better prepared and able to recreate situations which foster their own learning away from direct instruction. As teachers are the experts, it is our role to explicitly demonstrate and identify the strategies used for different exam questions because we recognise that this problem solving and decision making isn't always easy for students to learn independently (Pintrich, 2002).

To put this into perspective, consider when you (the subject expert) look at summer exam papers for the first time. There may be some questions which you feel are tricky or difficult and require thinking time to answer. Encouraging students to reflect before, during and after a task is ideal, but we should be mindful that one cannot teach what one doesn't know (Jiang et al., 2016), which suggests that some teachers may not possess the metacognitive ability to support students' metacognitive development. However, we all have an inner voice – it's allowing you to process this sentence and it has evolved substantially in the last five, 10, 15 years! As educators, we can support the development of students' inner voice to develop their metacognitive ability. This isn't just evident in students. As adults, we consistently modify and challenge our processing to improve our strategy and technique too.

The Sutton Trust–Education Endowment Foundation (2021) recommends modelling your own thinking to support metacognitive development in students. This development will reduce the need to spoon-feed, as we scaffold students to explore a new way of approaching problems, before, during and after a task. The concept of modelling isn't new, and some subjects will deliberately plan this strategy into their lessons. For example, conducting experiments in chemistry, observing technique in art, imitating and practising movements in drama or sports. However, the commonality between these examples is that the behaviour is observable and physical, whereas modelling your internal monologue and thought process with students may not be a commonly used strategy. This is where the 'curse of knowledge' appears – as experts, we may not instinctively verbalise our thoughts as they are almost intuitive to us, but to support our novice students to become experts, we need to share how we instinctively think and process.

When modelling our inner voice, there is a fine balance between scaffolding and 'deliberate difficulty' (Bjork & Bjork, 2011). This is where we provide some support (through modelling our internal monologue) while encouraging the students to practise their own thoughts by encouraging them to think independently. Bjork and Bjork (2011) propose that a level of difficulty when learning challenges the learner to form stronger connections and perform well. Over time, this internal monologue will support their own learning.

One consideration is that developing metacognitive skills in one subject may not be wholly transferable to another, due to the differing subject knowledge and specific skills. However, as students begin to develop metacognitive skills such as self-monitoring, goal setting or self-testing at a young age, this will transfer into a general competency as they become an older student. For example, Veenman and Spaans (2005) found a positive correlation between metacognitive skills in different domains were stronger in older students (15) than younger (12).

Walking-talking exams

One strategy that can model your inner voice while developing a student's inner voice is a walking-talking exam paper. It may be an activity you already do, especially around exam seasons, but you may not fully appreciate the benefits beyond showing students a real exam paper and modelling good answers for exam questions.

To do the walking-talking exam exercise, choose an exam paper that students may not have seen and give each student a blank copy of the paper along with the mark scheme. If you have access to a visualiser, this is the perfect exercise to use it. A visualiser will allow you to annotate the paper while verbalising your inner voice or to write model answers for students to see. We know from our understanding of working memory that verbal instructions combined with visual prompts are more effective than either on its own as humans can process verbal and visual information both independently or combined. This combination of visual and verbal information strengthens the develop-ment of schemata as students will acquire two coding methods for one concept (Clark & Paivio, 1991), known as 'dual-coding'. As you discuss the exam paper, talk through your strategy of how you will answer the questions. For example, you may encourage students to 'brain dump' throughout the whole paper, meaning they write down eve-rything they know about the question areas in note formation before they approach larger mark or essay questions in the paper. You may argue that this will enable them to gain more marks while recalling the least amount of knowledge and will utilise their time effectively. Another approach may be to encourage students to start on the topic or questions they find the most challenging.

While you are browsing the paper, ask students to think about how they feel about the paper. Are there any questions they're already planning to skip? What is *their* strat-egy? This will encourage them to start to become aware of their thought processes which are likely to be automatic and passing thoughts.

There are several methods you can now take. You can start with the question that the students have said they would most likely skip which would demonstrate that it isn't as difficult as they believed; you could start from the beginning of the paper and approach each question sequentially, or the method I suggest is to demonstrate your personal strategy as the expert of the subject and verbalise your inner thoughts, sharing your thought processing with each question. This will allow you to justify your reasoning and begin to model your inner voice, it is imperative that you model all thought processes which may be difficult at first, as these processes have almost become second nature to us as subject experts. For example, begin by reading the question and identifying the command verb, and explain what it requires you to do, then identify the exam board's 'Assessment Objectives' that this command verb meets, and how many marks are allo-cated to each command verb in this question type as per your subject and exam board. Let's demonstrate this with an example based on the AQA Psychology specification. The question is 'Outline and evaluate one explanation of attachment in psychology' which is 16 marks. My commentary would be:

This question has two command verbs – outline and evaluate. I know that 'outline' meets Assessment Objective 1 and in this question, it is awarded 6 marks. I know that Assessment Objective 1 means I write about theoretical and factual information about the topic and that 'outline' in this context means I need to give a brief account or summary of one explanation of attachment. The second command verb, 'evaluate' meets Assessment Objective 3 and is awarded the remaining 10 marks in this question. I know that Assessment Objective 3 means that I need to explain strengths, limitations or an overall judgement of the question area, usually using research to demonstrate this. I also know that because there is no scenario attached to this question, Assessment Objective 2 is not being assessed.

So, to answer this question I need to choose the explanation of attachment that I understand the best so that I can evaluate it effectively. I'm going to choose 'Bowlby's Monotropic Theory, as opposed to the Learning Theory of Attachment, because I understand Bowlby's theory in accurate detail, and I know a handful of evaluative points that I can easily write about using three to four PEEL paragraphs. This will ensure that I have the best chance of attaining the maximum 6 marks available for Assessment Objective 1 (outline) and the remaining 10 marks for Assessment Objective 3 (evaluate). As a subject expert and examiner, I know that the suggested timeframe for a 16-mark essay is 20 minutes to ensure I manage my time for the rest of the paper. This roughly equates to 3 pages of A4.

Before I write anything, I'm going to make a quick plan on the exam paper, using the planning box if one is provided. I do this because I know that to enter the level four mark-band, I need to produce a coherent and focused answer so I need to ensure my answer makes sense and that my evaluation points align with the information I've provided for my outline. I'll start by defining my chosen theory and giving brief outline of its five features, which will also help signpost to the examiner that I know the answer. In lessons, we have used the acronym 'ASCMI' to help me remember the five features… (I would then start to explain the answer to the essay, explaining why I have introduced specific concepts before others, why I have included specific evaluative points and why I have written them in my chosen order. As this is subject specific, it would not be beneficial for a non-psychology teacher to read this).

This example demonstrates the level of detail that is needed to show students how an expert thinks about and approaches an exam question. It may have been more detail than you would have thought about sharing with students. Following this, I would pause and ask the students if there is anything they think I've missed or if they have any questions about my approach. I would then continue to share my inner voice. I would include the information I set out in my essay plan. The visualiser will show them my notes live on the screen for them to see too. I'd explain how I'd start my essay and how I'd summarise Bowlby's theory, using the aforementioned five features without it being too brief or too descriptive to meet the requirements of the 'outline' command verb, and I may even explain what I would add to meet a 'describe' command verb instead. I would move on to evaluative points, explaining why I've chosen specific points over others and justifying my chosen order of evaluative points in relation to the mark-band language (coherent, detailed and effective). The aim is to write an essay live, which can be exciting as students can watch and hear how an essay is written while timing you and then instantly marking you with their mark scheme. From experience, students love being able to 'catch out' teachers by identifying content that is missed or incorrect. This opens a conversation on how to read mark schemes, and the nuances many have, which then enables students to understand how to assess themselves in future. This whole task may take around 30 minutes.

The second essay we approach together would encourage students to use their own inner voice, which I would support through questioning. For example, I would ask them 'what are the command verbs?', 'How will I allocate the marks?'. This can be a whole-class activity, where different students are questioned for their personal strategy, which can then lead to an open discussion with other students sharing their inner voice, strategy and verbally discussing their plan aloud. Teachers can support this discussion by asking students for the strengths and limitations of their plan and encouraging students to justify their approach in relation to the mark scheme and question requirements – all of which will encourage them to think about their own processing, strategy and awareness of their own knowledge.

In short, this strategy supports metacognitive development in students by strengthening students' inner voice. Our inner voice is always processing, evaluating and supporting our decision making. Encouraging students to observe and listen to experts model their own inner voice when approaching a problem means we can support students to develop their own.

Critical reading

A second strategy is critical reading, which encourages students to practise metacognitive thinking while they are engaging with wider topics in your subject. This strategy has a variety of benefits, such as students engaging with text beyond the specification and the act of reading. It will inevitably enable them to see how specialist language within your subject is used contextually, including how these words are pronounced, and can provide contemporary or synoptic links between topics.

Critical reading requires some preparation from the teacher. First, you need to source the text that you want the class to engage with. I tend to use current research that has been simplified for the general public, via reputable sources, but still includes academic language and themes. In some cases, when I'm stretching students, I will use academic journals. In the first few critical reading tasks, I deliberately choose research articles in topics that are familiar to students so that they are able to comprehend the research and spot the familiar research methods, terminology and concepts they will recall from their schema. The reason for this is to increase confidence through engagement, as presenting a student with a difficult text that is beyond the specification is daunting and will reduce confidence in their knowledge.

Once the text has been chosen, the teacher needs to read the article and write down the critical questions to ask as students read. I usually have my text in the centre of an A3 page, with my critical questions around the article in boxes. This means I can print out the document and each student will have their own copy to annotate and can see the questions that will be asked. This method also eliminates the pressure of a surprise question and allows students thinking time.

In the classroom, I use this activity as a consolidation task to enhance student learning beyond the specification, or at the start of a topic to begin making connections between prior knowledge and new learning. I explain why I have chosen this article and why it is relevant. It could be my personal interest in the field, and I'm modelling how I'd like them to source their own article to share, or it could be it's relevant to the current or previous topic which can be used as contemporary evaluation or a counter-argument in their extended essays.

The reading element can be conducted in two ways. In the first strategy, the teacher reads the text slowly, pausing at appropriate points to ask questions. In the second strategy, students volunteer to read and pause at appropriate points to enable the teacher to ask critical questions on the paragraph that was read. For example, in psychological articles, there is often an experiment that has been conducted, and the paper will include a methodology section which includes details on how participants were recruited and their demographic information. These are typically evaluation points that we explore within the psychology specification to be used in essays and so students should be able to answer critical questions on methodology and participant samples with ease. The challenge comes when we begin to question these elements further, to understand why the sample and methodology were used in the context of this new research study, unknown to students.

Critical reading allows the teacher to model critical thinking through reading and supports the development of metacognition by demonstrating the inner voice while reading a new text. It also has the bonus of developing oracy as students can be prompted and guided to develop their answers to create evaluative points verbally that can be corrected instantaneously rather than generic and simple written statements.

You can develop this strategy further so that students are guided and encouraged to source their own articles and conduct their own critical thinking independently, which they can share with the class. Instead of the teacher asking additional critical questions, the students will ask each other critical questions.

Ideas for the Classroom

- Walking-talking exam papers are an easy strategy to use to share your inner voice as an expert and to model how to devise a strategy and approach to tackling an exam paper. To fully benefit from this strategy, you will need a visualiser so that students can see what you are writing and a level of confidence in your own subject knowledge to be able to plan and write an essay under the watchful eyes of students. Mark schemes can sometimes catch us out too, so reading them prior to this activity will ensure that you feel confident to share your inner voice.
- Critical reading is another method you can use to model your inner voice, while also promoting reading and introducing contemporary and wider reading into

the lesson. To benefit from this strategy, you will need to source articles that are suitable for the activity. They can be sourced from a newspaper, an academic journal, a periodical, or any text that you feel is suitable for your students. While it may take some time to source and prepare appropriate texts, once you have done so, they will last.

Further Reading

This article explains the 'curse of knowledge' in more detail, including how it develops and how to overcome it:

Shatz, I. (n.d.). The curse of knowledge: A difficulty in understanding less-informed perspectives. *Effectivology* [online]. Available at: https://effectiviology.com/curse-of-knowledge/#The_psychology_and_causes_of_the_curse_of_knowledge

Pintrich (2002) explains the role of metacognitive knowledge in learning, teaching and assessing, while summarising the three types of metacognitive knowledge:

Pintrich, P. (2002). The role of metacognitive knowledge in learning, teaching, and assessing. *Theory into Practice, 41*(4), 219–225.

Paul Main (2021) gives a concise breakdown of Dual Coding Theory and Working Memory which is easy to understand and explores the benefits of developing your understanding to enhance your teaching:

Main, P. (2021). Dual coding: A teacher's guide. *Structural-learning.com* [online]. Available at: www.structural-learning.com/post/dual-coding-a-teachers-guide

References

Bjork, E. L., & Bjork, R. A. (2011). Making things hard on yourself, but in a good way: Creating desirable difficulties to enhance learning. In M. A. Gernsbacher, R. W. Pew, L. M. Hough, & J. R. Pomerantz (Eds.), *Psychology and the real world: Essays illustrating fundamental contributions to society* (2nd ed., pp. 59–68). New York: Worth.

Boyer, W. L. (1987). *College: The undergraduate experience in America*. New York: Harper & Row.

Camerer, C. F., Loewenstein, G., & Weber, M. (1989). The curse of knowledge in economic settings: An experimental analysis. *Journal of Political Economy, 97*(5), 1232–1254. doi: 10.1086/261651

Casselman, B. L., & Atwood, C. H. (2017). Improving general chemistry course performance through online homework-based metacognitive training. *Journal of Chemical Education, 94*(12), 1811–1821.

Clark, J. M., & Paivio, A. (1991). Dual coding theory and education. *Educational Psychology Review, 3*(3), 149–210. https://doi.org/10.1007/BF01320076

Entwistle, N., & Waterson, S. (1988). Approaches to studying and levels of processing in university students. *Journal of Educational Psychology, 58*, 258–265.

Jiang, Y., Ma, L., & Gao, L. (2016). Assessing teachers' metacognition in teaching: The Teacher Metacognition Inventory. *Teaching and Teacher Education, 59*, 403–413.

Jones, H., Black, B., Green, J., Langton, P., Rutherford, S., Scott, J., & Brown, S. (2014). Indications of knowledge retention in the transition to higher education. *Journal of Biological Education, 49*(3), 261–273. doi: 10.1080/00219266.2014.926960

Kim, S., Mahjabeen, R., & Seidman, E. (2019). Improving 21st-century teaching skills: The key to effective 21st-century learners. *Research in Comparative and International Education, 14*(1), 99–117.

Newton, E. L. (1990). The rocky road from actions to intentions. [Doctoral dissertation, Stanford University]. Retrieved from: https://creatorsvancouver.com/wp-content/uploads/2016/06/rocky-road-from-actions-to-intentions.pdf

Pintrich, P. (2002). The role of metacognitive knowledge in learning, teaching, and assessing. *Theory into Practice, 41*(4), 219–225.

Sadler, P. M., Sonnert, G., Coyle, H. P., Cook-Smith, N., & Miller, J. L. (2013). The influence of teachers' knowledge on student learning in middle school physical science classrooms. *American Educational Research Journal, 50*, 1020–1049.

The Sutton Trust–Education Endowment Foundation (2021). *Metacognition and Self-regulated Learning*. Available at: https://educationendowmentfoundation.org.uk/education-evidence/guidance-reports/metacognition (accessed 5 May 2023).

Tullis, J. G., & Feder, B. (2023). The 'curse of knowledge' when predicting others' knowledge. *Memory & Cognition, 51*, 1214–1234. doi: 10.3758/s13421-022-01382-3

Veenman, M. V. J., & Spaans, M. A. (2005). Relation between intellectual and metacognitive skills: Age and task differences. *Learning and Individual Differences, 15*(2), 159–176.

World Economic Forum (2023). *The Future of Jobs Report 2023*. Available at: www.weforum.org/agenda/2023/05/future-of-jobs-2023-skills/

4

Solving Poor Study Choices by Older Students

Elizabeth Mountstevens

An Educational Issue

As students near the end of their compulsory education we expect them to make decisions about their own learning. For example, this might be a GCSE student choosing a
particular revision strategy or an A-level student planning how to use their independent study time. The decisions they make can have a large impact on their final grade.
Research by Oakes and Griffin (2021) shows that study choices are a better predictor of
student success than their prior achievement.

Let us look at this in more detail by comparing two imaginary A-level students:

Student A is confident. In lessons they feel like they understand the content
and can answer the questions. They do not reflect on their work in detail and
when it comes to assessments, they have a quick look through their book the
night before. They do some independent study in addition to homework, but
mostly reading current affairs articles related to their subject.

Student B has the same prior attainment as student A, but in lessons they
regularly reflect and ask questions when there are areas they need to
understand in more detail. They focus their independent study on these areas
of weaknesses by completing extra practice questions. When preparing for
assessments, student B uses strategies such as retrieval practice.

Research into study choices and what we know about learning tells us that student B will
be more effective and that there are three problems that student A needs to overcome.

1   Student A is overconfident, which means they do not do enough independent
    study. Research carried out at the University of Pretoria, South Africa (Mathebathe &
    Potgieter, 2014) confirmed this link. Mathebathe and Potgieter found that over-
    confidence at the start of the course did not impact on performance, but when this

confidence persisted to the end of the course, or arose during learning, students did worse in their final assessments. This is likely to be because overconfident students think they already understand and therefore do not take the time to practise.

2   Student A is not able to identify strengths and weaknesses in their understanding. This will adversely affect their learning because they will spend time going over work they already understand and will not allocate their time to the tasks where they most need to improve.

3   Student A does not choose effective study strategies. Research on study strategies shows that many of the strategies that students use, such as highlighting and re-reading, are not effective (Dunlosky, 2013) for long-term learning. Students who use poor study strategies may spend a lot of time studying but will still underperform in assessments.

Overconfidence and an inability to identify strengths and weaknesses are both symptoms of poor calibration, which is a mismatch between a person's judgement of their performance and their actual performance. Supporting students to improve their calibration will help them to make better choices about what to study. Students also need to know how to study effectively. Understanding how learning happens and the strategies that are most effective will support them to make better use of their study time and improve their academic performance.

Your Approach

- Can you think of an example of a student A and a student B that you have taught? How successful were they in their final assessments? What do you think made one student more successful than the other?
- What feedback do you give students in your subject? To what extent does that help them to know how well they are doing? How do you support students who are overconfident or underconfident to be better judges of their own performance?
- How good are your students at identifying their strengths and weaknesses? How do you support them to do this?
- What advice do you currently give students about revision or study skills? Do you know if they use this advice to make effective study choices? What do you do if students are underperforming?

The Metacognitive Approach

As set out earlier in this book, metacognition is commonly divided into two parts: metacognitive knowledge and metacognitive regulation. Metacognitive knowledge is the knowledge we have about learning and ourselves as learners, while metacognitive regulation is how we control our thinking. Metacognitive knowledge is commonly divided further into three components: knowledge of self, knowledge of tasks and knowledge of strategies (Quigley et al., 2018). It is helpful to consider what a successful student would look like for each of these categories:

- Knowledge of self: Students with good metacognitive knowledge will have an accurate picture of how well they are doing. They will know the areas of the course where they are doing well and the areas they need to work on.
- Knowledge of tasks: Students with good metacognitive knowledge will know how the subjects they study are divided into different areas of knowledge or skill. They will be aware of the different types of questions they will come across in an exam or the different assessments they will do.
- Knowledge of strategies: Students with good metacognitive knowledge will know which study strategies are most effective and how to use them.

Improving our students' metacognitive knowledge will therefore help them to evaluate their performance and identify their strengths and weaknesses more accurately. They will also have a better idea of how they learn and this will support them to choose more effective study strategies. The rest of this section will outline some ways we can go about improving students' metacognitive knowledge.

Improving students' calibration

Calibration is the degree to which a person's judgements about their performance correspond to their actual performance (Nietfeld et al., 2006). Calibration can be absolute or relative. Good absolute calibration means a student can identify how many questions they can answer correctly. Good relative calibration means a student can identify which questions they are more likely to answer correctly. Both absolute and relative calibration are important when students make decisions about their studies. More accurate absolute calibration means students have a better idea of how they are doing overall; they can use this information to adjust the amount of time they spend on independent study. More accurate relative calibration means students are better at deciding which areas of the course they need to focus on; they can use this information to prioritise information for further study. It is possible for students to have good absolute calibration and poor relative calibration or vice versa.

Calibration is usually assessed by confidence judgements. Confidence judgements are when students are asked to estimate how well they have learned, or will learn, a particular topic. They can occur at three different points in the learning process:

1. Ease of learning (EOL) judgements are used before learning; students consider how easy a topic will be to learn.
2. Judgements of learning (JOL) are used after initial learning has taken place; students consider how successful they have been at learning it.
3. Retrospective confidence judgements (RCJ) are used after completing a test on the topic; students consider how well they have performed on the test.

Students use the results of their confidence judgements to make decisions about how easy future topics will be to learn and how much effort they will put into their learning. If their calibration is poor, they may overestimate or underestimate how much they have learned and fail to allocate the appropriate time for study.

Confidence judgements can be used to assess calibration but also to improve it by providing feedback. Fletcher-Wood (2017) describes the different levels at which feedback can be provided to students (see Table 4.1).

Table 4.1 Levels of feedback (adapted from Fletcher-Wood, 2017)

Level of feedback	Description	Example
Task	How well tasks are performed/understood	Which test questions a student has answered correctly or incorrectly
Process (Subject)	The main processes needed to perform/understand tasks	Which areas of a subject or which type of question students particularly need to improve on
Self-regulation	Self-monitoring, directing and regulating of actions	Whether the student correctly identifies questions they have done well on
Self	Personal evaluations (usually positive) about the learner	Whether the student is good at the subject or not

Feedback at the task, process and self-regulation level are all useful for students. Feedback on confidence judgements is feedback at the self-regulation level. Comparing the confidence judgements to the actual performance provides students with feedback on their calibration. They can use this to improve their judgements of future learning and make better use of their independent study time. Let us look at a couple of examples of this process: one example from a research paper and the second from my experience of using confidence judgements in science teaching.

The research paper: Nietfeld and colleagues (2006) investigated the effect of monitoring exercises on calibration and the academic performance of education psychology students. Students completed weekly monitoring exercises. The monitoring exercises asked students to reflect on their understanding, identify areas of the learning they had found more difficult and describe what they were going to do to improve their understanding of these areas. Students also answered three multiple choice questions, rating their confidence in the answers on a scale of 0 (not accurate) to 100 (accurate). The answers to the multiple-choice questions were discussed and students were asked to reflect on the accuracy of their confidence judgements. The effectiveness of the monitoring exercises was assessed by four tests containing multiple-choice questions with confidence judgements and the results compared to a second group of students who had the same classes but did not complete the monitoring exercises. The study found that the group who completed the monitoring exercises achieved significantly better results in the second and subsequent multiple-choice tests, suggesting that the monitoring exercises took about a month for an improvement to be observed but that this improvement was maintained throughout the course.

My experience: I teach science at secondary level. When my students complete an end-of-topic test, they also complete an exam wrapper. Exam wrappers are worksheets containing reflective questions that help learners to review their performance in a test or exam (Cambridge Assessment, 2023). In my class, students complete the first part of the exam wrapper directly after they finish their test. This part includes questions on the topic, how they prepared for the test and a relative confidence judgement. More information about the specific questions asked can be found in Table 4.2. The second part of the test review sheet asks students to reflect on the accuracy of their confidence judgement and set targets for the next topic.

Table 4.2 Exam wrapper questions

Questions completed directly after the test	• On a scale of 1 (easy) to 5 (difficult), how did you find this topic? • Describe something you found more difficult to understand. • What would you like to know more about? • How much revision did you do for the test? • How did you revise? • Which questions do you think you have answered well? • Which questions do you think you lost most marks on?
Questions completed after the test has been marked	• Are you happy with your test result? • Did you correctly identify the questions you answered well and those you lost marks on? • What do you think your target should be for the next topic?

Asking students to complete the first part of the test review sheet directly after the test captures students' immediate reactions to the test and the topic as a whole. It also provides a more detailed account of their revision because it is fresh in their mind. Information about their revision allows me to provide them with feedback on their revision strategies; this is feedback at the self-regulation level. It is also possible to use the relative confidence judgements to assess their calibration.

Completing the second part of the exam wrapper after the tests have been marked and returned provides students with feedback on their calibration. They can use their marks to see if they correctly identified the questions they had answered well and badly. They can then use all this information to set targets for the next topic.

Research has also been carried out on other ways to improve calibration accuracy. One of these, which is easy to apply to classroom practice, is to use collaboration between students (Winne & Azevedo, 2014). This may be because working with other students allows them to compare their performance, enabling them to better judge how well they are doing.

All the above methods improve calibration accuracy, and will enable students to identify the areas of the course where they need to improve. However, in order to improve they need to know about how they learn and the most effective study skills to use.

Teaching students how to learn

A lot of research has been done into effective study strategies. Dunlosky (2013) reviewed the research behind 10 techniques that are commonly used by students. His findings are set out in Table 4.3.

Table 4.3 Effectiveness of different study techniques (adapted from Dunlosky, 2013)

Technique	What is it?	How effective is it?
Practice testing	Self-testing of facts being learned	Very effective under a wide range of conditions
Distributed practice	Spreading out study activities over time	
Interleaved practice	Mixing different kinds of material in one study period	Promising but needs more work
Elaborative interrogation	Generating explanations for facts being learned	
Self-explanation	Explaining steps in a procedure or how facts are related to each other	
Rereading	Reading study materials again	Not as effective as other strategies
Highlighting and underlining	Identifying key ideas while reading	
Summarisation	Condensing information being learned	Difficult to do effectively
Keyword mnemonic	Associating an image with a particular word	Effectiveness limited to a small number of situations
Imagery for text	Associating an image with longer text being learned	

There are many reasons why students do not use the more effective study techniques (i.e., practice testing and distributed practice). One reason is that these techniques make students more uncomfortable because they highlight the areas that they do not know. It means that when testing themselves, students feel that they have learned less than they did having reread or highlighted their notes. The benefit of these effective study techniques is only apparent after some time has passed.

So how can we get students to adopt more effective study skills? The Education Endowment Foundation (EEF) has reviewed the evidence for teaching study skills and metacognition more broadly and recommends the following seven-step model: (1) activating prior knowledge, (2) explicit strategy instruction, (3) modelling of learned strategy, (4) memorisation of the strategy, (5) guided practice, (6) independent practice and (7) structured reflection (Quigley et al., 2018).

Prior knowledge can be activated when teaching study skills by asking students to reflect on the techniques they are currently using. This is particularly effective when done after an assessment, when students can see that their previous study strategies are no longer sufficiently effective.

Explicit strategy instruction involves not only describing the strategy used but also explaining why it is the best choice in the specific circumstances. This type of strategy instruction is much less common than implicit strategy instruction, which simply involves describing the strategy, but it has a much greater impact (Kistner et al., 2010). In terms of teaching study skills, explicit instruction might involve linking the strategies to the particular demands of a subject (e.g., for subjects that require a lot of application of knowledge, memorising facts is not sufficient and practising exam questions is essential), or it might involve explaining some of the science of learning to students. I take two approaches with my students. With older students, I provide them with the evidence from research that shows that these techniques are effective in the long term but will not necessarily feel as if they are working straight away. I also use resources from the Learning Scientists (2016) that explain how to use all of the strategies. For younger students, I use the analogy of tidying a wardrobe, which is suggested by Tricia Taylor (2020: 129): 'Retrieval practice is like tidying a wardrobe. Each time you open the wardrobe to look for something you tidy it up a bit. This makes it easier to find things next time. It's the same with memory. Each time you retrieve a memory, it makes it easier to retrieve it next time.'

As well as teaching the strategy, its use needs to be modelled. This is particularly important with younger students, who might be using the technique for the first time. Flashcards provide an illustration of the benefits of modelling. If students are simply told to use flashcards, they may just summarise their notes on the flashcard and then reread this to prepare for a test; summarising and rereading are study strategies with limited effectiveness. Teacher modelling can show students how to prepare flashcards with a question on one side and answer on the other. It can also demonstrate self-testing using flashcards by answering out loud before checking. Modelling can also be used to show the Leitner method of dividing cards into those which were answered correctly and can therefore be revisited less frequently and those which were answered incorrectly and therefore need to be revisited every day. Astolfi (2020) describes how she guides her students to use flashcards effectively.

Students should complete guided practice with the study strategy being taught. Initially, this should be done during a lesson so that the teacher can provide immediate feedback. As time goes by and students start to move into independent practice, it is still important to monitor their use. I do this in two different ways. The first is the exam wrappers described earlier in this chapter. The reflection sheets ask students to describe how they revised for a test and allow me to monitor and provide feedback. The second is to ask students to record the independent work that they do each week. I periodically review this information and can intervene if they are not using effective strategies.

Once again, let us look at a couple of examples of this process: one comes from a research paper and the second comes from my own classroom research into teaching study skills to year 12 chemistry students.

The research paper: Zhao et al. (2014) conducted a study on undergraduate chemistry students. The aim of the intervention was to help students to gauge and improve their learning strategies through metacognition. After their first exam on the course, students were given a lecture about metacognition and study skills. The timing of the lecture was chosen because it is at this point that students realise that their current strategies are not working well enough. After this initial instruction, students were given repeated reminders about the effective strategies throughout the semester. Workload made it challenging for students to complete all the work recommended, but the study did show an increase in the adoption of effective study strategies. The performance of the students on their end-of-course exams was better than previous cohorts (after similar performance at the start of the course), although it was not reflected in improved confidence in chemistry.

My experience: Three years ago, I carried out some classroom research on using metacognition to improve students' study skills (Mountstevens, 2020). Students studying A-level chemistry were divided into intervention and control groups. All groups had four 30-minute lunchtime sessions. The sessions were based on particular content they had learned during chemistry lessons. The comparison group completed exam questions on this topic and the intervention group learned a relevant study strategy (see Table 4.4). The format of the intervention sessions was:

1 Explicit instruction and modelling of the strategy.
2 Students applying the strategy.
3 Reflection on metacognitive prompts (e.g., what strategies did you use? What independent work would best allow you to improve?)

Table 4.4 Session content and metacognitive skill

Session	Content	Strategy
1	Mole calculations	Students were taught a problem-solving process (problem, parts, prior knowledge, proceed, post-mortem) and discussed different mathematical problem-solving techniques. They applied the techniques to mole calculations.
2	Ionic compounds	Students were presented with some of the evidence on retrieval practice and its challenges. They applied retrieval practice techniques to memorising the colours of precipitates.
3	Organic chemistry	A concept map was modelled, highlighting the importance of the connections between the items of information and students then completed their own.
4	Enthalpy experiments	Students were taught about the techniques of elaborative interrogation (why is this true?) and self-explanation (how does this link to what I already know?) (Dunlosky, 2013). They worked in pairs, asking each other these questions while they completed an enthalpy calculation.

Switching lunchtime sessions from exam questions to metacognitive discussions had a small positive effect on academic performance and a slightly larger effect on study skills. A possible mechanism for this change was that the sessions improved the effectiveness of independent work, which led to better academic performance. I also saw an improvement in students' calibration, so another possible mechanism is that students were better able to identify their strengths and weaknesses and prioritise their independent work.

Both the research paper and my own small-scale research suggest that it is possible to improve students' study skills by providing them with information about effective strategies and taking a metacognitive approach by asking them to reflect on how to apply these strategies.

Ideas for the Classroom

- Provide opportunities for students to reflect on their understanding. This can take the form of (1) exam wrappers after tests or assessments and/or (2) confidence judgements on classroom activities or retrieval questions.
- Give students feedback on the work they have reflected on that shows how well they are doing and their strengths and weaknesses.
- Support students to compare their reflections and the feedback they receive so that their calibration improves and they become better at judging their own learning.
- Explicitly teach students about effective study strategies by modelling the strategy and explaining why it is important to use ideas from the science of learning.
- Give students time to practise their study strategies in lessons.
- Monitor whether students are using effective study strategies by using exam wrappers or independent work logs.
- Provide students with feedback on their study strategies to support them to make effective choices.

Further Reading

For background information on exam wrappers:

Cambridge Assessment (2023). *Getting started with metacognition.* Available at: https://cambridge-community.org.uk/professional-development/gswmeta/index.html

For a summary of the different levels of feedback:

Fletcher-Wood, H. (2017). *What kind of feedback moves students on.* Available at: https://improvingteaching.co.uk/2017/11/05/what-kind-of-feedback-moves-students-on/

This is a good research paper on improving calibration:

Nietfeld, J., Cao, L., & Osborne, J. W. (2006). The effect of distributed monitoring exercises and feedback on performance, monitoring accuracy, and self-efficacy. *Metacognition and Learning, 1*, 159–179.

For a summary of the research into study strategies:

Dunlosky, J. (2013). Strengthening the student toolbox: Study strategies to boost learning. *American Educator, 37*(3), 12–21. Available at: https://files.eric.ed.gov/fulltext/EJ1021069.pdf

This is the Education Endowment Foundation's guidance report on metacognition:

Quigley, A., Muijs, D., & Stringer, E. (2018). *Metacognition and self-regulated learning guidance report*. EEF. Available at: https://educationendowmentfoundation.org.uk/education-evidence/guidance-reports/metacognition

For information on study skills that can be shared with students:

Learning Scientists (2016). *Six strategies for effective learning*. Available at: www.learningscientists.org/blog/2016/8/18-1

This is a good research article on teaching study skills:

Zhao, N., Wardeska, J. G., McGuire, S. Y., & Cook, E. (2014). Metacognition: An effective tool to promote success in college science learning. *Journal of College Science Teaching, 43*(4), 48–54.

This is an excellent example of how to teach students to use flashcards effectively:

Astolfi, C.(2020). Physics revision: How to guide students to write and use effective flashcards. *Impact, 10*, 26–27.

For my own work on teaching study skills:

Mountstevens, E. (2020). A metacognitive approach to improving academic performance and study skills in sixth form students. *Impact, 8*, 74–77.

References

Kistner, S., Rakoczy, K., Otto, B., Dignath-van Ewijk, C., Büttner, G., & Klieme, E. (2010) Promotion of self-regulated learning in classrooms: Investigating frequency, quality, and consequences for student performance. *Metacognition Learning, 5*(2), 157–171.

Mathebathe, K. C., & Potgieter, M. (2014). Metacognitive monitoring and learning gain in foundation chemistry. *Chemistry Education Research and Practice, 15*, 94–104.

Oakes, S., & Griffin, M. (2021). *The A level mindset – revised edition. 40 activities for transforming student commitment, motivation and productivity*. Carmarthen: Crown House.

Taylor, T. (2020). *Connect the dots*. Woodbridge, UK: John Catt.

Winne, P., & Azevedo, R. (2014). Metacognition. In R. Sawyer (Ed.), *The Cambridge handbook of the learning sciences* (pp. 63–87). Cambridge: Cambridge University Press.

5

Revision and Metacognition

Katie Holmes

An Educational Issue

Without explicit teaching, students often lack the skills and understanding when it comes to independent work, whether it's in class, during controlled assessment, when revising or doing home learning. Our students have reported that they struggle to concentrate, give up quickly when the work is challenging, and when at home become reliant on searching for the answer on the internet.

Very often we set students tasks to do at home, such as completing revision on the topic we have covered during the current term or revising for an upcoming assessment. But how confident are we as teachers that what our students are doing in their own time is effective? Do our students know how to complete the task you have set them? Are they working smarter, not harder?

Students often have a very negative perception of revision and home learning, referring to exams as stressful and hard, and to revision as boring (Howell & McGill, 2022). This is not necessarily because students don't have the ambition to do well, but simply because they do not know how to revise and work independently or because the methods that they have previously used were ineffective, so they see revision as a waste of time.

We need to think how, as educators, we can raise the profile of effective revision that can engage and support students towards independent study, not just from year 11 but from the start of their journey in secondary school, from year 7 onwards. We need to be able to motivate students to want to work independently and to want to strive to be the best they can be. By ensuring that the independent study students are doing is effective, we can improve student motivation and help them to become the best learners they can be.

There is not a 'one size fits all' approach for this, different methods suit students differently. We need to provide opportunities for students to discover which ways work for them and which ways do not. Without providing these opportunities for students, how are students going to understand how to work independently effectively? By modelling how to revise using different methods and modelling the thought process and thinking behind approaching tasks independently, we can begin to build students' confidence to work independently.

In this chapter, I will focus on revision strategies and skills that can be used both inside and outside the classroom. I will show how they can be embedded through a tutor-time curriculum. The core revision strategies I present can be applied by both staff and students in lessons and at home.

Your Approach

Students spend on average between two and three hours a week in tutor time. This is a significant amount of time that teachers can be using to tackle this key educational issue. I want you to think: How are you currently using this time? Can you use this time to help embed fundamental skills that will help prepare students to work independently?

By embedding time into the tutor-time curriculum, you can cover vital areas that will help students to become independent learners who can think metacognitively. This can include: how their memory works, how they can strengthen their memory, key revision strategies and how they can use them effectively, how to manage their time, and how to deal with the pressure of exams. Covering these areas will increase students' metacognitive thinking about how they approach independent work and revision. Students will learn how to select strategies that are best suited for them and will be encouraged to reflect on their learning process and progress. All of this can be applied across all year groups and subjects.

The Metacognitive Approach

Passive versus active revision

As teachers, we know that during curriculum time, when planning schemes of work, we embed end-of-topic or end-of-unit assessments throughout the year. Before these assessments, we will typically ask the students to prepare for them by revising in their own time.

One of the questions I want you to consider is: How confident are you that when a student goes home to revise for an upcoming test or assessment, they are completing the revision task effectively? The work that they do at home needs to promote active recall (Owen, 2022), so that students retain what they are learning and strengthen their long-term memory.

Is students' revision work promoting what we call 'active recall'? Or are they undertaking passive activities? If their revision is passive, it is going to have little benefit on the information they retain during their revision time (Dunlosky et al., 2013).

Defining 'passive' and 'active' revision

Students need to understand how to use their time effectively. We want students to move away from last-minute cramming and to understand the purpose of effective revision strategies and how to space and interleave revision (Webb, 2019). It is important that students are also aware of what passive revision is, and why this should be avoided.

> **Passive revision** often includes methods such as rereading, highlighting and rewriting (Howell & McGill, 2022: 65–66). While these methods can provide exposure to information, the lack of engagement and interaction with the information means that these strategies lack opportunities for active practice and the application of knowledge (Parent Guide to GCSE, n.d.).

> **Active revision** involves students actively engaging with material through a variety of different methods which require deeper thinking and application (Boyle et al., 2020). Examples of these methods are using flashcards, self-quizzing, brain dumps and mind maps (Howell & McGill, 2022: 68–81). These active revision methods, which focus more on processing and applying knowledge, deepen an individual's understanding of the material and strengthens their long-term memory.

When and how to use active revision?

It is important to think about how you can build active revision into curriculum time. Time for students to practise effective revision and for teachers to model the correct way to use revision strategies is vital for their understanding. Allocating revision time should not start a few weeks before students take their GCSEs. It is something that we should embed into the curriculum at the start of year 7, and continue throughout students' time at school. When students sit their GCSEs or A levels, they ought to be equipped with the study skills and independent learning habits that are required to complete successful revision.

Teachers are often reluctant to build revision techniques into curriculum time due to worries about an already-packed curriculum or because it eats into time spent on their own subject areas (Howell & McGill, 2022: 15). However, if you want students to retain information over long periods of time, to feel prepared and confident for exams and assessments, then it is important to build time to study and to model revision strategies into the curriculum. Teaching active revision skills can be implemented in many ways, such as through bell tasks, whole-class activities, pair work, or the teacher modelling and then monitoring independent revision within lesson time. As an example:

> During the lesson you can model to students how to use their knowledge organiser to create self-quizzing questions. You can use the 'I do, we do, you do' schema to do this. You can then ask students to create six self-quizzing questions and answers for home learning. The bell task in the following lesson can be for the student to answer their questions and check their answers, or to swap questions with a partner and answer their questions and then check the answers.

> In this way, the teacher is guiding the students on how to use a revision technique in a supportive way that they understand. Over time, as you build such exercises into your routines, there will become a point when students are capable of following all the steps independently at home as a revision strategy.

Why use active revision techniques?

Students need the security to know that what they are doing is beneficial and will lead to success. By modelling revision techniques, you can be more confident that students are using their time effectively.

Students are often more inclined to choose the less effective strategies when revising (Dunlosky et al., 2013), such as highlighting, rewriting and rereading, because they are passive strategies. Students feel more secure with these strategies because they are not having to think too hard. Furthermore, there is less chance that students will get a sense of failure using these strategies because they are not actively having to generate answers, so there is no opportunity to get something wrong. By encouraging students to use active strategies, and modelling them to students, you will support students to become more confident using active methods of revision. In turn, you will be promoting a culture where students are not afraid of getting something wrong, but rather they will see it as a way of addressing gaps in their knowledge in order to move forward.

Four Core Revision Strategies

What are the four core revision strategies?

It is important that students understand how to revise and are taught methods that are easy to follow, so that they can be used effectively and without confusion. Strategies that can be applied across a range of subjects are also extremely helpful. Simply telling students to revise is not enough. You need to provide clear instructions about independent learning and the revision tasks you set students. You need to be confident that they can select the right strategies (i.e., the active strategies), and can use them effectively. There are four core revision strategies which fulfil these criteria: flashcards, brain dumps, mind maps and self-quizzing (Gill, 2022: S1).

When and how do we use the four core revision strategies?

Having named the four core revision strategies, now we need to consider when and how these strategies can be applied to all the groups across many subjects. First, it is important that all the staff across the whole school deliver the same, consistent message on what strategies to use and how to use them. This can be achieved through tutor time and lesson time, as well as through the curriculum. The more these strategies are used in lessons across the different subjects, the more practice students get in using them, the more permanent they will become, and thus the more confident students will be when using them.

You may also want to think about when other subjects are using the core revision strategies and actually plan them into the curriculum time. For example, you can work with other faculties and plan to use the same strategies at the same period of time. This will mean that students are using the same strategy but applying it to different content and subjects at the same time, therefore increasing their exposure to the strategy, consolidating their expertise in using it, and improving the embedding of the new revision strategies.

Why do we use the four core revision strategies?

Having core revision strategies can be beneficial for students in a number of ways:

- **Consistency**: Having a set of core revision strategies ensures that all students receive consistent guidance and support. It eliminates any potential inconsistencies in teaching methods and ensures that students have a common framework to use. It provides clarity when discussing revision, thus improving the learning experience for all students.
- **Equity and inclusion**: Implementing the core revision strategies ensures that all students, regardless of their backgrounds and abilities, can access these revision techniques. The concise five-step method approach, inspired by the format in the *Teaching WalkThrus* book and the work of Tom Sherrington and Oliver Caviglioli (2020), is a good template to follow. Thus, helping to level the playing field, benefiting all students, regardless of ability or learning needs, and ensuring that every student has an opportunity to succeed.
- **Clarity and simplicity**: From experience, students can often feel overwhelmed when it comes to revision, mainly because they don't know where to start and there are too many different ways to revise. Mastering the four core strategies

gives students clarity about what is expected of them when revising and working independently.

- **Improved outcomes**: Implementing the core revision strategies over a longer period of time leads to improved outcomes for students (Benjamin, 2023). By providing students with effective tools and techniques, they are better equipped to review and consolidate their knowledge. They are able to reflect on their learning and think metacognitively, leading to increased retention and understanding of content. In turn, it should result in improved performance in exams and assignments, and reduced anxiety and stress regarding exams and revision (Inner Drive, n.d.).

Putting the Core Revision Strategies into Action

Flashcards

The first thing for students to understand is that creating flashcards isn't revision, and that it is important that the flashcards are used properly to promote active recall (Jones, 2019: 140–143). One of the most common outcomes is that students spend more time making the flashcards than using them. And when the flashcards are being used, they are not being used effectively.

So how should students use flashcards in a way that will promote active recall? They need to say out loud, or write down, what is on the flashcard, before checking their answer (Jones, 2019: 140–143). More often than not, students will say the answer in their head, or look at the answer before thinking of it and say/think 'oh yes, that's what I was going to say', but have they said it? Do they actually know that if they had to put pen to paper and write down the answer or say it out loud that is still what they would say? Unless students engage with the question and think hard to recall the answer or to write it down, as they would in an assessment, the exercise will not give them an accurate representation of the knowledge stored in their long-term memory.

Creating flashcards can be an activity done in class. As a class activity, the teacher is able to demonstrate how to do it as a home learning task. It is also important to provide class time for students to learn how to use them properly, so again, they know how to do this effectively. The active recall and the hard thinking must be the priority when using flashcards. You could do this in an activity in the classroom, for example in pairs. One student reads the question out and the other student answers it. If students are using flashcards independently, they can number the flashcards, write the answers down in turn and then only check their answers once they have answered all the flashcards. It is important that students do not just visit the flashcards a couple of days before the exam, or even make them a couple of days before the exam. You want to encourage students to be regularly making flashcards as they complete topics so that when it comes to assessment, they are already made and are a ready-to-use revision tool.

Students should always answer a flashcard at least three times before moving on, and this exercise needs to be done regularly. For example, using the Leitner box system will allow students to use spaced retrieval by visiting the flashcards over a number of days, allowing them to return to the questions they frequently get wrong rather than the ones they answer correctly (Jones, 2019: 143). With flashcards being simple and easy to follow, it is also something that students can use at home by asking someone else to quiz them. As clear and concise answers are already supplied on the reverse, the other person does not need any knowledge on the subject to be able to help the student with the revision.

Brain dumps

Brain dumps engage students in a type of retrieval practice, allowing them to actively retrieve information from their long-term memory and to consolidate knowledge. The purpose of a brain dump exercise is for students to write down as much relevant information as they can on a subject, including concepts, formulas and key points about a specific topic or subject (Agarwal & Bain, 2019: 56–61). But to be an effective revision aid, it is important that there is absolute clarity on what students should be writing down and that students understand the task before starting.

Brain dumping helps students to reinforce their understanding of the topic they are covering and to identify knowledge gaps. Students need to understand that brain dumps are meant to be quick and comprehensive; students do not need to worry about making their writing perfect. The effectiveness of completing this revision technique is about the process of actively recalling and summarising the information from memory so that students can visually see exactly what they can recall from memory and where the gaps in their knowledge lie.

Mind maps

Mind maps are a visual representation of information, helping students to create a mental image of concepts and relationships (Blunt & Karpicke, 2014). When students are creating mind maps, they are actively visualising the information, which is going to enhance their ability to recall it later on. Although this strategy involves the least amount of active recall, it's an effective way for students to organise their thoughts and revise information, which in turn can help them to identify gaps and prioritise further revision.

Students can create effective mind maps independently. They can begin by selecting a topic or subject that they want to revise, for example, a specific subject like English, or a particular topic, for example, *Romeo and Juliet*. Students write the main topic in the centre of their page and begin their mind map by drawing main branches out from the central topic. These represent different subtopics that are related to the central topic in the middle of the page.

For example, if students were creating a mind map on *Romeo and Juliet*, they can identify different subtopics such as the different acts within the play, the characters and the key themes. This is all crucial information that students need to know about the topic.

From each of these subtopics, students can branch off in further detail. For instance, under characters, students can create further branches listing all the main characters, and add other branches for descriptions or key details that they need to know about the characters.

An effective mind map refrains from using too much writing and using long sentences. The note-like form makes the information easier to recall and more memorable. As students add further information to their mind map, they can also connect and link ideas by drawing lines. This shows the relationship between different pieces of information and illustrates to the student how they are connected. For example, students may draw a line linking the characters to the acts that they appear in, or from the act to the key theme.

Once students have created a mind map, they can review it to ensure that they haven't missed any important information by comparing it to their knowledge organiser. When it comes to using the mind map for revision, it can be used as a visual guide to help recall information, to jog the student's memory and to reinforce their understanding of the subject. If students create a mind map on a full topic, they can also use it for reflection to 'RAG rate' their understanding on the content, so that they can prioritise what they need to revise further.

By engaging in the process of creating and reviewing mind maps, students are actively retrieving and reinforcing the information into their long-term memory, making it more likely to be retained and easily recalled when required.

Self-quizzing

Self-quizzing can encourage metacognitive thinking by allowing students to reflect on their thinking and their learning processes. It can be done with or without knowledge resources (Howell & McGill, 2022: 72–74), in class or at home as independent learning. Students can create their own practice questions or use online platforms or questions already prepared by teachers. The self-quizzing technique allows students to reflect on their performance, so that they can gain an insight into their strengths and weaknesses on a topic. Self-quizzing can also be used to replicate the conditions of an actual test or exam, and so by practising with quizzes, students become more familiar with the format of assessment, the structure and types of questions that they may encounter in an exam. As another revision strategy that helps students to assess their understanding, self-quizzing is a useful tool to highlight gaps in their knowledge, indicating what they need to review further. It therefore helps them to prioritise their future revision topics.

Self-quizzing can be teacher-led or student-driven. This revision strategy starts with the student identifying the knowledge that they want to quiz themselves on. Students can use knowledge organisers, textbooks or other materials to help them generate questions. However, it is important that they are able to identify the correct answer easily. When I use this strategy with students, I recommend that they create both the questions and the answers so that they can quickly check their own answers in future without having to waste time. If you give students knowledge organisers at the start of the topic, it can be used to create banks of questions that students can refer to alongside the knowledge organiser.

Self-quizzing is based on using a knowledge organiser. The students spend around 5–10 minutes reviewing the content of a topic and create 10 questions based on this content. Students then cover up the knowledge organiser and answer the questions from memory. You need to be careful here, because if students have only just written the questions, they are not retrieving the information from their long-term memory – they are only retrieving from working memory, which is less effective. It is important that students attempt all of the questions and take their time in writing down their answers. Once all the questions have been answered, students can go back to the content and self-mark their answers in a different coloured pen, allowing them to see what they have got right and where the gaps in their knowledge lie. The final stage of the process is crucial because it ensures that students review their knowledge and revisit the areas in which they have gaps. Any questions they did not answer correctly should be revisited next time they do a self-quiz. For example, if a student answers five out of 10 questions correctly, the five questions they could not answer correctly would be repeated in exactly the same way on their next quiz (Howell & McGill, 2022: 73).

Self-quizzing is a highly effective study technique which helps to increase memory retention, promote active recall and develop metacognitive skills. By incorporating regular self-quizzing into revision routines, students can build effective study habits, enhancing their understanding, identifying knowledge gaps and strengthening their long-term memory (Owen, 2022).

Tutor Time

What is tutor time?

Tutor time provides an opportunity to create a curriculum where these strategies can be taught and embedded. The curriculum should ensure that students develop a knowledge of a range of different strategies, including which strategies work best, and when and how to incorporate them into successful independent learning. The curriculum can be mapped over a number of years, but ideally it should start as early as possible. Starting the curriculum in year 7 and working through to year 13 is going to be most beneficial for students. As Doug Lemov states, practice does not always make perfect, but it does make permanent (Lemov et al., 2012). By making time for students to understand how their memory works, how they can effectively learn and consolidate knowledge, and giving them time to practise revision strategies, it is more likely that students will develop effective study habits. I recommend a curriculum that is developmental over the years, where students are exposed to the same information in different ways, but also to new information that is beneficial to the current situation within education. For example, a tailored year 11 programme that would run in the term before mock exams would focus on creating revision timetables, prioritising revision, dealing with exam stress and coping with a bad exam experience.

When and how to use tutor time?

There are many ways that revision strategies can be implemented in the tutor time curriculum. While there are many other statutory requirements that need to be covered in tutor time, not all teachers will have consistent time allocated throughout the year. It's also a big job for staff to plan as it is a curriculum which is developed throughout all years. So, it's important to consider when you think this should be delivered to students and how often it needs to be delivered for it to be beneficial.

An example of how this can be run is through a termly curriculum plan, in which all students are delivered one term's worth of sessions once a week, which equates to around 12 sessions. These sessions can primarily focus on providing students with information on effective study habits and independent learning, and allowing students to reflect on how they work independently and how they can improve their study habits to become more effective. But students also need time to practise what you are teaching them. For example, if a revision strategy is being taught in one of the curriculum sessions, not only do you need to model it to the students, but they also need to be given time to practise the techniques before being expected to use them independently at home. Therefore, it is necessary to allocate a separate amount of time every week during tutor time for students to work independently. This will also provide time for tutors to have one-on-one discussions with students about their revision – what's going well and what they need support with – and to promote more discussion about independent learning and their methods of revision to get students talking and thinking about them.

However, all this being said, it is also important that tutors are aware of the content they are delivering and are able to effectively communicate a consistent message to students. One way to achieve this is to voice-record PowerPoints so that there is less reliance on the individual tutor delivering the sessions and all students receive the same, consistent message. In this scenario, tutors can instead concentrate on facilitating discussions and activities, which also happen in the tutor-time sessions. Nevertheless, tutors do need to know and understand the content of these PowerPoint sessions, so staff need effective training regarding what students will be learning in the tutor time curriculum. In this way, they can do their best to support their tutees. Furthermore, knowledge of the curriculum will support tutors to embed these strategies in their own teaching, which will further support student understanding of how to use these strategies in alternative contexts.

Why do we use tutor time?

All teachers want their students to learn – it's our goal in the classroom. We want students to be able to feel confident in what they have been taught in lessons, to be able to ask questions if they don't understand and to know what steps to take following the lesson to consolidate their knowledge and check their understanding independently. As teachers, we want to be confident that students are selecting the right strategies outside lessons and using their time effectively when working independently. By modelling these revision strategies in lessons and during tutor time, and providing time for students to practise them, we are equipping students with valuable techniques for independent study, such as reviewing, testing and refining their knowledge. Through modelling, these students gain an insight into how they can improve their work effectively. Students can observe how teachers identify strengths and weaknesses in their work, how they identify gaps in their knowledge, and how the process moves forward. In this way, students become more aware of the thinking and learning process, which in turn develops their metacognitive abilities (Webb, 2021: 31).

Revision is an essential part of the learning process. It helps students to strengthen the schemas in their long-term memory (Webb, 2021: 21). It allows students to learn from their mistakes and to understand that failure, and getting things wrong, is actually a crucial part within the learning process. If students lack resilience to failure, they are likely to hesitate to engage in particular topics and content, sticking to what they know and feel comfortable with so that they feel that sense of success. However, it is the content that students don't know which they really need to focus on. If they can develop a growth mindset by learning from mistakes, students will be much more likely to challenge themselves further.

Developing study habits is just as important as learning study strategies. There are going to be times when students know what to do and they know how to do it, but they struggle to create the right environment that allows them to work productively with minal distractions. It's important to look at these areas and to discuss how effective habits and environments can help to promote effective learning, such as by reducing distractions, creating the right environment to study and organising their time productively. A lot of pressure is put on students with regards to performance in exams, and so teachers need to provide students with ways of dealing with the pressure, and guide them in what to do if an exam didn't go as planned. Inner Drive is an organisation that researches effective learning techniques. They provide many resources that promote good study habits and effective learning and publish research and blogs on these topics (see their website at www.innerdrive.co.uk).

Figure 5.1 provides an example of an outline of a tutor time curriculum that addresses memory, study skills and study habits. All year groups start with sessions about memory and how important it is. It's vital, through the delivery of the curriculum, that students understand why they are doing something and the benefits that it is going to have. When students understand the purpose, they are more likely to be motivated to carry out what you are asking of them (Wentzel & Brophy, 2013: 217–246).

Figure 5.1 An outline of a tutor time curriculum

	Year 7	Year 8	Year 9	Year 10	Year 11	Year 12	Year 13
Session 1	How does our memory work	How does our memory work	How does our memory work	CLT and the forgetting pit	Common questions that we want to answer	Metacognition and how memory works	Monitoring progress
Session 2	Why is it important to improve memory	How can you improve your memory	The learning brain	Improving long-term memory	Mindset – the psychological benefits of mock exams	Mindset	Spaced and retrieval practice
Session 3	Independent learning strategy 1 – Knowledge organisers & why we need them	Reading strategies	15 ways to improve memory	Improving mindset and practical optimism	Independent learning strategies 1 – Using flashcards for retrieval	Habit creations and common mistakes	Interleaving and dual coding
Session 4	Using knowledge organisers	Independent learning strategy 1 – Self-quizzing & knowledge organisers	Independent learning strategy 1 – How to create flashcards	Independent learning strategy 1 – How to create flashcards	Independent learning strategies 2 – Using past exam papers	Independent learning strategies – Cornell Notes & Reflection	Organising and managing learning effectively
Session 5	Reading strategies	Independent learning strategy 2 – Reflection strategies	Independent learning strategy 2 – Self-quizzing	Independent learning strategy 1 – How to use flashcards (Leitner system)	9 ways to manage revision stress	Independent learning strategies – Reading strategies	Preparing for exams and building up to the exam period
Session 6	Motivation	Motivation	Independent learning strategy 2 – Self quizzing	Reflection & self quizzing	Habit creations	Managing revision and revising smarter	Plenary session

1/2 Term 1

Session 7	Studying with the brain in mind – Multitasking	Studying with the brain in mind – Procrastination and learning environments	Organise and effectively manage learning
Session 8	Studying with the brain in mind – Sleep and music	Studying with the brain in mind – handling stress	Monitoring progress
Session 9	Independent learning strategy 3 – Mind maps	Independent learning strategy 2 – Brain dumps	Revision timetables
Session 10	Independent learning strategy 3 – Mind maps	Revision timetables	Building up the exam period
Session 11	How to revise	Revision timetables	Retrieval practice questions
Session 12	Plenary session	Plenary session	Plenary session

1/2 Term 2

Ideas for the Classroom

- Review your schemes of work and the timings of assessments. Consider what you are doing to prepare the students for these assessments other than teaching them the content and applying it. If you can, build in time that focuses on revising the content you have taught, and plan the time to model effective revision strategies.
- Think about the revision strategies you are currently using to guide your students. Are all strategies clear for the students to understand and are you certain that the students are using them effectively?
- Make the strategies that you expect your students to be using clear and concise.
- Build in time for students to reflect on their knowledge during lessons, and help them to prioritise their own revision, helping to ensure that students revise what they ought to and not just what is easy.
- Review how tutor time is currently spent. Could you be doing something more beneficial? Think about how you can use the tutor time curriculum to embed whole-school revision strategies and create effective habits around independent learning and developing metacognitive learners.
- One of the most important points is to model effective study strategies to students. Ensure that you are taking the time to model these strategies to students and give students the time to implement these new skills.

Further Reading

When looking for strategies to apply in the classroom, Kate Jones' books on retrieval practice are full of great ideas on how to use different activities to promote active recall in the classroom:

Jones, K. (2021). *Retrieval practice: Resource guide: Ideas & activities for the classroom.* Woodbridge, UK: John Catt.

Dunlosky's strengthening the student toolbox in action is a book that gets you thinking about effective revision strategies versus ineffective revision strategies, along with the learning memory model:

Gill, A. S. (2022). *Dunlosky's strengthening the student toolbox in action.* Woodbridge, UK: John Catt.

The revision revolution is full of ideas on creating an effective revision culture in school, and shows how to implement it in curriculum time:

Howell, H., & McGill, R. M. (2022). *The revision revolution: How to build a culture of effective study in your school.* Woodbridge, UK: John Catt.

This book is a useful guide to understanding how to use metacognitive strategies in the classroom:

Webb, J. (2021). *The metacognition handbook: A practical guide for teachers and school leaders*. Woodbridge, UK: John Catt.

The *Inner Drive* website is full of informative blogs, with clear infographic illustrations which look at study habits, how to create the right environment when revising, how to use flashcards, multi-tasking, procrastination, dealing with exam stress and much more:

Inner Drive (blogs & website): https://blog.innerdrive.co.uk/

References

Agarwal, P. K., & Bain, P. M. (2019). *Powerful teaching: Unleash the science of learning*. San Francisco, CA: Jossey-Bass.

Benjamin, Z. (2023). Revision techniques: A teacher's guide. *Structural Learning*, 24 April. Available at: www.structural-learning.com/post/revision-techniques-a-teachers-guide (accessed 3 May 2023).

Blunt, J. R., & Karpicke, J. D. (2014). Learning with retrieval-based concept mapping. *Journal of Educational Psychology, 106*(3), 849–858. doi:10.1037/a0035934.

Boyle, A. et al. (2020). *Deeper thinking*. Pilot Report February 2020. London: Education Endowment Foundation. Available at: https://educationendowmentfoundation.org.uk/projects-and-evaluation/projects/deeper-thinking (accessed 14 June 2023).

Dunlosky, J., Rawson, K. A., Marsh, E. J., Nathan, M. J., & Willingham, D. T. (2013). Improving students' learning with effective learning techniques. *Psychological Science in the Public Interest, 14*(1), 4–58. doi:10.1177/1529100612453266.

Gill, A. S. (2022). *Dunlosky's strengthening the student toolbox in action*. Woodbridge, UK: John Catt.

Howell, H., & McGill, R. M. (2022). *The revision revolution: How to build a culture of effective study in your school*. Woodbridge, UK: John Catt.

Inner Drive (n.d.). The link between test anxiety and uncertainty. *Inner Drive* [blog]. Available at: https://blog.innerdrive.co.uk/test-anxiety-and-uncertainty (accessed 9 June 2023).

Jones, K. (2019). *Retrieval practice: Research and resources for every classroom*. Woodbridge, UK: John Catt.

Lemov, D., Woolway, E., & Yezzi, K. (2012). *Practice perfect: 42 rules for getting better at getting better*. San Francisco, CA: Jossey-Bass.

Owen, M. (2022). Active recall: The most effective high-yield learning technique. *Osmosis* [blog], 21 February. Available at: www.osmosis.org/blog/2022/02/21/active-recall-the-most-effective-highyield-learning-technique (accessed 14 June 2023).

Parent Guide to GCSE (n.d.). Active vs passive revision – picking the right methods! *Parent Guide to GCSEs*. Available at: www.parentguidetogcse.com/members-area/active-vs-passive-revision-picking-the-right-methods/ (accessed 14 June 2023).

Sherrington, T., & Caviglioli, O. (2020). *Teaching WalkThrus: Five-step guides to instructional coaching*. Woodbridge, UK: John Catt.

Webb, H. (2019). Revision techniques: Interleaving and spacing. *SecEd*, 3 April. Available at: www.sec-ed.co.uk/best-practice/revision-techniques-interleaving-and-spacing/ (accessed 14 June 2023).

Webb, J. (2021). *The metacognition handbook: A practical guide for teachers and school leaders*. Woodbridge, UK: John Catt.

Wentzel, K., & Brophy, J. (2013). *Motivating students to learn*. New York: Routledge. doi: 10.4324/9780203108017-15.

6

The Role of Metacognition in the Art & Design GCSE Externally Set Assignment

Paul Carney

An Educational Issue

It is extremely difficult to draw long-term conclusions from recent trends in examination data (NSEAD, 2022), due to the impact of Covid-19 restrictions on education. From my own experiences and conversations, however, GCSE art and design teachers are reporting that it is getting harder and harder to achieve high results in the subject. There are many reasons for this: the recent addition of the higher attainment grades (Ofqual, 2018) have added increased pressure on both teachers and pupils to produce ever more highly skilled coursework at a time when curriculums are being squeezed; resources are more restricted; and students seem to arrive less prepared for secondary art education, are less resilient and less motivated (Fabian Society, 2018). Another reason, I believe, is the high-stakes accountability nature of secondary art and design education, which is resulting in more tightly controlled, teacher-led methods of teaching (NIFDI, 2023) in Key Stage 3 and early Key Stage 4.

The curriculum approach that most schools favour is the gradual release method, where pupils receive tightly-controlled tuition at the beginning of their course of study and this control is gradually relieved over time as students' expertise grows. Except, this only usually happens with a minority of higher-attaining students. Accountability is so great that schools daren't allow too much autonomy in the externally set assignments (ESA). Middle and lower attaining students are heavily directed into prescribed ESA outcomes via teacher-prepared resources and materials.

The externally set assignments in GCSE art and design examinations are, I believe, the most challenging and creative activities students undertake in the education system. The ESA constitutes 40% of the final grade and is an examination of students' ability to autonomously produce a personal and original piece of creative art, prepared over a period of approximately one term, executed in a 10-hour sustained period and produced in examination conditions. The underlying principle of the assignment is to respond independently to starting points in supervised, unaided conditions (AQA, 2015). Yet, the knock-on effect of this high level of teacher control is that students are increasingly unprepared to meet the demands of the externally set assignment at the end of Key Stage 4.

Part of the demand of this assignment is that there are no right or wrong answers to it, and every individual response is exposed and scrutinised to assessment objectives that identify how the student has applied their conceptual understanding of other artists' work, how they have experimented and creatively manipulated art materials, how they have constructed and developed an original response to the starting point and the overall quality of the final piece they have produced. What is being asked of the students during this period is the management and execution of a wide range of highly complex processes, all of which are meant to be produced independently. Students are given a choice of seven, highly demanding, open-ended questions to select from. If they have been taught well, most students should be perfectly capable of responding to any of these questions independently. After all, the ESA is such an important component of the syllabus that you can reasonably expect teachers to equip students with the knowledge and skills they need to answer it.

What happens more often than not is that students are not ready for the test. This is evident from the way teachers analyse the question paper before giving it out to students and produce lengthy, logistical analysis of how students should respond to it. This includes creating presentations, providing artist names and potential starting points, stipulating time frames and strategies for what should be completed by what date and to what level. I've worked with many secondary schools on their ESA preparation and some of the demands and expectations I've seen teachers place on their students are completely overwhelming. Their response often manifests itself in abject apathy to the assignment itself. Visit any GCSE art-related social media group during ESA season and there are always plenty of panic-stricken teachers desperately seeking support to get their students working. Too often students simply switch off, they seem disinterested and are demotivated by the whole process, rather than being inspired to create an autonomous piece of artwork.

I'd agree that much of this behaviour is because of the pressure teachers are under to get results, but it is also partly because the students are not properly prepared to respond to the ESA independently. So how might we do this better? Well, we need to analyse curriculum progression so that we can identify how pupils are progressing towards being ready to independently respond to what is arguably the most challenging aspect of the GCSE syllabus. After all, if I asked art teachers and subject leads to show me how their curriculum delivers increased knowledge and practical skills, I'd expect to be readily shown examples of plans, tables and progression maps. We should surely, then, expect similar evidence for other, equally critical components of the course.

Sadly, this is not usually the case. In recent years, the main effect of the Department for Education's and Ofsted's drive for knowledge-rich curriculums has resulted in a greater emphasis on easily visible, tangible, semantic forms of learning at the expense of less obvious, high-quality thinking and metacognition (Ofsted, 2023). Now, I don't want to undermine knowledge and skills. They are some of the component parts of high-quality curriculums and high performance in GCSE art and design. You'd rightly want your higher-attaining students to demonstrate greater knowledge and skills, after all. However, there is much more to a GCSE syllabus than this. Pupil autonomy – the freedom to produce creative outcomes that reflect their own thoughts, beliefs, ideas and experiences – is at the heart of the subject. Furthermore, it is the teacher's role to mould and shape their students' ability to exercise their thinking in ways that are original and more sophisticated. These form the the basis of the higher GCSE grade descriptors (AQA, 2015), which define high attainment as:

> Demonstrating an exceptional ability to critically understand and apply information from sources to suit purposeful, independent investigations; to thoughtfully refine ideas, and effectively select and experiment with appropriate media, materials and techniques; to record ideas relevant to intentions and present personal and meaningful responses with confidence and conviction.

Your Approach

So, if I now asked you to show me how your curriculum develops pupils' cognitive thought processes, develops their critical understanding, improves their ability to act purposefully, become independent and create art thoughtfully, and develops their ability to effectively select and record information-relevant intentions or make purposeful and meaningful responses, could you do that?

Where can I see evidence of students learning to know and understand what separates good ideas from bad ones, how to manipulate and mould their ideas for a purpose, and how to make appropriate decisions and choices when solving problems and approaching tasks?

How are pupils learning to make appropriate choices when making them? How are they learning to identify, select, edit and extract information from sources, and when they do, how do they learn to take purposeful courses of actions?

In short, where do your students learn how to think intelligently and act appropriately when they make decisions?

The Metacognitive Approach

If students have only experienced following their teacher's instructions to raise skill levels, producing literal interpretations of subject matter, or copying and mimicking, then they are not equipped to cope with the demands of the GCSE syllabus, let alone become independent, thinking artists and designers. This is why metacognition is so important. Metacognition is a thought process. It is the cognitive ability to evaluate and process relevant information that results in the most effective actions. It is higher-order thinking around how we best select, acquire, utilise and apply appropriate knowledge. In highly structured, teacher-led environments, there is limited use for this kind of thinking – metacognition becomes largely redundant. In high-attaining departments, students learn metacognitive strategies that help them to make good decisions and take appropriate actions.

Metacognition is a component of self-regulation, but whereas metacognition is a thought process, self-regulation is a broader series of actions and behaviours. So, in this chapter we are specifically looking at how to improve the thought processes that drive the potential actions students might take, rather than follow-up actions or behaviours.

Metacognition itself is split into two areas – knowledge of cognition and regulation of cognition. Knowledge of cognition is our existing level of knowledge; it is what we already know. Regulation of cognition is how we evaluate and regulate our future thinking. It refers to strategies and tasks we complete and so informs our actions. But there are significant areas of overlap and, in any case, they often link or lead into each other quite easily. To make this more accessible, then, I've related the different areas of metacognition to areas of the ESA.

Knowledge of cognition

When students are faced with answering complex questions such as those posed in the ESA, the first thing they need to do is to utilise the knowledge of cognition metacognitive strategy. Remember, this is where we get students to identify what they already know about tasks or problems such as these. The knowledge of cognition domain asks students to think and recall things they've done like this before, comprehending what it is they are being asked to do, and clarifying what alternative strategies they can use to answer it. It also asks them to be aware of their knowledge of self – what are their existing capabilities, preferences and aptitudes that they can bring to this task? These aspects of knowledge of cognition are called knowledge of self, knowledge of task and knowledge of strategy, but remember, they are derived from what students already know, which implies that students should have a firm understanding of tasks such as these prior to encountering the ESA.

- Knowledge of self – Knowing and understanding what I already know and can do in relation to a task. This should also include my own preferences and prior knowledge of successes and weaknesses when working.
- Knowledge of task – Awareness of task expectations and assessment objectives. What is the question asking me to do? What do I know about tasks like these? What is relevant or appropriate for this task, and what isn't?

- Knowledge of strategy – What is the time frame for the task? What strategies do I know that I can use to answer this task? How have I approached things like this in the past? What worked well? What stages do I need to go through or demonstrate to answer it successfully?

Knowledge of self

Knowledge of self is perhaps the most important aspect of metacognition in Key Stage 4 art & design, since so much of the syllabus is self-directed. In the ESA, you want students to work to their strengths, to demonstrate their existing aptitude and capability, and so knowledge of self is critical. Not only do you need students to be able to be self-aware of their levels of practical skill, you want them to know which artistic styles and artists they lean towards, which approaches they favour and which areas of art they work best in. You also want them to be self-aware of the levels of time and commitment they are going to give to this task, because that will determine what they can realistically achieve. If they aren't going to do any work at home or outside the lessons during the period, then their final idea should be set accordingly. Are they aware of how they like working, things that help them to work effectively, or conversely, things that distract them?

Knowledge of task

You will probably do 'mock exams' in Key Stage 4, of course, and this will go some way to preparing your students' knowledge of cognition. But, unless they are familiar with metacognitive strategies to answer ESA-style tasks, where questions are often posed as starting points, rather than necessarily being posed as a formal question, they will still struggle when faced with the ESA. A typical ESA question is little more than a starting point, but often these starting points are buried in a complex, highly technical paragraph that many find difficult to understand. For example, here's a question from the Assessment and Qualifications Alliance (AQA) externally set assignment paper from 2018:

> Artists have featured interiors in their work as the setting for stories, great events or domestic life. Vermeer painted household interiors and Hogarth used interiors as settings for moral stories. Laurie Simmons creates photographs of staged dolls' house interiors which explore ideas of gender stereotyping and Sarah Jones photographs domestic interiors to explore relationships. John Monks creates atmospheric paintings of interiors of neglected historical buildings. Heidi Bucher's work 'Skinnings' used gauze soaked in latex to make casts of interiors. Research appropriate sources and create your own response to interiors. (AQA, 2018)

First, it is not really clear what I'm being asked to do. Apart from anything, the question has a reading age of 18 years and a significant proportion of your year 11s will have a reading age of around 14 years or less (GL Assessment, 2020). As a professional, I can easily see that the main focus of the question is the final six words of the statement: 'create your own response to interiors'. But this isn't easy to isolate, let alone understand how I should do that. How do I respond? What are interiors?

Again, if students were familiar with metacognitive strategies, they would know how to look for the main focus of the question, to decipher that first, then to use dictionaries and thesauruses to better understand the language being used and what is being asked of them. They would know what a response was and how to formulate the appropriate next steps to tackle it. These aren't incidental aspects of GCSE art and design teaching – they are imperative. And what's more, they are strongly linked to skills students learn in GCSE English and history examinations. I'd strongly advise you to work with colleagues in these departments to better understand how students learn to decode and decipher examination questions in these subjects because it will help both teacher and student if cross-curricular connections can be made.

Knowledge of strategy

In my mind, knowledge of strategy is closely linked to the planning phase in the next section. The difference, however, is that at this stage of the thought process, students are considering their existing knowledge of strategy, whereas the planning phase looks at how we carry out strategies.

What I hope students know, before they even receive their ESA paper, is a range of possible ways they can approach the brief itself. For example, the way projects are approached most often is by following the design process – first, we research the brief, then we record, then we ideate, then we experiment with different solutions and materials, before finally executing our idea. The design process closely relates to the four GCSE assessment objectives I outlined earlier and that you will no doubt be familiar with. But there's no reason why we have to follow this traditional order. Your students should be familiar with the ways in which they can invert it. Instead of researching the brief first, they may begin by recording visual forms from observation, then move into investigating sources, before developing ideas and experimenting with materials. Or, they can begin by exploring materials, then by developing ideas, then observing and recording, before investigating and perhaps modifying designs further.

Students will have preferred ways of working. I myself prefer to construct an idea first, or sometimes just record from observation, to see what comes out of my studies. I'm not good at exploring and experimenting. However, other artists are, and this is the way they work. In best practice curriculums, pupils learn different ways to approach complex projects. They develop a repertoire of approaches and can adjust and vary them for purpose. It's far better that your students have prior knowledge and experience of this before they tackle the ESA, to facilitate more effective use of metacognitive, strategic thinking.

Regulation of cognition

- Planning – Planning procedures and orders of operation (do this first, then that, etc.)
- Monitoring – How much evidence do I need to provide for different aspects of the task and how much time should I spend on them? Is my strategy working? Am I on the right track?
- Evaluation – Produced after the task has been completed. Did I answer the question fully? What would I change if I were to do this again?

Once we can approach tasks with greater prior knowledge, we can begin thinking about how best to move forward in our regulatory state. Too often in the ESA, it's the classroom teacher who takes over the planning and monitoring of student performance, which is counterproductive to doing it well. The problem teachers face, of course, is that they may give students short, week-to-week deadlines coupled with a list of 'non-negotiable' tasks to complete, but too often students don't complete them and fall behind. In my experience, though, no amount of nagging and cajoling on my part makes students complete work they don't want to do.

The skill here is to only plan for what is possible and no more. Get students to make a diary of the available classroom time over the course of the ESA. Then ask them to realistically add additional time they will spend working outside the class. Finally, get students to visualise how long pieces of work take to complete. If they have 16 hours of classroom preparation time, and it takes them three hours to complete one sheet of artists' studies, then it's pointless demanding they complete four, no matter how poor you think the final grade will be as a result. If you try to demand more coursework than is possible, you will overwhelm the student and they will do nothing. The important thing is that you teach them how to do this themselves! They have to be taught how to make effective plans and how to self-monitor their own progress. They need to be able to evaluate what is essential and relevant and what isn't. They need to know how to gauge if the plans they've made are realistic in the time frame they have available or within their capabilities.

Some students also need to know when enough is enough, because very often they do a lot more than they need to, and spend longer on, say, researching than they do on developing the idea. The ability to effectively plan, monitor and evaluate your progress over time in this way is a metacognitive strategy that you have to teach from year 7 onwards, and this comes out of planning units of work that require them to plan, monitor and evaluate. It isn't something you leave until the final term of year 11, when it is too late to learn it. There's no reason why you cannot design short projects in each year of Key Stage 3 that demand sequentially more complex, independent planning.

You will, of course, be familiar with evaluation as a common art room process. It is important, and not to be undermined, but in the context of answering an externally set assignment, it isn't especially relevant because it isn't a component part of the assessment. There's no need to produce in-depth teacher assessments of the learner's ability to use metacognition, but it is useful to have a framework of performance. These have been defined as:

- Tacit – At this basic level, learners are engaged in cognitive thought processes, but they are not consciously aware of metacognitive strategies.
- Aware – Students are in the early phases of cognitive evaluation but they are still muddled and disorganised.
- Strategic – Students use implicit metacognitive strategies on a regular basis.
- Reflective – Metacognition is a conscious, organised and constant process that is used to monitor ongoing work and reflect on what has been completed.

Teachers who are most effective in implementing metacognition strategies use three fundamental principles:

1 They embed metacognitive instruction in the content matter to ensure connectivity.
2 They inform learners about the usefulness of metacognitive activities.
3 They incorporate further training to ensure the continuing application of metacognitive activities.

(Veenman et al., 2006: 9)

So, it's not enough to simply embed generic metacognitive activities. You have to teach learners why they are useful. By informing them of their purpose, you make learners exert the extra effort they need to implement them. All of this requires additional training on your part, of course. If you're going to implement metacognition into your curriculum, you will need to know and understand how to do it effectively. So look for CPD opportunities or explore ways in which you can develop metacognition in the subject.

Ideas for the Classroom

I'd like to outline a few ways in which you might incorporate metacognition in your classroom. 'Going meta' is a term coined by educator Lee Shulman (2002). It refers to the process of getting your anxieties and concerns out in the open before a difficult task begins. A small research group with maths anxiety (Ramirez & Beilock, 2011) wrote about their fears before taking a maths exam. They performed better in the exam than the group who did not first write about their fears. Identifying their concerns prior to the commencement of a task and seeing themselves as learners with certain proclivities, capabilities and aptitudes empowers students and helps them to overcome any doubts they may have.

Flow charts are diagrams that represent workflows or processes. I've used them very successfully in the past as a metacognitive tool for improving the efficiency of learners. I begin by thinking of the most common questions students ask me again and again. For example: Which materials should I work in? A flow chart can help to support students' decision-making process by providing a framework for their thought patterns. In this instance, they help students to make informed choices so that they produce artwork in materials they are most confident and capable in using. You can devise flow charts for other common problem areas too, such as 'Where do I go for help when I'm stuck?' or 'Where do I get ideas from?' Figure 6.1 provides an example of a flow chart.

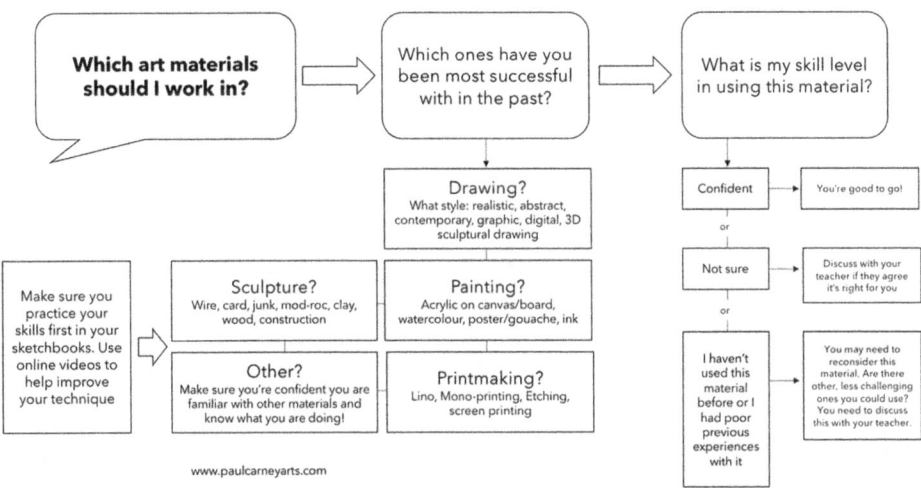

Figure 6.1 An example flow chart

I first saws comics being used by the brilliant metacognition expert, Professor Kate Wall of the University of Strathclyde (Wall et al., 2017). She demonstrates how teachers can help primary-aged children to articulate their thoughts and feelings before and during difficult tasks. A simple comic strip, cartoon, or illustration is provided that depicts an appropriate scene, such as a student sitting at a computer struggling to find research information. Blank thought bubbles and speech bubbles are positioned above the student's head. The image is discussed with students, which should help them to recognise and recall the situation as something familiar to them. The teacher asks them to write a response in the thought bubble: How does this difficult situation make you feel? What are you thinking in moments like this? The speech bubble is then used to articulate a solution: How would you overcome this anxiety? Where would you go to solve it? In this way, comic strips can be used to highlight and overcome familiar problems (see Figure 6.2).

Figure 6.2 Using illustrations to articulate thoughts and feelings around tasks

Further Reading

If you'd like to read more on this subject, I can recommend you visit the webpage of Professor Kate Wall at the University of Strathclyde which lists her academic papers. https://www.strath.ac.uk/staff/wallkateprofessor/

I'd also highly recommend:

Burns, N. (2023). *Inspiring deep learning with metacognition: A guide for secondary teaching.* London: Sage/Corwin Press.

This book is the source of many of the strategies I have discussed in this chapter.

I found this book, *Using reflection & metacognition to improve student learning,* to be especially easy to read yet highly informative:

Kaplan, M., Silver, N., Lavaque-Manty, D., & Meizlish, D. (2013). *Using reflection and metacognition to improve student learning: Across the disciplines, across the academy* (New Pedagogies and Practices for Teaching in Higher Education). Sterling, VA: Stylus Publishing.

I hope you now have a deeper understanding of the important role metacognition plays in the art room, especially in the externally set assignment. I do believe that, with the right teaching and instruction, metacognition can play a pivotal role in student improvement.

References

AQA (2015). *GCSE Art and Design specification (8201, 8202, 8203, 8204, 8205, 8206)*. The Assessment and Qualifications Alliance. Available at: www.aqa.org.uk/sub jects/art-and-design/gcse/art-and-design-8201-8206 (accessed 20 October 2023).

AQA (2018). *GCSE Art and Design (Fine Art): Component 2 externally set assignment (June 2018)*. The Assessment and Qualifications Alliance. Available at: https://filestore.aqa. org.uk/sample-papers-and-mark-schemes/2018/june/AQA-8202X-QP-JUN18.PDF (accessed 20 October 2023).

Fabian Society (2018). *Primary Colours: The decline of arts education in primary schools and how it can be reversed*. London: Fabian Society. Available at: https://fabians.org.uk/ wp-content/uploads/2019/01/FS-Primary-Colours-Report-WEB-FINAL.pdf (accessed 20 October 2023).

GL Assessment (2020). *New study highlights the importance of reading to the whole school curriculum*. London: GL Assessment. Available at: www.gl-assessment.co.uk/press-office/press-releases/new-study-highlights-the-importance-of-reading-to-the-whole-school-curriculum/ (accessed 20 October 2023).

NIFDI (2023). *Basic philosophy of Direct Instruction (DI)*. Eugene, OR: National Institute for Direct Instruction. Available at: www.nifdi.org/what-is-di/basic-philosophy.html (accessed 20 October 2023).

NSEAD (2022). *Examinations & trends: The challenges ahead*. National Society for Education in Art and Design. Available at: www.nsead.org/news/newsroom/ examinations-2022/ (accessed 20 October 2023).

Ofqual (2018). *Get the facts: The GCSE reform*. The Office of Qualifications and Examination Regulations. Available at: www.gov.uk/government/publications/get-the-facts-gcse-and-a-level-reform/get-the-facts-gcse-reform (accessed 20 October 2023).

Ofsted (2023). *Research review series: Art and design*. The Office of Standards in Education, Children's Services and Skills. Available at: www.gov.uk/government/publications/ research-review-series-art-and-design (accessed 20 October 2023).

Ramirez, G., & Beilock, S. L. (2011). Writing about testing worries boosts exam performance in the classroom. *Science, 331*(6014), 211–213.

Shulman, L. (2002). Excerpts from an interview with Lee Shulman, President of the Carnegie Foundation for the Advancement of Teaching. Discussions of Metacognition section. Recorded July 2002 Annenberg Learner/thinking about metacognition website.

Veenman, M. V. J., Van Hout-Wolters, B. H. A. M., & Afflerbach, P. (2006). Metacognition and learning: Conceptual and methodological considerations. *Metacognition & Learning, 1*, 3–14.

Wall, K., Higgins, S., Hall, E., & Gascoine, L. (2017). What does learning look like? Using cartoon story boards to investigate student perceptions (from 4 to 15) of learning something new. In M. Emme & A. Kirova (Eds.), *Good question: Arts-based approaches to collaborative research with children and youth* (pp. 211–227). Victoria, BC: The Canadian Society for Education through Art.

7

Solving the Problem of Feedback

Marco Narajos

An Educational Issue

There are occasionally pupils, or even whole classes, who struggle to make the progress that we would expect, despite our endeavour to provide high-quality instruction and the frequent use of formative assessment. As teachers, we seek to employ different strategies to help learners develop after assessing their progress, but these do not always lead to visibly improved attainment. The teacher's frustration with this is most palpable when marking work and noticing the same mistakes that had previously been identified and fed back to the pupil returning to plague a pupil's work almost seasonally.

Given that there are many ways to use classroom and planning time productively, it is no surprise that feedback can come lower down on a busy teacher's priority list, especially in subjects where teachers feel pushed for time to cover the entire syllabus. If teachers or learners considered the provision of feedback as a performative act, or something that is only needed for accountability purposes, then the quality of feedback given is unlikely to lead to much learning.

At its best, seeing feedback as something that is only needed for accountability would mean it is delivered regularly, and relevant stakeholders in education (including senior leadership, governors and inspectors) can be satisfied that activities that support learning are taking place. After all, learning itself cannot be directly measured, but proxies indirectly correlated with learning are more easily observed. At its worst, poor-quality feedback takes up valuable classroom and planning time that could be used for direct instruction, assessment, practice and other activities for learning, while also harming learners' performance.

Consider the following two cases where feedback may even harm learning outcomes. Many teachers will recognise the learner who is pleased to receive feedback that highlights positive aspects of their work but who then does not work as hard in the next assessment. We also recognise another type of learner who receives feedback focused on poor aspects of their work, whose motivation and engagement suffer, preventing learning. It is easy to interpret both scenarios simply: that the first child became complacent and the second became even more demotivated. However, these interpretations ignore a wealth of empirical research that suggests that the way feedback is given has important effects on learning and metacognition.

It is possible to frame the scenarios as poor choices from the students; this does not benefit anyone other than perhaps a teacher's ego. However, in the spirit of professional development, we can consider these problems as an *interaction* between the learner's (developing) metacognition and the teacher's feedback. The interaction resulted in undesired changes in the learner's self-regulation, which is, in itself, a determinant of performance and learning. In this framework, the learner's approach to feedback is just as important as the feedback itself. Likewise, the feedback itself has the potential to affect learners' approaches to feedback.

A metacognitive and motivated learner attempts tasks, seeking feedback appropriately with the goal of using the feedback for improvement. Motivated but poorly metacognitive learners appear to ask for feedback readily during a task, but actually seek further guidance, support or instruction before engaging with tasks in an attempt to avoid making mistakes in the first place. In the second approach, learners do not seek feedback to improve their learning; they seek to perform in ways that are congruent with their self-belief or how learners see themselves. In such cases, simple feedback that provides the outcome or corrects the pupil's work is unlikely to support metacognition. Learners like these would benefit from feedback that places the onus on students to evaluate their own work in a scaffolded and expert-led way.

Your Approach

1 In what format or medium do you provide feedback to your pupils?
2 In what ways do pupils engage with your feedback and how do they show their engagement?
3 How do pupils use your feedback to plan their approach to work set?
4 How do pupils use your feedback to help them monitor their own performance during a task?
5 How do pupils use your feedback to evaluate the strategies they used in a task?

Metacognitive Solution

What is feedback?

This chapter focuses on feedback from teacher to pupil, which is called 'teacher feedback' or simply, 'feedback'. Here, I define 'feedback' as information provided to a learner about the learner's performance that is intended to cause learning or to improve performance. Feedback is often done as part of a formative assessment process, which also involves the process of determining the quality of a learner's performance.

Some astute readers may already have thought of solutions to the two cases where teacher feedback can harm learning. Most commonly, alternatives to teacher feedback include 'peer feedback' and 'self-feedback'. In its strictest sense, 'peer feedback' differs from 'peer marking'. If pupils swapped answer sheets with their partner to mark each other's quiz and nothing else, this is 'peer marking'. If, after marking, a peer informs the learner of areas of strengths and development and specific topics that the learner may wish to revise, then this is 'peer feedback'.

We can view 'self-feedback' as the information that a learner gains from assessing their own performance. It is intended to cause learning or improve performance. A learner who marks their own quiz is self-marking and self-assessing. The learner who receives their marked test paper back and rightly or wrongly announces 'I'm terrible at this subject' in a self-deprecating way is voicing out their internal perception or identity as a learner but is not doing 'self-feedback'. The same is true for the learner who deter-mines they are 'doing well at this subject', informing their own self-esteem and motiva-tions, but without learning or improving future performance. In contrast, the learner who makes mental or written notes on areas of strength and development to inform their future work is doing self-feedback as part of self-assessment.

It is also important to note that giving feedback – from teacher, peer or self – is not eve-rything. Learning and teaching processes are exceptionally complicated as they happen in innumerable contexts spanning different learners, teachers, abilities, ages, languages, cultures, policies, curricula and purposes. We know that people can teach themselves a skill, such as solving Rubik's cubes, without peer or teacher feedback. Equally, many learners experience successes during undergraduate education which often consists of direct instruction and little formative assessment or feedback. Feedback does not have to take place at every learning event for learners to make improvements over time. How-ever, failing to give feedback at all in a school classroom over a year is likely to reduce the potential learning outcomes.

I make the case that the way feedback is delivered affects pupils' metacognitive devel-opment. Given that the way we deliver feedback is something that we teachers generally have a lot of control over in our classroom, it is worth examining the range of feedback approaches we have at our disposal – and trying them out in our own contexts.

The case for whole-class feedback

My approach to teacher-delivered feedback is in accordance with the model of feedback as the information provided to learners after an assessment of pupils' work (Hattie & Timperley, 2007), which is the most established way of viewing how feedback relates to learning in schools. In this model, the teacher uses information from assessment to cause learners to gain information about their understanding, skills, performance, attainment or progress. The largest beneficial effects of feedback are thought to relate to pupils engaging successfully with the information and influencing the metacognitive aspects of their learning.

Many argue that there is too great a focus in school policies on the quantity and format of marking and feedback, rather than emphasising delivery that maximises the depth of pupil engagement with feedback itself. However, as several lines of research evidence suggest, not all feedback is created equally. Indeed, the Education Endowment Foundation conclude that spoken feedback interventions have a slightly higher impact than written feedback interventions do (Newman et al., 2021).

There are several ways to describe 'types' of teacher feedback: the number of recipients (individual, small group or whole-class), the medium (spoken or written) and the timing (immediate or delayed). It is also useful to describe the type of information the feedback represents, such as whether the focus is on the quality of performance (the task level), the strategies used during the performance (the process level), or the way that a learner plans, monitors and directs their actions (the self-regulation level).

According to Hattie and Timperley (2007), feedback at the process level and self-regulation level are most likely to produce a benefit in learning outcomes. However, in written feedback or individual feedback, the likelihood of teachers providing this level of information for each pupil is low. In reality, the mistakes that pupils make within a class and between classes are predictable and have obvious patterns. When we write feedback, especially if we are also correcting neatness, organisation, spelling, punctuation and grammar, it is not always clear to pupils which feedback is most salient.

It would certainly be expected that where policies exist to provide regular individual written feedback as part of 'book-marking', teachers with large class sizes will be unable to write written feedback of a sufficient quality for each student. When the teacher asks pupils during a lesson to engage with the feedback by correcting their work or completing a short task, the teacher is unable to determine whether pupils are developing their skills in planning, monitoring and evaluating their own work, because pupils are working individually in their books. It is also nearly impossible to have individual dialogues in the class during directed improvement and reflection time (DIRT), yet a dialogue is frequently needed to ensure pupils are thinking about their work and how it compares to the success criteria.

During any lesson, there is a range of opportunities for feedback of different kinds to be delivered. Commonly, spoken feedback is given during sequences of direct instruction, retrieval practice or guided practice. It is standard practice in many schools to provide individual, written feedback when marking homework, classwork or formal assessments. Individual feedback given in classrooms, in either spoken or written form, is predominantly at the self level or the task level and is less effective than feedback at the process level or self-regulation level (Shute, 2008).

Of course, every context is different, so this is not to say that the teaching practices detailed above are detrimental to learning. As Dylan Wiliam wrote in 2018, 'Everything works somewhere; nothing works everywhere'.

A metacognitive approach to whole-class feedback

In my metacognitive approach to whole-class feedback, the teacher's act of marking as part of formative assessment for 'responsive teaching' becomes separate from the process of giving feedback. Teachers deliver feedback in a way that explicitly instructs learners to evaluate their own performance and consider how they planned and monitored their learning activities. Learners become motivated to do this when they are not given a simple 'outcome' (like a grade or score), when they all have opportunities to experience success and areas for improvement, and when they are provided with tools to appraise the quality of their work, such as success criteria, exemplars and model answers. It is a versatile approach and can be used in different ways and it requires only a little training.

The assessment and feedback events may take place within the same lesson or in different lessons, but feedback in this approach has the following characteristics:

1   The feedback is delivered to the whole class.
2   The feedback is predominantly at the process level or self-regulation level.
3   The feedback prompts pupils to identify relevant success criteria and compare their work against the standard.
4   The language used in the feedback prompts pupils to respond in a way that explicitly models metacognitive processes.
5   The feedback highlights salient patterns and mechanisms relating to areas of success and for development, identifying changes made and to be made.

In my practice, I find it helpful to make notes of what I will cover during the feedback, but it need not be arduous, nor should it be a script. It could be as simple as a photocopy of the work that pupils were doing that the teacher annotates during the marking process. For purposes of accountability or for early career teachers who want evidence for their portfolios, it is also possible to use a whole-class feedback proforma sheet or use a pre-existing one. Regardless of the recording of the teacher's thinking process, it is intended to be used in a dynamic way; we cannot predict how pupils respond and we should not be attempting to cover everything that could come up to preserve pupils' cognitive load for the task of engaging with the feedback. Importantly, when an environment is set up where pupils are happy to receive feedback, it is often these moments where answering relevant questions can be particularly powerful.

In the following examples, I will model the language that should be used when giving feedback metacognitively to a whole class. There are two examples, each differing slightly based on age group, subject and teacher's experience with this method. The scenarios are fictional but are based on real-life examples from English secondary schools.

Example from English

Last lesson, Year 8 pupils read an extract from author H.G. Wells and were asked questions about the ways in which Wells focuses the audience's attention and what Wells conveys about the nature of time travel. The students in a Key Stage 3 English class wrote their answers during the lesson and handed the work in to be marked. The teacher has read through the students' answers in their exercise books and compiled successful work by taking photos of their books.

Table 7.1 An example of teacher feedback in an English lesson

Features	Examples of what the teacher says
Whole class	Today, Year 8, we are doing something different. I will give you your exercise books back. I have marked your homework, but I haven't written anything in them because I want you to have the opportunity to assess your own work too.
	I will show you some excellent examples from this class that we're going to look at to find ways we can improve our own work. Get ready. You need a green pen.
Process or self-regulation level	The most successful students highlighted five key quotes from the passage and annotated it directly about the senses, objects and feelings in the quotes. Check if you did that and give yourself a tick if you did that. Aly, what senses did you write about? Ben, which objects did you choose? [students who did this]
	Hands down! Why might it be a good idea to select key quotes before writing anything? Let's hear from Clara [student who did not do this].
Comparison with standards	I won't say whose this was, but I am showing it to you [on the screen] because there are some things on here that are working at a very high level and there are also things that this person and everyone else can learn from.
	They have written here about the use of atypical imagery. What do I like about this? Are they using connectives? Are they using PEEL? Now can you check if you have used connectives and PEEL as well? What about linking to the question?
Metacognitive modelling	I'm now going to talk you through how I would go about making quick and large improvements in your work. While I am talking, make a note of what things you have already done and what things you can still do to improve because I will ask you to re-write your answers at the end of the lesson.
	When I choose a quote for a point, I am looking at word choice. What are the connotations of words used? Is there a repeating motif across the whole extract? I can't just be looking at the sentence alone. What else should I be doing, Dean?
Salience of whole-class patterns	From my marking, I saw that the question 'what Wells conveys about time travel' was a particular challenge. Most of you identified that this was Victorian science fiction but few of you related this to class struggles and the idea of a conflict between 'man and nature'. Now, write another PEEL paragraph on this idea.

In the example in Table 7.1, the teacher introduces the whole-class metacognitive feedback approach for the first time. Students may need a lot of reassurance this time because of the worry that they are not doing the right thing. It is particularly useful to give pupils tools they can work with, such as a checklist of things they need to look for and to identify areas of strengths and for development. Depending on the class and the time dedicated for feedback, the teacher may conclude the activity by asking pupils to complete a similar task again or to write a reflection that includes specific goals, such as 'To improve my work, I should plan my essay by analysing selected relevant quotes carefully for the use of imagery'. Next time they are faced with a similar task, it can be a good idea to ask pupils to look through their previous reflections and targets to remind them that the purpose of the whole-class feedback strategy is about them recognising how they can improve their learning outcomes in that subject.

Example from science

Last lesson, Year 11 pupils completed an end-of-topic test on homeostasis and response. The teacher has marked all the test papers as usual with simple ticks and crosses. The class scored poorly in the test and the teacher wants to ensure everyone pays attention to the feedback. A total was calculated and recorded in the teacher's personal mark book before the feedback lesson. The class has previously used this metacognitive strategy.

Table 7.2 An example of teacher feedback in a science lesson

Features	Examples of what the teacher says
Whole class	Year 11, purple pens out. Your job today is to check if I have marked your papers correctly, so I haven't written a score on your test paper today in case there are any changes. I will put up the mark scheme for each question on the screen. At the end of the lesson, you can tell me if I should have given you any extra marks and why.
Process or self-regulation level	In the last part of question 1, you had to compare the nervous system and endocrine system. Hands up if you circled the word 'compare' because it is a command word. Emma [who had a hand up], what does that mean we should use in our answers if it is a 'compare' question?
	This question here asks you for the symbol equation for respiration but only a few of you got that right. What reaction have many of you confused for respiration? [photosynthesis] What is the last thing you need to check after writing any chemical equation? [equation is balanced]
Comparison with standards	This is the mark scheme for this extended writing question. It is a challenging mark scheme because you have to give yourself a level first, before scoring yourself. Check yours now to see what level you are and count the number of correct points you made to decide on your score.
Metacognitive modelling	Many of you lost marks in simple knowledge recall questions. Hands up if that applies to you. If that applies to you, I want you to write some notes now on how you can remember it in future. Maybe there's a good mnemonic for it. I saw Farid write down, 'glucaGON because the glucose is GONE' on his test paper. If you think you would use that, write it down. Hands up if you've made flashcards of these? However you want to do it, you need to find a way to make sure these things stick because they are easy ways to pick up some more marks.
	Can you write down how many more marks you would have scored in the exam had you just gone back and double-checked your answer?

(Continued)

Table 7.2 An example of teacher feedback in a science lesson *(Continued)*

Features	Examples of what the teacher says
Salience of whole-class patterns	Percentage change questions always come up in exams and they always catch students out. Most of you got both marks, an improvement from last time. If you look at your previous reflections now, can you see if percentage change is something you had to work on last time? We're at a point now in the course where 100% of the class should be getting these easy marks.

In this scenario, the teacher finds positive things that pupils may have done and asks them to put their hands up if this is something that they did. It is an easy and low-stakes way for pupils to show engagement and it can also be used to demonstrate a class culture of personal improvement by asking pupils to show hands if they fell into a particular trap. It also identifies pupils that you may wish to direct questions at, which allows the class to have conversations and genuine dialogue about the assessment and feedback. For example, there may be an opportune moment to discuss with pupils about the pros and cons of specific mnemonics and why some are more memorable than others. When pupils are engaging in their work with the motivation of finding an extra mark, it can also open a discussion about the success criteria or mark scheme. Sometimes, mark schemes are controversial, even among experienced teachers, so a debate can be common in some classrooms during feedback time, but the real learning is how pupils will change their future actions to improve their learning outcomes.

The feedback given in this case is little to do with giving pupils the correct answers from the mark scheme, although of course this is important. Rather, the feedback prompts pupils to make attempts to improve their learning in a genuine and inquisitive manner. This occurs through a range of techniques, including direct commands, metacognitive questioning, and exposing learners to model and peer examples. This kind of metacognitive feedback rarely occurs with written feedback alone.

Ideas for the Classroom

- While you are training a class, it can be worth giving some written feedback alongside, especially for pupils who may struggle with spoken feedback due to English as an additional language (EAL) needs or special educational needs and disabilities (SEND).
- Find a hassle-free system for taking photos of pupil work and incorporating it immediately into a document that can be displayed on a screen. It will likely depend on your context, your ability to use a device in school and your internet connection.
- It is worth explicitly training a class in this method, giving them the reasons why you are using this method of doing feedback.

- You may wish to use a whole-class feedback proforma to make notes on for the very first time. These are freely available online and you can modify them for your own purposes.
- Consider buddying up with someone who can observe you doing this. A typical feedback segment is only around 15–20 minutes long. It is worth getting their feedback on your feedback!
- Do speak to your pupils about the feedback they receive from you and other teachers. Do they like having written feedback? Why? What do they use it for?
- Adjust this method to suit you and your class. You might want to try a version of this strategy for live marking or peer-marking.

Further Reading and References

Collin, J., & Quigley, A. (2021). *Teacher feedback to improve pupil learning*. Guidance Report. Education Endowment Foundation.

This is an evidence-based guidance report that includes a review of current best practices and suggestions for implementation.

Hattie, J., & Timperley, H. (2007). The power of feedback. *Review of Educational Research, 77*(1), 81–112.

This is the seminal text for understanding the role of feedback in learning in schools and includes a framework for thinking about characteristics of effective feedback.

Newman, M., Kwan, I., Schucan Bird, K., & Hoo, H. T. (2021). *The impact of feedback on student attainment: A systematic review*. Education Endowment Foundation.

This is a systematic review of the effect of feedback specifically on attainment, including meta-analyses and subgroup analyses of different types of feedback across a range of contexts.

Shute, V. J. (2008). Focus on formative feedback. *Review of Educational Research, 78*(1), 153–189.

This is a seminal text that defines the formative use of feedback, reviews literature on types of feedback and describes a variety of models to explain the varying effectiveness of feedback.

Wiliam, D. (2018). *Creating the schools our children need*. West Palm Beach, FL: Learning Sciences International.

This is a book written with a US audience in mind but it has highly transferable ideas about improving curriculum and pedagogy and how to implement new strategies at the classroom level.

8

Metacognitive Monitoring

Sarah Dowey

An Educational Issue

Metacognitive monitoring involves our ability to be able to accurately judge our own cognitive processes. This ability plays a central role in the three-part metacognitive process of planning, monitoring and evaluating learning. If we think of planning as the actions that learners need to do before a task to prepare for it (such as working out which strategies to use to help them memorise facts for an upcoming assessment) and evaluation as the consideration of how to approach a similar task, which takes place after task completion, then monitoring is the vital part of the process that comes in between. Thus, metacognitive monitoring involves students being aware of their thinking throughout a task, which also helps them to work out their progress during the task. This process is shown in Figure 8.1, which was developed as part of a Task Completion Process Model I designed as part of my doctoral research into metacognition.

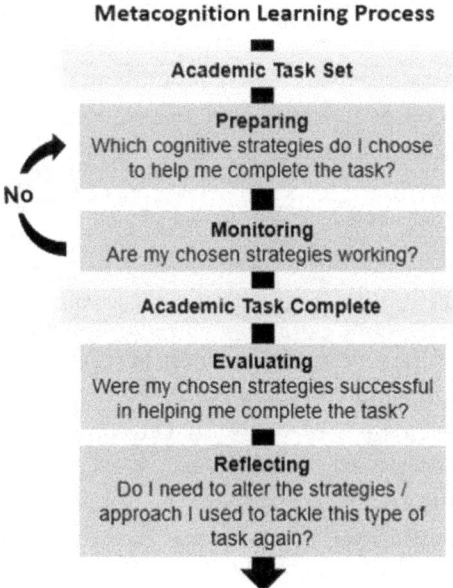

Metacognition Learning Process

Academic Task Set

Preparing
Which cognitive strategies do I choose to help me complete the task?

No

Monitoring
Are my chosen strategies working?

Academic Task Complete

Evaluating
Were my chosen strategies successful in helping me complete the task?

Reflecting
Do I need to alter the strategies / approach I used to tackle this type of task again?

Figure 8.1 The metacognitive process model (taken from the Task Completion Process Model)

However, monitoring on its own is not enough. For students to really benefit from this part of the process they also need to be able to control their actions to alter or finesse their chosen approach if it is not working effectively. For example, if a student had been set 20 words to learn independently for homework, they may begin by planning for this by deciding to use the look, cover, write, check method to help with memorisation, as it is a strategy they've used in the past. Each night they practise learning the 20 words using this method; however, after four nights, they keep getting the same five spellings wrong. Although the student has demonstrated metacognitive planning skills, it is the monitoring of progress and how they respond that will have most impact on the final outcome. The student may decide to keep using look, cover, write, check and hope that by the time it gets to the test that they have learned the last five words. However, now that they have realised that they keep getting the same five spellings wrong, they may decide to try another approach to help learn them, such as de-chunking or mnemonics. In isolating the five words from the ones they have already learned, they have monitored their progress and then gone back to the planning stage to help them select different strategies to memorise the vocabulary. In doing so, they have taken control of their own learning.

The benefit of facilitating students to monitor and take control of their own learning during the metacognitive process is that it helps them to keep a much tighter grasp on their own progress and shape their learning journey to develop more successful outcomes (Muijs & Bokhove, 2020). Yet, helping students develop their metacognitive monitoring skills can be tricky. High-stakes tests take place within strict and challenging time restrictions. Although these conditions need to be replicated within the classroom to help students prepare for terminal exams, this pressure can lead to students having a blinkered approach, where they focus on reaching the finish line as quickly as possible, rather than as effectively as possible. Other barriers include a lack of student understanding about how to monitor and control both their learning and their learning environment. In this next section, we will look at how to develop students' metacognitive monitoring, along with some practical strategies to use in the classroom.

Your Approach

- Do you give students the time and opportunity to reflect on how successfully they are tackling a task during the completion of the task?
- Which strategies do you use to encourage students to monitor their learning/ success during a task?
- Do you teach students a range of strategies that they can use to tackle a task, so that they have alternative strategies if the ones they have utilised are not effective?
- Do you explicitly model the monitoring process?
- Do you explicitly teach and model time-management strategies?

The Metacognitive Approach

Metacognitive strategies differ from cognitive strategies. Teaching students how to monitor and control their learning requires us to use both types of strategies for maximum impact. Metacognitive strategies are used to help learners focus on and manage the metacognitive process, for example, asking students to rate their success during a task, or to think about what they need to change in order to improve their progress. Cognitive strategies are learning strategies that students select and use to help them complete a task, such as creating flashcards with key words and definitions to help them revise subject terminology for a test. In this section we will consider how to develop your use of metacognitive strategies in the classroom to help your students hone their monitoring skills.

Metacognitive questioning

Questioning is a cornerstone of effective pedagogical practice for good reason. It is a tool that can be used to effectively check and develop students' disciplinary knowledge, make links to prior learning, aid retrieval practice, and increase student participation. However, teacher use of metacognitive questioning is also an effective way of both instigating and encouraging students to monitor their learning. In the Educational Endowment Foundation's (EEF) guidance report on metacognition (Quigley et al., 2018), the second of their seven recommendations advocates teachers to explicitly teach students metacognitive strategies for each of the three stages of the metacognitive process (the EEF's model of the metacognition process consists of three stages: planning, monitoring and evaluating). To achieve this, it suggests using a questioning approach to prompt students to think about what they need to do at each stage of the metacognitive process. It also gives worked examples of what this might look like when a teacher is modelling the creation of a self-portrait, such as 'Are all of my facial features in proportion?' and 'Is there anything I need to stop and change to improve my self-portrait?'

This approach can be applied to any curriculum subject or task. More generic questions to support metacognitive monitoring can include asking students to consider:

- Am I still on task/answering the question?
- Is my chosen strategy working?
- Do I need to change my strategy?
- Am I working successfully?
- Have I encountered any problems?
- How do I overcome any problems?
- Will I finish this on time?
- Do I need any extra support?
- Can I complete this independently?
- Is this too easy/difficult?
- Am I meeting the success criteria?

There are, of course, many ways that you can deliver these questions in your lessons and the time spent on the intellectual planning of how and when you will use targeted questions to support your students to monitor their own learning is just as important as the questions themselves. As with any new learning, teaching students how to monitor their own learning will need to be heavily scaffolded/supported when it is first introduced, until students gain confidence and expertise. Students need to be able to do this automatically as part of their metacognitive process.

You may also want to be judicious in your questioning and build up the repertoire of questions you use with your class gradually to focus on monitoring progress in a specific skill or area. So, rather than asking students if they are meeting the success criteria, you may identify a particular strand of the criteria and ask students to monitor this at different points as they work on the task. For example, you may be working with your class on completing a long-form response or essay that requires them to utilise several different skills to develop a successful response. To begin with, rather than asking students to monitor their success in hitting every aspect of the mark scheme, you can begin by isolating one skill, such as using relevant textual evidence to support a viewpoint, and use questions that prompt students to monitor only that skill. For example:

1 Have I used **evidence** from the text to support my ideas?
2 Is the **evidence** I have chosen relevant to the task I'm completing/question I'm answering?
3 Is the **evidence** too long/short?
4 Is this the best piece of **evidence** I can use to support my idea?
5 Have I included enough different pieces of **evidence** to support my ideas?

In this example, you can see that I have structured the metacognitive questions so that each one supports a higher level of challenge than the one before it. Students should move on to the next question only when they have satisfactorily answered the one before it and made any necessary changes to help them get back on track. If the answer to question 1 is 'No', then there is not much point in them moving onto question 2 until they've gone back and added evidence to their response. Equally, if a student has judged accurately that they are using evidence to support their ideas, they would then benefit from working through the other questions to monitor just how successful they are in using evidence effectively.

In addition to choosing your metacognition questions, you also need to carefully consider timing. As discussed earlier in this chapter, the monitoring process needs to take place when students are in the throes of completing the task, not when they have finished it. The five questions I listed above can also be posed to students after they have completed the task and be used to evaluate their success. The answers they give can then be used to create targets for the next time they complete a similar task. However, the purpose of monitoring is to give students the opportunity to assess their progress during the task: to direct them towards making any necessary adjustments; to improve their response before they finish; and to foster independent thinking. Timing is important here. You need to give them sufficient time to have tackled enough of the task so that they have something to monitor their success on, but not so little that they do not have enough time to make any adjustments. You may also want to repeat the process more than once during a task, particularly when you first begin, building in 'monitoring moments' or 'pause points' where students work though the metacognitive questions you have created.

Ultimately, all our students will need to complete assessments in terminal exams at some point in their academic careers, such as GCSEs and SATs, without our support or feedback. If we only teach them how to assess success on completion of a piece of work, then we are denying them the opportunity to know how to monitor and change their responses for the better before the exam paper is taken away from them and it is too late to change anything. Realising, after they have walked out of the exam hall, that they have not included enough evidence to support their ideas is not going to help them gain a better exam grade. Realising it as they monitor their response and then adjusting their approach accordingly will.

Providing prompts

The first time that students tackle monitoring they will probably need some extra support to help guide them and keep them on track with the process. Although we want our students to be able to work autonomously – and the EEF lists teaching pupils how to work independently as another of its guidance recommendations – they will initially need more support with this novel skill until they develop their confidence and expertise, and then this support can be reduced.

One way of doing this is by providing visual prompts and cues that students can use to direct them to both monitor their work and control their response to how well they are doing in order to increase progress. Visual prompts and cues can be to use paper resources that they can stick into their books and refer to later, prompts on the board, or even classroom displays. For example, if we go back to the question that I want my students to ask themselves so that they can monitor their use of evidence to support their ideas during the writing process, I can base this resource on the five questions I want them to ask themselves (see Table 8.1).

You can see from this example that the resource not only prompts students into monitoring their use of evidence, but it also directs them towards what to do to change their work and develop it further. The first time you try something new, like this, I recommend modelling it to them so they understand how you, as an expert learner, would use the resource to monitor and control your own writing (there is more on teacher modelling to support monitoring in the section below). As students become more proficient at monitoring themselves, I gradually fade out this support so that students work towards asking themselves these questions without being prompted.

Table 8.1 An example resource

Question	Answer	Changes
Have I used **evidence** from the text to support my ideas?		
(If 'No', what changes will you make? When 'Yes', go to the next question)		
Is the **evidence** I have chosen relevant to the task I'm completing / question I'm answering?		
(If 'No', what changes will you make? When 'Yes', go to the next question)		
Is the **evidence** too long / short?		
(If 'Yes', what changes will you make? When 'No', go to the next question)		
Is this the best piece of **evidence** I can use to support my idea?		
(If 'No', what changes will you make? When 'Yes', go to the next question)		
Have I included enough different pieces of **evidence** to support my ideas?		
(If 'No', what changes will you make? When 'Yes' to all of the questions, you are effectively including apt quotations to support your ideas - well done!)		

Thus, the next time they complete a writing task I may just have the question on the board for thesm to refer to, but I will still control the timing of the lesson so that students have to stop what they were writing, read through their work and consider these questions before moving on. Depending on the context of the class/ lesson, I may also repeat this process at least once before they finish the task. The next time, I can put the questions on the board and direct students to them at the start of the task, but not control the timing so that it is up to the students when and how to use the prompts. Finally, I remove the prompts and at the end of the task I discuss with the students how and when they used monitoring to support their writing.

Depending on the task and the needs of your class, there are a multitude of different prompts you can create to direct students' monitoring skills. For example, I had a class (well several classes, actually) that needed to develop their academic writing skills so they could express themselves more effectively and progress. To support them with the vocabulary they needed, I created a display of academic vocabulary that they could use and some bookmarks that I placed on their desks with sentence stems, phrases and words they could use. I then modelled how to use this vocabulary in their writing, and I did see some progress in their writing. However, several students were still not developing their writing despite the prompts and I realised that this was because once I set them on with a task, they were so focused on completing it that they were not monitoring their writing during the process. To address this, I created 'pause points' during the lesson, where they read through what they had written so far and highlighted when they had used academic vocabulary and circled words they needed to improve, which they then changed before they moved on. In taking time to monitor and control the use of academic vocabulary, I found that students' writing improved, and responses became more fluid as students thought about their word choices as they wrote, rather than waiting for me to give them feedback. I then took the bookmarks away from them (though they could ask for them if they needed the prompts). To begin with, I saw that they were then looking at the display a lot more as they were writing, which was great as it showed they were monitoring their work throughout the task. As we moved through the term, they barely looked up at the displays and still they used academic vocabulary. Before the end-of-unit assessment, we had a discussion about how they monitored their work to use academic writing. Their comments included:

- 'I don't even have to think about it now, I just do it.'
- 'I'm always thinking about if this is the best word to use and if it isn't what a better one is.'
- 'When I'm writing, I imagine a teacher is reading it as I write, so I think about what they would say to me, like, "Is there a better word you could use than that?" and I try to think of the words on the bookmark and use the better word.'

In this example, prompts were used to support students' academic writing. However, the prompts were most effective in helping students to progress when they were monitoring their use of them throughout the writing process. Eventually, self-monitoring became so embedded in their practice that they no longer needed the prompts and could work independently.

Teacher modelling

Teacher modelling is probably the most effective strategy teachers can use to develop their metacognitive thinking, so it is no surprise that it has also been referenced in other chapters within this book. Consequently, this section will only relate to teachers modelling as a way of encouraging students' monitoring skills, and I will keep it brief!

Explicit teacher modelling is a way of sharing your knowledge (as an expert learner) with your students so that they understand how you approach monitoring your work and why you have chosen to do it in that way. They can then better understand the rationale behind monitoring and develop a clearer understanding of the benefits of monitoring and how to use it in their own work to judge and control their progress. Again, this forms the basis of another recommendation from the EEF guidance report on metacognition (Quigley et al., 2018) and builds on Vygotsky's research into the Zone of Proximal Development (ZPD) (Vygotsky, 1967).

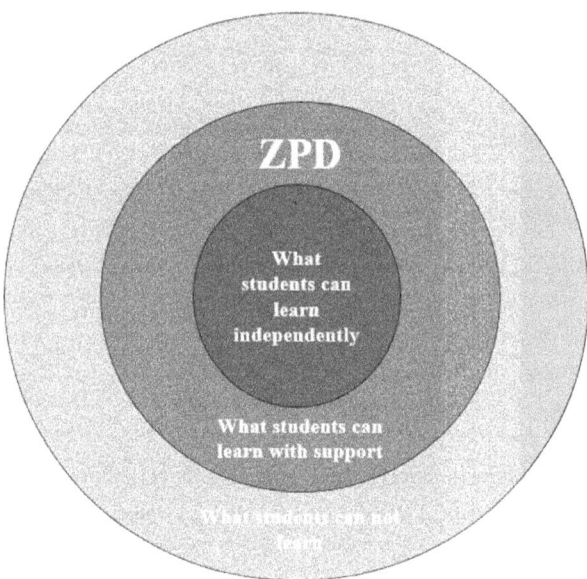

Figure 8.2 A model of Vygotsky's Zone of Proximal Development

The ZPD charts the gap between a task the learner can complete independently and one they are unable to complete, as shown in Figure 8.2. For students to negotiate this gap in learning, Vygotsky proposed that learners use the assistance of a More Knowledgeable Other (such as a more knowledgeable peer or teacher) to help them learn how to complete a task independently. When modelling monitoring to students, teachers are working as the More Knowledgeable Other, sharing how they make judgements and changes to their work as they complete a task. In the example I gave earlier about supporting students to use academic vocabulary, I modelled how to monitor my word choice as I wrote an analytical response to the task set. Throughout this process I paused and questioned students about word choice and explained to them why I was monitoring my work like this (so I could express myself more precisely and fluently) and the changes that we made as a response of their answers to my questions. Questions included:

- Is this the best word I can use here?
- What alternative word could I use so that I'm not repeating my vocabulary?
- Is this word/phrase too informal?
- What word/phrase could I use instead?

- If I can't think of a better word, what resources can I use to help me?
- Is this word accurate in this context?
- Have I spelt this word correctly?

During the process, I also explained that while this might feel quite slow and time-consuming at first, as students became more proficient at it, they would also become quicker. I also explained that it was worth spending the time to create a more crafted and thoughtful response as it would help them to develop and progress as writers, so that they understood the rationale.

Focus and time management

As teachers, we can sometimes fall into the trap of assuming that students already have the tacit knowledge that we take for granted as expert learners. So, it is worth considering if students have been explicitly taught how to regulate and monitor their focus and time management skills, especially when they are not working in a classroom environment.

Research into the optimal amount of time we can focus does not offer a definitive time frame, with results ranging from approximately 10 minutes to 90 minutes. This makes sense as the amount of time we can focus varies from person to person depending on factors such as sleep, interest in the task, motivation and self-control. However, although focus can diminish the longer we spend on a task, we can help students develop their concentration by teaching them strategies they can use to monitor and control this aspect of their learning.

Strategies include teaching students how to:

- Create a work environment that is free from distractions, such as putting mobile phones on aeroplane mode so that notifications are disabled during 'focus time'.
- Structure timed activities with regular breaks. Using timers and apps that automatically factor in break time, such as the Pomodoro technique, are useful as they prompt students when to concentrate and when to take a break, helping them to monitor the time they spend focusing.
- Use interleaving and spaced practice, which provide students with opportunities to monitor their progress over a longer period (EEF, 2021).
- Have a clear goal in sight and monitor progress towards the goal, such as scoring at least 18 out of 20 in their next spelling test and using self-testing to review progress made so that a different approach can be chosen if they are not on track for meeting their target.

Before you begin teaching these strategies, you may want students to monitor how they manage their learning, so that they can reflect on their study habits and make changes to support their learning. Question prompts that students can reflect on can include:

- Do you have a quiet place to study?
- When you're studying/working on a task, do you focus only on the task, or do you get distracted by your mobile phone?
- Do you listen to music, watch TV or chat to your friends while you are studying?
- Do you take regular breaks?
- How long can you concentrate on a piece of homework before your mind starts wandering and you become distracted?
- Do you know if you're becoming distracted?
- Do you have a goal when you start your work?
- Do you space out your work, or try to fit it in all at the last minute?

It goes without saying that such monitoring questions are designed to support a dialogue in which students think about how they learn and can choose from more effective study habits. It needs to be more than just a record of what they are doing well, or not so well. Encouraging students to share with each other (as More Knowledgeable Others) the strategies that work for them and how they monitor and regulate their concentration during independent study will also make for a richer and more useful discussion – and you might learn a new strategy too!

Teaching students how to monitor and manage their time during a task is also an important skill. Ineffective time management can potentially be a barrier to students self-monitoring as the pressure of timed conditions can cause students to hurtle towards the end without really thinking about how they are getting there. Alternatively, they may prioritise the wrong task, spending too long on it so that they are not focusing on what has the most impact. For example, planning an essay response before writing it is an important skill that helps students consolidate and organise their ideas. However, if in an exam they only have 30 minutes to complete the assessment and spend 15 minutes of this time planning their response, they will not have time to complete the task effectively. Although planning is important, it is also important that the student does not become so absorbed in planning that they fail to monitor the time and complete the other component parts of the task.

As with the other examples given in this chapter, time management is a technique that can be taught, modelled and prompted by you so that students can consider how to use their time during a task. You can support them to do this by teaching them how to:

1 Break down the task into component parts.
2 Prioritise and order component parts.
3 Allocate the time to spend on component parts.
4 Monitor their time.
5 Adhere to time deadlines.

Once students have begun to work on the task, you can initially use a timer to let students know when it is time to move on to the next component part of the task and to prompt them to start on it. It is probable that students may struggle with this at first if they are not used to monitoring their use of time as closely. However, it can also provide useful feedback that you can use to help students improve their time management. For example, if a student spends too long planning, what techniques can you work with them on to reduce planning time (such as using notes and abbreviations, or a planning frame) to help them move on from this component so that they have sufficient time to complete the rest of the task.

Ideas for the Classroom

- Ensure students have been explicitly taught a repertoire of cognitive strategies they can utilise when undertaking a task/learning (this will allow them to change or adjust strategies during the monitoring process if they need to).
- Use metacognitive questioning and talk to encourage and direct students towards monitoring their progress.
- Consider having written monitoring prompts to begin with, which can be gradually removed.
- Plan time ('pause points') and activities for students to monitor their progress in class.
- Explicitly model how to monitor progress when working on a task and the changes you make because of your monitoring.
- Explicitly model the monitoring of time management and focus/concentration.

References

Education Endowment Foundation (EEF) (2021). *Cognitive science approaches in the classroom: A review of the evidence.* Available at: https://educationendowmentfoundation.org.uk/education-evidence/evidence-reviews/cognitive-science-approaches-in-the-classroom (accessed 20 October 2023).

Muijs, D., & Bokhove, C. (2020). *Metacognition and Self-Regulation: Evidence Review.* Education Endowment Foundation.

Quigley, A., Muijs, D., & Stringer E. (2018). *EEF Metacognition and self-regulated learning: Guidance report.* Available at: https://educationendowmentfoundation.org.uk/education-evidence/guidance-reports/metacognition (accessed 20 October 2023).

Vygotsky, L. S. (1967). Play and its role in the mental development of the child. *Soviet Psychology, 5*(3), 6–18.

9

Modelling Metacognitive Mathematics for Understanding

Dave Tushingham

An Educational Issue

In the lockdown of 2020, school closures meant that there was an urgent and immediate need for teachers to adapt the carefully planned and practised methods of delivery that they had cumulatively spent tens of thousands of hours perfecting. No longer were teachers able to ask students to show their mini whiteboards to check for understanding or talk to the partner next to them about a concept. At best, techniques needed adapting, at worst they were no longer usable. Within the online classroom, particular teaching techniques, such as 'Turn and Talk', 'Radar/Be Seen Looking' and 'Least Invasive Intervention', were suddenly a lot less effective or impossible to use in their current guise (Lemov, 2015). Some techniques became more impactful and therefore more important to relearn. They looked different in their delivery online, and we urgently needed to become experts in a new style of using these techniques.

The techniques that we were relearning how to use might include 'Name the Steps', 'Wait Time' and 'Exit Ticket'. Because teachers were not in physical classrooms, the approach to practising teaching needed to adapt and for many teachers, more time was devoted to planning and practising how these techniques might look in the online classroom. This happened particularly through the input part of the lesson. Modelling examples was an example of pedagogical practice that was more suitable to teachers' online development, and teachers were able to choose more carefully the examples they use to explain concepts. Teachers had more time to think more deeply about the curriculum they use and why it is sequenced how it is, building stronger subject knowledge links themselves and therefore offering better explanations to their students. Modelling examples would become our core, our pivot, our vehicle for developing a successful online learning environment.

> A model of carefully planned explicit instruction is likely to be more successful in terms of learning than leaving students to their own devices under a model of partial guidance. (Barton, 2018)

Students need explicit instruction to be able to build their own, correct schema. Novices think backwards and need to have their attention focused on the right areas, offering clear explanations for the steps in the problem and what they need to do for success. Expert learners need the opportunity to think about their learning and make links between pieces of knowledge. Experts think forwards. Experts need opportunities to work independently. Students need opportunities to experience desirable difficulties and overcome them (Robbins, 2021). Learning needs to be effortful (Barton, 2018). Explicit instruction, whether it be through recorded lessons or in live online lessons, teaches students how to think critically about the examples they are given. We must be mindful of cognitive load while learning new, complex subject-specific knowledge, but explicit instruction of modelled examples offers students the opportunity to think metacognitively about the subject-specific knowledge they are expert in as well as making links between pieces of knowledge and solving problems. It gives them the opportunity to think about why they made the decisions they made, where their own misconceptions and gaps are and how they might overcome them. With carefully chosen modelled examples, there will be opportunities for all students to think deliberately about their metacognitive thinking within the subject-specific explanations that are delivered. All students are experts in some pieces of subject knowledge and with carefully chosen examples, all students can practise metacognitive thinking at parts of a modelled example without experiencing cognitive overload.

Being subject experts is different from being expert thinkers. There is a strong correlation but there is a distinction. Through teaching students how to think metacognitively within explicit instruction, we are developing an independence in our students, but students need the knowledge of how to successfully think metacognitively if they are to be efficient in making subject-specific links and practise using their subject knowledge effectively. They need to know metacognitive techniques, how to use them and then have time to practise them in isolation, without cognitive overload. They need to be able to give the techniques their full attention. Metacognition and metacognitive strategies need to be taught. Students need knowledge of how to think metacognitively just as they do when learning a new subject-based concept. Lockdown demanded that we rethink the strategies we use for learning with an immediacy, and it took students into a new environment, which demanded they work more independently without well-planned scaffolds to do this effectively.

Teachers were novices at how to teach this important knowledge and how to generate opportunities for impactful practice in the new online classrooms. We were all novices, who were, in many ways, learning how to learn in the 'new normal' together. And with time, we would have strategies that enable students to think separately about metacognitive strategies before being expected to apply independent thinking to new subject content without appropriate scaffolding. Applying what I know about classroom teaching into an online environment so that students have the best chance of success was the goal, and my personal experiences on how this can be achieved provide the narrative for this chapter.

Your Approach

This chapter looks at how we can teach metacognitive behaviours online within a traditional teaching model. The chapter considers how we can increase students' knowledge of what a metacognitive learner looks like and support students to become more expert in skilfully applying metacognitive behaviours to their learning to support the acquisition of new knowledge. It will also look at how we teach metacognitive thinking alongside new subject-specific content in a way that supports students to quickly become expert learners. The chapter offers an interpretation of what teaching metacognitive thinking might look like in the online classroom, exploring how we model new concepts to our students, how we support them to start their deliberate practice, and how we collect and use feedback and retrieval strategies to strengthen metacognitive thinking in the classroom.

Although many of the examples and writing in this chapter are chosen by a secondary mathematics teacher, the suggestions made are largely transferable across a range of subjects and school settings. The online techniques are also transferable into the classroom; much of what is discussed here is from us transferring 'Teach Like a Champion' techniques that have been successful in the classroom to online learning (Lemov, 2015). Understanding what is the same and what is different between classroom and online application helps us to become more expert in teaching metacognitive thinking.

Teaching metacognitive thinking and teaching subject knowledge should be considered separately before students get the opportunity to practise applying metacognitive thinking to subject-specific examples. Like any knowledge, isolating the steps required to successfully apply metacognitive strategies, before applying them to more complex problems, supports the learner's journey from novice to expert. Novices are 'more likely to experience cognitive overload as attention is swamped by new information' (Didau, 2019). Experts are 'less likely to experience cognitive overload as attention is buttressed by memorised "chunks" of knowledge' (Didau, 2019).

The urgent need created from a lockdown did not afford the profession this opportunity. We remain aware of this moving forward. And now that we are back in the classroom, we have created both online and classroom lessons for students that explicitly teach metacognitive strategies. The chapter looks at modelling metacognitive techniques and subject-specific content separately at first, and then bringing them together in subject-specific examples to support students in becoming more expert in their subject and becoming more expert learners.

To do this, we will attempt to answer the following questions:

- Why does it matter?
- What does explicit teaching of metacognitive strategies look like online and when does it happen?
- Metacognition in subject-specific modelling: What does this look like in the online classroom?
- How do we choose the right examples for metacognitive learning?

- What is metacognitive teaching not?
- What are the barriers to teaching metacognitive behaviours?

> Once information is in our working memory, we can think about it. (Enser & Enser, 2020)

To understand what these two approaches look like in practice, the chapter is divided into a series of questions, designed to elicit reflection and to challenge the disposition of the reader, offering strategies for teaching behaviours and giving the reader ideas that can be practised in the new, online classroom. This chapter offers an interpretation of how you may explicitly teach metacognitive behaviours, and although these ideas are led by evidence, the ideas in this chapter do not tell you *the* way to explicitly teach meta-cognitive strategies. It does not tell the reader the best approach to use. But the evidence used to inform these ideas acts as the lightbulb.

> Bradley Busch, a psychologist from Inner Drive, has wisely phrased that, 'On our own, we are all separately bumbling around lost in the dark to our own experiences. With research, we at least have a lamp and a map to help guide us'. (Jones & Macpherson, 2021)

The evidence guides what you will read in the rest of this chapter. However, while we will explore techniques, the chapter does not confirm them.

The Metacognitive Approach
Why does it matter?

For this chapter, I shall be working with definitions from Jennifer Webb in *The Metacog-nition Handbook* (2021) for metacognition and metacognitive learners.

> Metacognition is a set of behaviours which maximise the potential for and effi-cacy of learning. (Webb, 2021)

> A metacognitive learner is one who has knowledge and control over cognitive skills and processes. They understand how learning happens and they are able to actively and independently apply this understanding to help them learn in the most effective way, and to sustain that learning into the future. (Webb, 2021)

As Jade Pearce succinctly put it in her session on the GLT book club podcast (Rainbow & Tushingham, 2022), metacognition is so much more than just learning how to revise. It is learning how to write an answer, how to plan, how to link knowledge together. It needs to be applied in all subjects as this practice will look different in different subjects. Metacognition is learning to think like an expert in your subject area. Being an expert metacognitive thinker makes it easier for the learner to find links between pieces of knowledge and practise using their knowledge, and to become more skilful in the subject they are studying. In her book *What Every Teacher Needs to Know* (2022), Jade Pearce refers to the seven steps for explicitly teaching learning strategies that are detailed in the 2018 Education Endowment Foundation report (Quigley et al., 2018). With careful planning and adaptation of the strategies we use in the classroom, these steps can be effectively applied to the online classroom too. They are:

- Activating prior knowledge
- Explicit strategy instruction
- Modelling of the strategy
- Memorisation of the strategy
- Guided practice
- Independent practice
- Structured reflection

> The EEF toolkit ranks metacognition and self-regulation as the second highest impact strategy of all classroom practices, sitting just behind feedback. (Webb, 2021)

What might explicit teaching of metacognitive strategies look like and when does it happen?

> understanding metacognition is only part of the process – and implementing and sustaining approaches that support metacognitive thinking and independent learning can be really challenging. (Education Endowment Foundation, 2023)

I believe that we all learn in largely the same way. As individuals, we face unique challenges, experiences and emotional barriers when acquiring new knowledge, and approaches need to be adapted to best support the individuals we teach, but our brains retain knowledge in the same basic way regardless of the content we are learning. It does not discriminate in this, whether we are learning online or face to face in the classroom. Metacognitive knowledge and processes can be taught using the same explicit teaching model that we use for teaching subject-specific knowledge. Inspired by *The Revision Revolution* (Howell, 2022), I believe that the knowledge and processes required can be delivered through a metacognitive curriculum for students, taught throughout their time in their educational setting. In a secondary setting, for example, this might be a tutor time programme where each year group learns a different strategy. Year 7 may look at self-quizzing, year 8 at mind mapping, year 9 may use flashcards, year 10 brain dumps and year 11 Cornell notes. The teaching of techniques may be revisited across the years as a form of retrieval practice. Year 7 may also learn about retrieval practice explicitly through a whole-school policy where every class uses low stakes quizzing and they may have a homework platform that they are trained to use as well as other opportunities to learn and practise using metacognitive processes.

Self-quizzing is an example of a technique where students think metacognitively. In our setting, students are given a knowledge organiser and have a self-quizzing timetable that they follow. They answer a set of questions independently and then check their answers, marking them in green pen. Any incorrect answers are repeated until they have answered all questions correctly.

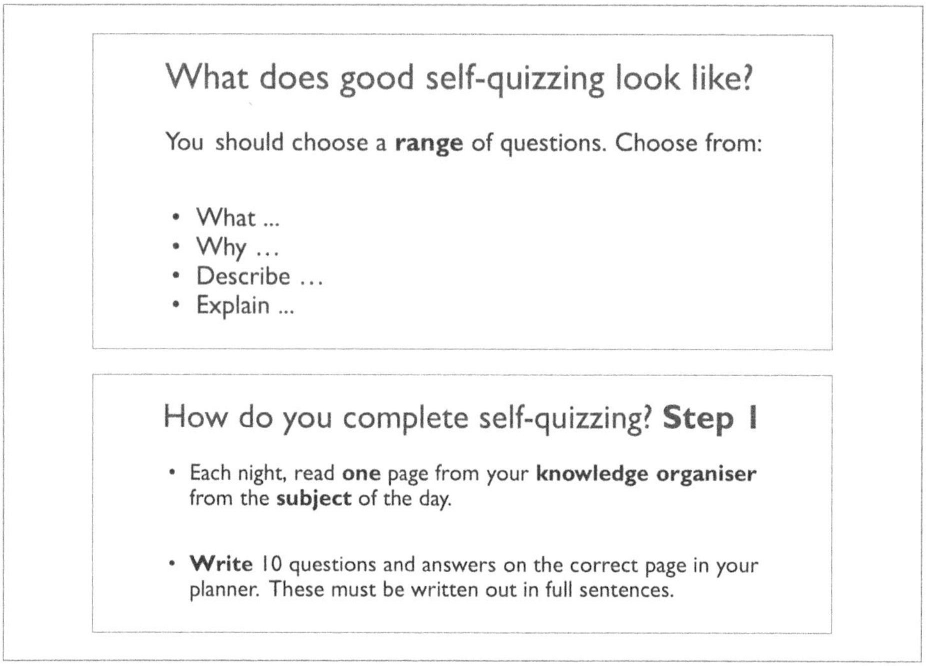

What does good self-quizzing look like?

You should choose a **range** of questions. Choose from:

- What ...
- Why ...
- Describe ...
- Explain ...

How do you complete self-quizzing? **Step I**

- Each night, read **one** page from your **knowledge organiser** from the **subject** of the day.

- **Write** 10 questions and answers on the correct page in your planner. These must be written out in full sentences.

Figure 9.1 Slides from the instruction self-quizzing video (used with permission from Josie Shelton)

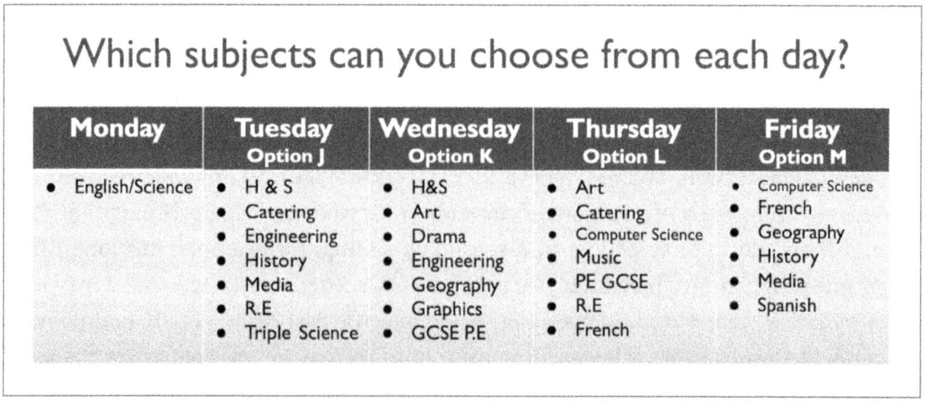

Which subjects can you choose from each day?

Monday	Tuesday Option J	Wednesday Option K	Thursday Option L	Friday Option M
• English/Science	• H & S	• H&S	• Art	• Computer Science
	• Catering	• Art	• Catering	• French
	• Engineering	• Drama	• Computer Science	• Geography
	• History	• Engineering	• Music	• History
	• Media	• Geography	• PE GCSE	• Media
	• R.E	• Graphics	• R.E	• Spanish
	• Triple Science	• GCSE P.E	• French	

Figure 9.2 An example of a self-quizzing timetable (used with permission from Josie Shelton)

Contents	
Homework timetable and expectations	Page 2
Login details	Page 3
Knowledge organiser – practice book example	Page 4
FAQs	Page 5
Knowledge organiser – homework guidance	Page 7
Sparx Maths homework – Sparx book example	Page 9
Year 8 English Monday Night	Page 13
Year 8 Science Tuesday Night	Page 17
Year 8 German Wednesday Night	Page 21

Figure 9.3 Contents from a knowledge organiser

Set 1 Music 5/1/23	Piece of information	Definition
1	Djembe	A West African drum used for communication
2	Rhythm	An interesting pattern of beats
3	Pulse	The beat of the music
4	Crochet	One beat
5	Quaver	½ beat
6	Dynamics	The volume of the music (loud or quiet)
7	Texture	The layers of the music (thick or thin)

Figure 9.4 Screenshots from an instructional video and resource, offering a glimpse into the explicit teaching of self-quizzing to year 7 students (used with permission from Zoe Giblin)

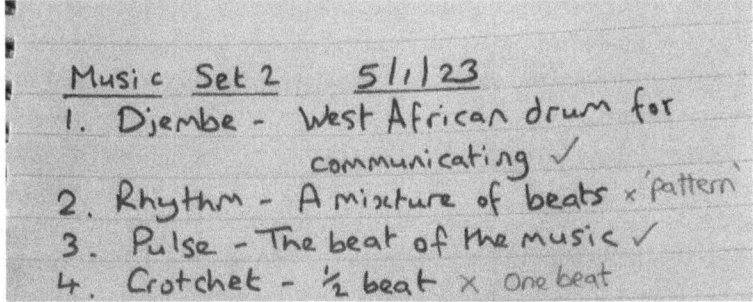

Figure 9.5 Screenshots from an instructional video and resource, offering a glimpse into the explicit teaching of self-quizzing to year 7 students (used with permission from Zoe Giblin)

The 'I do, we do, you do' model lends itself to online learning through instructional videos or through a live lesson format. It can be used to teach metacognitive strategies in the same way that it can be used to teach subject-specific knowledge. First, the teacher models using the process themselves, using foundational subject knowledge in the process so that students are not thinking hard about the subject knowledge as well as the metacognitive process. Teacher expertise for metacognitive thinking can be variable as the knowledge is outside their subject-specific domain. This is another reason why the modelling is delivered in the form of an instructional video from an expert. It ensures that every student has access to the same high-quality instruction. In the live online lesson, the teacher completes a second example with the student, where students support the teacher in their thought process. This can be through the chat function or Cold Calling students and students being unmuted to answer questions. A culture of error needs to be built for questioning to become effective in generating accurate data on student understanding. In a recorded lesson, the student may be working asynchronously and the teacher will check for understanding, collecting the data via quiz forms, emails or screenshots. Appropriate *Wait Time* is added to the video or lesson so that the students have time to 'have a go'. Once the teacher is confident that the students have understood the process and why it works, the students engage in deliberate practice of the skill, in the online classroom, independently, but in the company of the teacher. In a live lesson, students and teacher may use the chat function to ask questions; in a recorded lesson, this may be done using email. The teacher is available to offer scaffolding, as they would in a lesson in their subject. They may 'close the feedback loop' if common misconceptions are appearing by re-teaching part of the lesson (Lemov et al., 2012). Thai can be an additional shared recording or a live model using a visualiser. At the end of the session, students are required to practise the process further independently as part of a homework task. They can submit their work electronically through screenshots, pictures or online quizzes. They are advised that they will now be asked to use the technique in future lessons in their subjects as part of subject-specific homework.

For example, when teaching the process of self-quizzing, the teacher may be explaining to a year 10 online history class what they should be looking out for when answering an 18-mark question: 'You are likely to need a paragraph on this and so you will need to be able to retrieve two or three of these key ideas.' They may show a set of self-quizzing questions that provide the knowledge required to answer the question in sufficient detail. At this stage, we expect students to be able to use the self-quizzing process successfully because it has been explicitly taught in year 7 and has been used in other subjects, but, assuming no prior knowledge, the process of self-quizzing can be revisited briefly in the context of the 18-mark question. They are already beyond the novice stage of self-quizzing, and forming these subject-specific links will help them to very quickly become experts at self-quizzing, so this input is deliberately brief. The teacher may only need to highlight and model a few key features or misconceptions for self-quizzing, reminding students to revisit their incorrect answers, for example.

Once the teacher is satisfied that the students have understood what the process of self-quizzing looks like in history, the students can have a go themselves. This can be through a homework assignment that prepares them for the next lesson's retrieval quiz. Once the skill is automatic for the students, the students are then in a position to use it in their subject with newly taught knowledge, when called upon by the subject teacher. The subject teacher can then teach subject-specific knowledge and expect students to use the process they have learned without having to teach the technique of self-quizzing. Students can now simply be asked to complete their independent self-quizzing in preparation for the next retrieval task lesson. The teacher adapts to any arising need for further teaching of the self-quizzing process as they collect their retrieval data. By the end of the process, the students should be in a position where they understand the process, why it works and are well practised in its effective use, as well as having learned the intended subject knowledge.

Although the metacognitive technique is explicitly taught when students are novice self-quizzers, as they become experts, the process of self-quizzing should no longer be modelled to them. Guidance should be given as to which pieces of information to explore and when; knowing which knowledge to self-quiz on requires expert knowledge. Students are guided on what the most powerful knowledge is for their self-quizzing questions, but ultimately, they should be able to use the technique with these chosen questions independently.

> Self-regulation is hard: students must already know what they're doing.
> (Fletcher-Wood, 2022)

> Metacognition is not something which is *done* to students, such as a pop quiz or live modelling. Metacognition is something which students do *themselves*.
> (Webb, 2021)

Figure 9.7 is an example of how a teacher might model a set of self-quizzing questions in a year 10 history class. Note how the model looks the same in structure as the explicit metacognitive lessons taught in year 7 with the content adapted to offer multiple responses to questions in preparation for an 18-mark GCSE History question.

Metacognition in subject-specific modelling: what does this look like in the online classroom?

> Metacognition and self-regulation approaches to teaching support pupils to think about their own learning more explicitly, often by teaching them specific strategies for planning, monitoring, and evaluating their learning. (Education Endowment Foundation, 2023)

We want to integrate students' thinking about how they are learning with what they are learning. We often think of the metacognitive process as coming in later in the

1	Elizabeth's 1	Why did some people question whether Elizabeth was the legitimate queen?	Her father had annulled his marriage to Anne Boleyn
2	Elizabeth's 1	Give TWO problems that Elizabeth's gender posed:	Couldn't lead an army in battle / expected to do what her husband wanted
3	Elizabeth's 1	Mary I died without an heir. What does this mean?	She did not have any children to take the throne after her
4	Elizabeth's 2	How much debt did Elizabeth inherit from Mary?	£300,000
5	Elizabeth's 3	Give THREE features of Catholic belief:	Latin bibles / priests wear vestments / Pope head of the church
6	Elizabeth's 3	Give THREE features of Protestant belief:	English bibles / Monarch head of the church / plain churches
7	Elizabeth's 3	Who were the Puritans?	Extreme Protestants
8	Elizabeth's 5	Why was Elizabeth's Religious Settlement known as the Middle Way?	It contained Catholic and Protestant beliefs
9	Elizabeth's 4	Name TWO Catholic superpowers:	Spain and France
10	Elizabeth's 4	Name TWO highly Catholic parts of England:	The North and the West

Figure 9.6   An example of self-quizzing in history (used with permission from Ed Durbin)

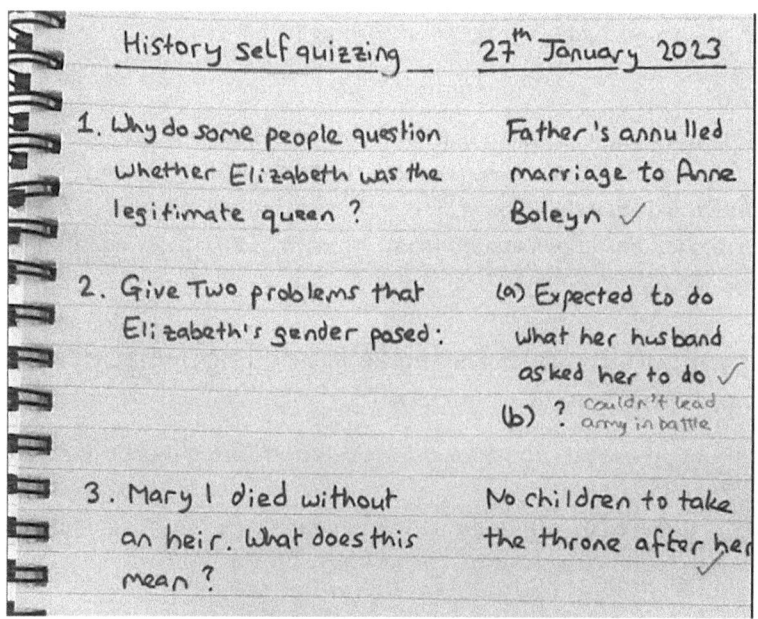

Figure 9.7   An example of how a teacher might model a set of self-quizzing questions in a year 10 history class

learning episode. It is easy to think that once students have understood a process, they can then reflect on the learning that has taken place within that process. Craig Barton suggests that in 'Reflect, Expect, Check, Explain', during the input stage of a learning episode, when using an 'I do, we do, you do' model, students should be reflecting on the process, making predictions about what would happen if one aspect of the example was altered. They then check if their prediction was correct, explaining why they were correct or incorrect (Barton, 2020). It is the structured reasoning – the making connections and reflecting on predictions – that helps students to become more accomplished metacognitive learners, linking pieces of knowledge together with increased skill and precision (Webb, 2021). Although this reflective process may be more clear-cut in mathematics, reflecting on how the examples are similar and different and reflecting on the similarities and differences that you'd expect in an excellent answer holds true for other subjects too.

But when do we narrate the subject knowledge and processes to students and when do we narrate our thinking and choices for doing something in a certain way? There will be times when it makes sense to narrate our thoughts first and sometimes it makes more sense to share the knowledge first and then talk about why you did what you did. The order in which you narrate the thinking and the knowledge will depend on the knowledge that you are sharing and how expert you are. Although it is important to explore this further, scripting the detail in your narration necessitates time and strong subject knowledge, both of which require thought beyond this chapter. The examples in Table 9.1 simply offer a starting point for these reflections for a live lesson.

When using the 'I do, we do, you do' model, there is a natural lag between narrating the process for an example and making links between examples. During the 'I do' phase of modelling, I would explain the process to students, with the students simply watching. They would be expected to write nothing and to have their full attention on the model being used in the example. It is harder to use the 'Teach like a Champion' technique of *Radar* online, but the expectation is still there and habits in lessons should support the online classroom culture.

Table 9.1 Examples of narrating subject knowledge in a lesson

Making connections between examples	I do	We do	You do	Deliberate practice
Narrating the process	Teacher narration	Cold Call/mini whiteboard check using unmute button/chat function	Reteach or deliberate practice	Check responses for subject-specific quiz questions
Narrating the thinking	–	Narration	Cold Call/mini whiteboard check using unmute button/chat function	Check responses for metacognitive quiz questions

In the 'we do' part of the process, students would be Cold Called to check for understanding for the process, either as a mini whiteboard check for understanding using the chat function or for a deeper check for understanding using Cold Call and the unmute button. Introducing this second, 'we do' example gives the first opportunity to explore the links between examples. For this reason, I would narrate the link without asking for input so that the students are able to observe the thinking process.

In the 'you do' phase of the model, students would share answers but students have not yet had the opportunity within the modelling to offer their thoughts regarding links between examples, so I would Cold Call or use the chat function after the sharing of student answers to explore the links they have found. These questions would be structured to guide their exploration of the links. If the check for understanding showed subject-specific misconceptions at the 'you do' phase, I would repeat this phase. If the students show metacognitive misconception, I would offer a new example for students to explore links. I would then use a quiz where students independently practise the processes and independently practise finding links between the questions they complete. I would monitor the answers centrally as they submitted them on a quiz form. If there are misconceptions in either the process or the links, we would stop the practice early and address the misconceptions. In other words, the feedback loop is shortened (Lemov et al., 2012).

The 'I do, we do, you do' approach works and feels better for expert learners. For novice students, more scaffolding may be required and so there may be more examples in the 'I do' phase of the modelling. It is likely that for novice students the knowledge is less complex or the processes have fewer steps, making it easier to add more examples and giving more opportunities to explore links between the examples. The links that are found may be simpler, so you may see and plan for more repetition in the links shared, reducing cognitive load and increasing retrieval success and motivation. The prompt questions in Craig Barton's book are an excellent starting point for planning a sequence of metacognitive questions to ask students (Barton, 2020):

> Reflect: What have they pointed to and asked?
>
> Expect: What do I think the answer is?
>
> Check: What is the answer?
>
> Explain: Do I understand why?' (Barton, 2020)
>
> Using Cold Call throughout your lesson not only holds students accountable but also reassures them that we value their presence and their contributions. (Lemov, 2015)

Learning the process of thinking at the same time as learning new knowledge can lead to unintentional cognitive load. So if students become confused, rather than making the learning easier, it may be the teaching method that is not being implemented well. Techniques such as colour in the examples, tone, layout and organisation of the example can help to ensure that the multi-faceted approach is a complementary one. I use an informal tone when explaining my thinking and a more formal tone for explaining processes. Colour is used to highlight similarities or link pieces of information. It is not used unless it has a cognitive purpose. Adding colour without meaning can add to cognitive load. Students may wonder why it is there or be distracted by the aesthetics or the example. Some narration may overlap, and this is not an exact science of course, but delivering the narration with this tone in mind helps to distinguish between the types of modelling that are happening throughout the examples.

When considering the cognitive load for a student and what we can do to minimise external noise so that the student's attention is on exactly what it needs to be, there may be no narration whatsoever. Some examples need narration, as watching a process alone is not a sufficient scaffold for the student to understand what is happening and why, but often the example will be better understood when the teacher is working through silently. The same ideas mentioned above can apply when this happens.

As I proceed working through the example, my use of colours and annotations take on more importance. Colours can also be used to distinguish between subject-specific thinking and metacognitive thoughts. For example, the process can be in black pen, the annotation explaining the process can be in green and the questions exploring metacognitive thought can be in blue. Rather than using annotation, I can simply highlight or point at different parts of the process or underline the key elements in appropriate colours before I complete the process and begin my narration. Adopting a consistent approach is key to students being able to understand the role of colour. Then they will be able to grasp the key ideas more quickly.

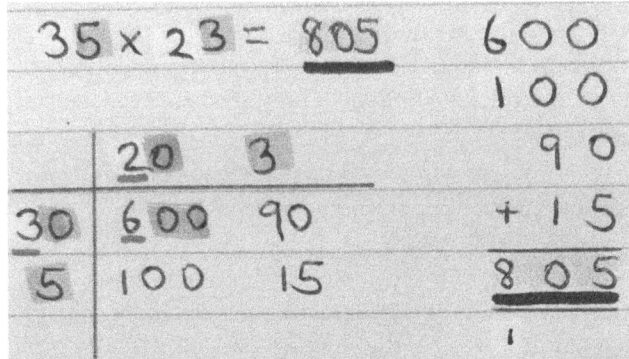

Figure 9.8 An example of colour coding in maths to convey process

How Do We Choose the Right Techniques and Examples for Metacognitive Learning?

When modelling subject-specific knowledge in mathematics, examples are created so that the 'I do' is similar to the 'we do' with one variable changed. During the modelling process, the thinking process is narrated with the students in mind. For novice students, the narration will focus on metacognitive behaviours where students are expected to check their work or consider common misconceptions in their predictions. Questions will be scaffolded and more specific to support students to frame their thinking. For more expert students, the students may be encouraged to make more complex predictions on what they think might happen in the next example. The students will then work through the 'we do' example, with the teacher checking for understanding and moulding the thinking process. As discussed, the check for understanding will look different depending on whether the lesson is live or recorded. During this part of the lesson, students will be asked to consider a range of carefully planned metacognitive questions. Why did they make the choice they did? What other possible answers are there? Is one method more concise or efficient than another, and why? Students may be encouraged to consider the boundary examples and why a particular answer cannot be correct. During the model, students will be expected to write down their reflections. There are lots of benefits of asking everybody to write down their thinking, as described in 'Teach Like a Champion'.

> Students remember significantly more of what they are learning if they write it down. (Lemov, 2015)

If Lemov's statement is true, students are more likely to remember the metacognitive processes that they have engaged with if they write them down.

> In the classroom we can promote this journey from guided to independent talk by doing the following things.

- Explicitly speaking out loud our thought process when we model tasks in front of the students
- Giving students written prompts and asking them to speak to themselves out loud before, during and after a piece of work. (Webb, 2021)

> At this point, students are able to apply metacognitive principles independently and are actively thinking through the kinds of questions which have previously been spoken to them and by them. (Webb, 2021)

When teaching metacognitive behaviours to novices, we should think about how we scaffold the process in the same way we might think about scaffolding subject-specific knowledge. Novice students 'look backwards' (Didau, 2019), so they will benefit from more precise, scaffolded questions. They will need the thinking process to be broken down into small steps:

- Why did I not choose the number three here?
- What would I do here if I found an error?

- What step should I go back to if I need to have another go without starting again?
- What do I need to change to ensure that I don't make the same mistake next time?

More expert students will require and desire the opportunity to explore links between pieces of knowledge:

- What happens if I double these numbers?
- What might the examiner report say here?
- Why do I make this misconception?

If we get this right, we will most likely have a high success rate and increase student motivation. If we are going to practise metacognitive strategies through problem solving with students, we want to choose knowledge that does not put a load on the working memory, applying a similar rationale to the explicit teaching of metacognitive strategies.

> This technique of asking yourself 'why?' may be better suited to some students rather than others. (Watson & Busch, 2021)

When choosing examples, it is important to think carefully about the links that you want your students to find and other links that the students may find, as well as possible misconceptions with the links that may be seen. Some examples may look like they link in a certain way when in fact they do not link in this way at all. This is fine, as long as they are introduced at the right time so that you can recognise this along with your students. If it builds understanding, great, but if it breeds misconception, then it's not the right example for that stage of the learning episode. I plan my examples so that I avoid links between questions that introduce new knowledge. In this way, I reduce cognitive load. If the links highlight misconceptions, I very deliberately introduce these misconceptions. For novice students, the links will be less complex and there will be more repetition naturally, due to the examples they see. If I want them to see more complex links, I will be more structured in the narration I give to support students in finding them. For more expert learners, I choose examples that offer opportunities for further exploration and desirable difficulties. For example, I link other pieces of prior knowledge with the examples. When planning what I want the students to find, I must be prepared for them to find unexpected, wonderful links that I have not thought of. These moments are the hardest to teach, especially in the online classroom, but they are often the more interesting and enjoyable moments too, as I learn and grow in my own knowledge.

> We very often show how to create a successful piece of work but we don't always show them how to quality assure it when they have finished. (Webb, 2021)

We want to use the most effective technique for learning the content being taught. Different techniques work better in different topics and different subjects. How well they work is based on a number of complex factors – the depth and breadth of the content, opportunities to link to already acquired knowledge, the subjectivity, to name a few. I won't pretend to be an expert in which techniques work best and when. As the expert in your field, you will have a much better idea about which techniques will have the greatest impact with your students and when!

Ideas for the Classroom

Which parts of this chapter can you relate to? Which ideas do you think will have a positive impact on your students' ability to think critically about their learning? Which sections resonate less well with you? Why? Which ideas will be easy to implement? Which ideas can you try tomorrow? Which parts do you disagree with? Which elements will be more challenging to embed as learning habits? Why? Below are some ideas to get you started on this reflective journey.

- There are similarities and differences between online and classroom teaching. We need strong knowledge of what they are so that we can choose effective teaching strategies and plan how to use them online.
- We can explicitly teach metacognitive strategies online.
- When students are more expert in using a metacognitive strategy, we can ask students to use the strategy when engaged in subject-specific examples.
- We should look to build habits for success by using specific, consistent routines (Fletcher-Wood, 2022).
- Novices think differently from experts. Accordingly, we must plan questions to check for and deepen understanding of metacognitive strategies.
- We should carefully scaffold metacognitive thinking for novices. We should use more open questions for experts.
- When using metacognitive strategies when practising more complex questions, we should use foundational knowledge material to avoid cognitive overload.
- Everyone can learn to think metacognitively. Metacognitive behaviours need to be taught to all students so that engaging in these behaviours independently becomes habitual.

What is metacognitive teaching not?

To understand what it means to teach metacognitive thinking to our students, we need to be mindful of what metacognition is not:

- Metacognition is not a bolt-on.
- Metacognition is not a fad.
- Metacognition is not a skill exclusively taught to experts or taught at the end of a learning episode.

What are the barriers to teaching metacognitive behaviours?

To be able to teach metacognitive thinking, we need to be aware of the barriers to meta-cognitive thinking and have strategies to overcome them. Table 9.2 lists some of these barriers and suggests some useful strategies.

Table 9.2 Barriers to thinking metacognitively in the online classroom and how to overcome them

Barrier to thinking metacognitively in the online classroom	How to overcome the barrier
Teacher subject knowledge	Impart knowledge through reading, professional development training and provide opportunities for teachers to plan modelled examples and practise collaboratively.
Teacher knowledge of how to teach metacognitive thinking	We can confuse metacognitive thinking with deep subject thinking. Isolate the skill. Offer CPD that is specific to metacognitive practices.
Popularity with some teachers	Teachers are more likely to buy into an idea that has proven to be successful and when they know how to complete the process (see managing change) (Kotter, 2012).
Behaviour and school culture can make metacognitive conversations challenging to do	Embed a culture of metacognitive thinking in your school/classroom through consistent use of routines.
You can't teach someone to revise; they do this independently	Just because our students are learning how to be independent learners, it does not mean they need to discover how to do this independently. Use explicit instruction to teach students how to think independently.
Time	By teaching metacognitive strategies well, you save time in the long run as students become better at forming links and finding their own misconceptions.
How do we know that our students are thinking?	Build the culture and the active participation follows. You can measure thinking through output. In the periods of silence, trust that thinking is taking place. Interrupting to measure thinking can be tempting if the learning is not visible, but it is often counterproductive as students need time to think.
Confidence in our approach	The ideas in this chapter are an interpretation of how you can teach metacognitive thinking in the online classroom. Using a structured approach reduces cognitive load for the teacher and builds learning habits for the students since they know what to expect.
	Learning is not binary; it is complex and messy. But by ensuring consistency in delivery, and displaying humility when giving feedback and when adapting approaches, you are more likely to succeed.

> Being alert to the positive side of making mistakes and following the sequence of acknowledging them, thinking through how to do things differently, also keeps us nimble. (Myatt, 2016)

This chapter represents one method of how you can teach metacognitive thinking in an online classroom. This is not to say that the approaches are the right ones, but using consistent approaches, developed through research and experience, and by adopting a humble and curious approach to regular feedback, you are more likely to succeed when using metacognitive strategies. I envisage this chapter dating quickly as we respond to the new online learning environment. I therefore look forward to learning from others as we, as a community, become more expert at teaching in the online classroom.

If they are to teach metacognitive strategies effectively, the methods I have described in this chapter require teachers to be experts both in their subject and in how humans think. It requires teachers to be expert enough that they can combine the two skills and teach metacognitive thinking through the delivery of subject-specific knowledge. There is a need to teach students metacognitive processes independently so that they know how to think metacognitively and how to apply the skills to their subject-specific learning. There is space to do this in an online curriculum. We had to be reactive to the immediate, urgent change brought about by the Covid-19 pandemic, but we need to isolate the subject-specific and metacognitive skills before asking students to combine them. Explicitly teaching metacognitive knowledge comes before applying the knowledge to subject-specific learning.

So, to become an expert metacognitive teacher, it seems there is much to consider. Maybe too much. My own cognitive load is stretched. Designing such a curriculum is complex and it takes time to train staff. Impact is difficult to measure, particularly in online teaching. Teaching is such a rewarding and complex vocation, and it will take a lifetime and more to be the expert I strive to be for my students. I am on a journey, and every day I am learning more about how metacognitive strategies can complement explicit instruction. As I progress on my journey, I look forward to learning much more and becoming more expert in my understanding of the knowledge and skills that are needed to apply effective metacognitive learning strategies.

This would be a good time to reflect on your own learning and to think about what you can take away from this chapter. The examples in Table 9.2 may act as a starting point. Good luck and thank you for joining me on this wonderful journey!

Further Reading and References

Inspired and informed by:

Bambrick-Santoyo, P. (2018). *Leverage leadership 2.0: A practical guide to building exceptional schools.* San Francisco, CA: Jossey-Bass.

Barton, C. (2018). *How I wish I taught maths: Lessons learned from research, conversations with experts, and 12 years of mistakes*. Woodbridge, UK: John Catt.

Barton, C. (2020). *Reflect, expect, check, explain: Sequences and behaviour to enable mathematical thinking in the classroom*. Woodbridge, UK: John Catt.

Burns, N. (2023). *Inspiring deep learning with metacognition: A guide for secondary teaching*. London: Sage/Corwin Press.

Chiles, M. (2020). *The CRAFT of assessment: A whole school approach to assessment for learning*. Woodbridge, UK: John Catt.

Didau, D. (2019). *Making kids cleverer: A manifesto for closing the advantage gap*. Carmarthen, UK: Crown House Publishing.

Didau, D. (2021). *Making meaning in English: Exploring the role of knowledge in the English curriculum*. Abingdon, UK: Routledge.

Education Endowment Foundation (2023). *Mobilising metacognition: A starter kit to support teacher understanding*. [Blog]. Available at: https://educationendowment foundation.org.uk/news/eef-blog-mobilising-metacognition-a-starter-kit-to-support-teacher-understanding (accessed 24 May 2023).

Enser, Z., & Enser, M. (2020). *Fiorella and Mayer's generative learning in action*. Woodbridge, UK: John Catt.

Fletcher-Wood, H. (2022). *Habits of success: Getting every student learning*. Abingdon, UK: Routledge.

Howell, H. (2022). *The revision revolution: How to build a culture of effective study in your school*. Woodbridge, UK: John Catt.

Jones, K. (2019). *Retrieval practice: Research & resources for every classroom*. Woodbridge, UK: John Catt.

Jones, K., & Macpherson, R. (2021). *The teaching life: Professional learning and career progression*. Woodbridge, UK: John Catt.

Kotter, P. (2012). *Leading change*. Boston, MA: Harvard Business Review Press.

Lad, N. (2021). *Shimamura's MARGE model of learning in action*. Woodbridge, UK: John Catt.

Lemov, D. (2015). *Teach like a champion 2.0: 62 techniques that put students on the path to college*. San Francisco, CA: Jossey-Bass.

Lemov, D. (2020). *Teaching in the online classroom: Surviving and thriving in the new normal*. San Francisco, CA: Jossey-Bass.

Lemov, D., Woolway, E., & Yezzi, K. (2012). *Practice perfect: 42 rules for getting better at getting better*. San Francisco, CA: Jossey-Bass.

Mansworth, M. (2021). *Teach to the top: Aiming high for every learner*. Woodbridge, UK: John Catt.

Mattock, P. (2019). *Visible maths: Using representations and structure to enhance mathematics teaching in schools*. Carmarthen, UK: Crown House Publishing.

McCourt, M. (2019). *Teaching for mastery*. Woodbridge, UK: John Catt.

McGrane, C., & McCourt, M. (2020). *Mathematical tasks: The bridge between teaching and learning*. Woodbridge, UK: John Catt.

Morgan, J. (2019). *A compendium of mathematical methods*. Woodbridge, UK: John Catt.

Myatt, M. (2016). *High challenge, low threat: Finding the balance*. Woodbridge, UK: John Catt.

Pearce, J. (2022). *What every teacher needs to know: How to embed evidence-informed teaching and learning in your school*. London: Bloomsbury.

Pershan, M. (2021). *Teaching math with examples*. Woodbridge, UK: John Catt.

Pink, D. (2018). *Drive: The surprising truth about what motivates us*. Edinburgh: Canongate Books.

Quigley, A., Muijs, D., & Stringer, E. (2018). *Metacognition and self-regulated learning: Guidance report*. Education Endowment Foundation. Available at: https://educationendowmentfoundation.org.uk/education-evidence/guidance-reports/metacognition (accessed 25 October 2023).

Rainbow, R., & Tushingham, D. (2022). What Every Teacher Needs to Know with Jade Pearce. *GLT & Friends Book Club* [Podcast], 4 October. Available at : https://www.youtube.com/watch?v=Jz6z42u3b7Q (accessed 6 October 2022).

Robbins, A. (2021). *Middle leadership mastery: A toolkit for subject and pastoral leaders*. Carmarthen, UK: Crown House Publishing.

Sherrington, T. (2020). The art of modelling… it's all in the handover. *Teacherhead – Zest for Learning… into the rainforest of teaching* [Blog], 28 November. Available at: https://teacherhead.com/2020/11/28/the-art-of-modelling-its-all-in-the-handover/ (accessed 24 October 2022).

Watson, E., & Busch, B. (2021). *The Science of learning: 99 studies that every teacher needs to know* (2nd ed.). Abingdon, UK: Routledge.

Webb, J. (2021). *The metacognition handbook: A practical guide for teachers and school leaders*. Woodbridge, UK: John Catt.

10

Metacognition Together: The Power of Challenge Talk and Contrast

Michael Walsh

An Educational Issue

Metacognition has in many recent publications been characterised as a teacher-led approach with explicit strategies provided for students. However, while the Education Endowment Foundation (EEF) Teaching Toolkit recognises the significant potential impact of metacognition in educational attainment, it also highlights a problem: 'it can be difficult to realise this impact in practice as such methods require pupils to take greater responsibility for their learning and develop their understanding of what is required to succeed' (EEF, n.d.).

This chapter will argue that alongside explicit teaching, teacher modelling and the development of strategies, pupils also need to develop an understanding of what Flavell (1979: 907) describes as 'everything that you could come to believe about the nature of yourself and other people as cognitive processors'. Designing suitably challenging tasks and socially situated metacognition through talk is a means to achieve this and provide greater responsibility to students.

Your Approach

- How do you design lessons and questions to encourage metacognition?
- What role do you see for talk in metacognition?
- How do you use classroom peers to support students to become more aware of their thought processes?
- How do you slowly transfer responsibility for metacognition from the teacher to the students?
- How do you support pupils to develop their ability to monitor and evaluate collectively as well as individually?

The Metacognitive Approach

One of our aims when developing a metacognitive approach is to support students to become more consciously aware of their thinking. We are therefore seeking the Goldilock's level of the 'just right' challenge that causes students to pause and encourages planning, monitoring and reflection but is not so difficult that it is beyond students' reach and decreases their engagement and motivation. In the 'Summary of recommendations' of the EEF's *Teaching and learning toolkit: Metacognition and self-regulation* (n.d.), point 4 states: 'Set an appropriate level of challenge to develop pupils' self-regulation and metacognition'. It recommends the following:

- Challenge is crucial to allow pupils to develop and progress their knowledge of tasks, strategies, and of themselves as learners.
- However, challenge needs to be at an appropriate level.
- Pupils must have the motivation to accept the challenge.
- Tasks should not overload pupils' cognitive processes, particularly when they are expected to apply new strategies. (EEF, n.d.)

In setting an appropriate challenge we need to ensure the task or questions are sufficiently familiar to provide opportunities for students to build on their prior knowledge, while also sufficiently thought-provoking to require accommodation and new ways of thinking. A challenge for educators is to recognise what is intrinsically challenging for students.

You may wonder what that looks like? An example from a *Let's Think in English* (www. letsthinkinenglish.org) lesson may help. The lesson is entitled 'Poetry or Prose' and supports students to develop their ability to classify   in this instance, the key question is how do we know when a text is a poem? To set a challenge, we must sequence our task or questions carefully. So in this lesson, students start by accessing their prior knowledge via the question: What do we expect poetry to look like? A very common response from year 7 students is whether it rhymes and the way it looks on the page (structure). Once students have shared their list of the characteristics of poetry, they are then invited to apply their classification list to two texts and decide if the texts are poems or not.

We then come to the cognitive conflict or challenge. Students are presented with William Carlos Williams' poem 'The Red Wheelbarrow' (www.poetryfoundation.org/poems/45502/the-red-wheelbarrow). The text is selected because it does not have a clear rhyming scheme, so students can't take the easy option and say it is a poem because it rhymes. Furthermore, when the students are presented with the poem, the line breaks are removed, so they read it as one continuous line. This denies them the other key feature of their poetry scheme: structure. Students typically feel that the text is poetic, but they must move beyond the easy explanation and dive deeper when considering what make it a poem/poetic.

How does such a challenge help in encouraging metacognition? Table 10.1 shows how a year 10 class responded to this question.

Table 10.1 Student responses to 'The Red Wheelbarrow'

	(The teacher re-reads William Carlos Williams' poem, 'The Red Wheelbarrow')
Teacher	So, there was more disagreement this time. So let's see if it is poetry or prose? Did any table manage to agree?
	(The teacher takes feedback and finds that three groups have agreed it is poetry but two are unable to agree)
Teacher	So, let's start with those who think it's a story. *(Some students raise their hands)* Explain to us.
Student A	In a story they are using 'the', so it must have been mentioned before. There's something that comes before this part.
Teacher	Interesting. Does anyone else agree?
Student B	I thought it was a story as there was a crisis, like so much depends upon. If the red wheelbarrow is not there, what would happen?
Teacher	Can poetry have a crisis? *(Lots of 'yeahs' from the class)* But the crisis makes you think it's a story?
Student B	Yes, that and there's lots of description and the adjectives. And the fact they say it's white chickens not the chickens. It's descriptive.
Student A	Yes, there's a plot. There's a story happening.
Teacher	So, you've found two of the features we agreed could be in a story. Any other thoughts on the phrase 'so much depends upon'?
Student C	I think it's a poem but I like a story too, but the reason why I think it's a poem is it has a clear rhythm.
Teacher	What's the clear rhythm?
Student C	Each line has 11 syllables.
Teacher	Is that so? Did anyone else notice a pattern. *(The class begins to count and there are murmurs of agreement)*
Teacher	Yes, we will come back to you. What about over here. *(The teacher moves to groups that haven't spoken yet)* Remember when I was moving around you said 'I just think it's a poem' despite most of your group saying it's a story. Did you get any closer to understanding why you had the feeling it was a poem?
Student D	Probably it's the rhythm. The first line and second line. They don't sound like they should be one long sentence but they should be two different lines. They create two different lines in my mind.
Teacher	Two different lines in your mind... *(Student B is keen to speak again)* Student B, you said you found what Student A said very convincing but you didn't think it was a story but a poem. Could you explain that now?
Student D	I think it depends where this piece of text comes from. If it's from the middle or the start.
Teacher	So would it help if I told you whether there was more text to accompany this and where it came from within a text? *(The class nod and agree)* Well, this is it; the complete text. Is that helpful? Does it change things? *(The class breaks out into spontaneous small independent discussions)*
Student E	I think it's a poem because the two lines link.
Teacher	Could you explain the link?

(Continued)

Table 10.1   Student responses to 'The Red Wheelbarrow' *(Continued)*

Student E	The second last word in each line is a colour. So like, in the first line it's red and the second line is white. And both last words have two bits... like wheelbarrow (stresses second syllable) and chick-ens (*Student E stresses the 'ens'*).
Student F	Yeah, maybe everything stands for more than it is. Like the red wheelbarrow and the white chickens aren't just wheelbarrows and chickens. I think it's a poem. I think you need to read between the lines.
Teacher	That's an interesting idea. (*Some students nod*) Something to consider when we start the next activity. Can I have a quick show of hands ... who now thinks it's poetry? (*More hands go up than initially shown*) Who now thinks it's a story or prose? (*Fewer hands go up*) Who changed their minds during the discussion? (*Four hands are raised*)

If we accept that monitoring and evaluating our thoughts are key components of metacognition, then we are more likely to become consciously aware of thinking when it is challenging. Furthermore, as evidenced in the transcript in Table 10.1, we are also more likely to become consciously aware of our thinking when we can compare and contrast our thoughts with others. The students in this example are not merely thinking 'Is my response correct?', they are having to critically evaluate their own ideas in the light of other ways of thinking. By its very nature, this process makes students more likely to monitor and evaluate their thinking.

Question prompts

You may notice in the transcript in Table 10.1 that the teacher choses to adopt a neutral stance. This approach may seem at odds with some recommendations that teachers should model their own thoughts to evoke and encourage metacognition. However, teacher input is key. Teachers can evoke metacognitive opportunities through timely, carefully considered questions, such as:

- Can you explain what you mean by...?
- Tell us a bit more about...?
- What led you to think that?
- What do you think about X's point?

Such apparently simple question prompts are encouraging pupils to pause in their interpretations, to monitor, evaluate and, if possible, develop their thoughts further. We view students' responses as being directed to another, typically a teacher, but sometimes a peer. However, for many students the first audience of their utterances is themselves. By giving words to their inner, fleeting, half-formed thoughts, students can articulate and hear their own ideas and become more consciously aware of how they think.

Only once they are aware of their own thinking are students able to monitor, review and evaluate.

Here it is important to draw a distinction between 'talk for learning' and 'talk for performance'. Talk for performance is when students are presenting at an assembly, in a debate, etc. We would expect a structured presentation with a formal register. In contrast, 'talk for learning' recognises talk as a tool to assist learning and has an immediacy as students give words to their emerging thoughts. For some students, they can articulate their inner thoughts in a fluent, structured way. For others, their utterances may be marked by hesitations, repetitions and informality. Yet often these are the very markers that indicate the students are thinking hard and are more likely to lead to the conscious awareness of their own thoughts that encourages metacognition. In the 'Summary of recommendations' of the EEF's *Teaching and learning toolkit: Metacognition and self-regulation* (n.d.), point 5 emphasises the need to: 'Promote and develop metacognitive talk in the classroom'. It includes the following recommendations:

- As well as explicit instruction and modelling, classroom dialogue can be used to develop metacognitive skills.
- Pupil-to-pupil and pupil-to-teacher talk can help to build knowledge and understanding of cognitive and metacognitive strategies.
- However, dialogue needs to be purposeful, with teachers guiding and supporting the conversation to ensure it is challenging and builds on prior subject knowledge. (EEF, n.d.)

But what if students overlook a possible answer, interpretation or metacognitive strategy? The teacher can model their own thinking and explain their interpretations, highlighting the key lines and words that contribute to this understanding. Alternatively, they can provide a gentle nudge:

A class I taught last year would always argue _____. Why might they say that?

Here the teacher provides a scaffold by suggesting a premise but not the reasoning behind it. The students are encouraged to step into the mind of another and consider why they might think this way. This provokes another cycle of monitoring and evaluation as the students consider this new premise and compare it with their previous thinking.

Pause for review and neutrality

Teachers can explicitly support pupils to become more metacognitively aware of how their thinking has changed by providing an opportunity to pause and consider if their thinking has changed. The teacher can take the temperature of the room by listing the different answers, responses or interpretations evoked and asking pupils to consider which one they most agree with. If teachers are seeking to develop pupils' self-efficacy, they may first encourage a 'blind vote' by asking pupils to close their eyes and raise their hand in support of the interpretation they agree with. They can then follow up by providing feedback to the class regarding the collective response rather than saying 'It seems most of you agree with point X. In your groups, can you explain why?'

Once pupils share their responses in classes, it is normal for teachers to offer an evaluation. For example: 'I like the idea...' or 'I'm not sure if that links to the previous three stanzas...'. However, one of the aims of metacognition is to develop pupils' evaluative capabilities. In the light of this, one might agree that there are times when teachers should be less explicit in their feedback and encourage pupils to critically evaluate the ideas that have been shared.

In *Let's Think in English* lessons, pupils are encouraged to evaluate their own ideas and the ideas of others. However, to create an environment where this is likely to happen, teachers may need to revise their use of praise. When a teacher praises or validates a response, it is less likely pupils feel the need to monitor and evaluate the ideas that have been shared. Teachers who adopt a neutral stance can encourage pupils to be active agents in monitoring and evaluating ideas, and once more provide further opportunities for pupils to develop self-efficacy.

Metacognitive prompts

Metacognition should be a thread that runs throughout a lesson with the ebb and flow of thoughts being shared. It supports students to be more consciously aware of how they and others think. Identifying rich metacognitive opportunities in lessons can be helpful, but it may be best to avoid seeing metacognition as an add-on moment in a lesson. As the EEF guidance suggests, we should offer pupils opportunities to 'reflect on and monitor their strengths and areas of improvement, and plan how to overcome current difficulties' (EEF, n.d.). Supporting students with metacognitive prompts and encouraging them to track and consider how their ideas change and to reflect on the tasks undertaken, are helpful. Such prompts might include:

- Our first thoughts were...
- We've now realised...
- It was difficult/easy to....
- If I was to do this again, I would...
- Some further questions I have are...

A helpful technique to support pupils to take a bird's eye view of their learning experience is to ask them to consider the strategies they used in the lesson. You may ask pupils to imagine that they will address another class which is going to study the same text and to consider what advice they would give them. However, you need to explain that they can't explicitly reference the text in hand. This encourages pupils to move beyond the specific and to start to generalise and identify transferable strategies.

Some schools see value in 'metacognition walls', which provide prompts. These are working walls, where pupils can populate the wall with post-it notes listing the metacognitive strategies they've discovered. However, these strategies are continually reviewed and adapted in the light of new findings.

Summary

In his pioneering and ground-breaking work on metacognition, Flavell (1979: 907) identified metacognitive knowledge as having 'three major categories of these factors or variables—person, task, and strategy'. He defined the person category as '...everything that you could come to believe about the nature of yourself and other people as cognitive processors' (Flavell, 1979: 907).

It is this understanding of yourself and others that is so central to the *Let's Think in English* programme and is informed by Vygotsky's social constructivism (Vygotsky, 1962). It could be argued that metacognition is more than the sum of strategies learnt, but rather is a developing consciousness, awareness and habit of the mind that monitors and evaluates input. Developing pupils' self-efficacy is a tricky task but it can best be achieved by balancing the need for explicit guidance and teacher modelling with opportunities for pupils to be responsible for their own learning. Challenge and opportunities for talk are central to this.

With time, students and classes may attain the academic benefits of metacognition, as identified by the EEF. But if we recognise it as a habit of the mind, we may also help them to reach the other goal identified by Flavell: 'to make wise and thoughtful life decisions' (Flavell, 1979: 910).

Ideas for the Classroom

Here are some prompts to start to develop metacognition through talk in your classroom.

- Plan for challenge. Can you set low-entry but high-ceiling tasks and questions that engage and challenge all students? It may be helpful to consider setting questions or tasks that can be seen in many ways or evoke two different responses. Where are the rich opportunities for metacognition in your subject. What might students find difficult about this topic/schema?
- Encourage students to give words to their thoughts. Provide time and guidelines for students to work in small groups so they are accountable. You may wish to number the students so each has an opportunity to talk. Try to create a collaborative environment where students are free to share their thoughts without immediate fear

of being right and wrong, and ensure that their ideas and thoughts can be refined throughout the lesson.

- Consider your role in supporting evaluation. Can you find opportunities where you put the onus on the students to evaluate the ideas that have been shared by asking them to vote and justify their choices? Perhaps you can encourage students to make the argument for a different train of thought from their own? At the end of a lesson, you can provide time for student testimonials, where groups identify the students who helped them to understand the lesson. The emphasis should be on *how* the students helped them.
- Can you provide metacognitive prompts or sentence starters that support students? What language is helpful to encourage metacognition in your classroom.

Further Reading

Flavell, J. H. (1979). Metacognition and cognitive monitoring: A new area of cognitive-developmental inquiry. *American Psychologist, 34*(10), 906–911.

This article offers an overview of the Foundations of metacognitive theory.

Education Endowment Foundation (2021). *Metacognition and self-regulation: Guidance report*. EEF. Available at: https://d2tic4wvo1iusb.cloudfront.net/production/eef-guidance-reports/metacognition/EEF_Metacognition_and_self-regulated_learning.pdf?v=1689843802

This is the definitive guide to metacognition in the classroom.

Let's Think in English (n.d.). [Website]. Available at: www.letsthinkinenglish.org

Let's Think in English is a teaching programme that helps primary and secondary children develop the higher-order skills they need to be successful in English. The website provides brilliant resources to support metacognition in the English classroom.

Vygotsky, L. (1962). *Thought and language.* (Edited by E. Hanfmann & G. Vakar). Cambridge, MA: MIT Press.

For more in-depth thinking about constructivism in education, Vygotsky is the author to read.

References

Education Endowment Foundation (n.d.). *Teaching and learning toolkit: Metacognition and self-regulation. EEF.* Available at: https://educationendowmentfoundation.org.uk/

education-evidence/teaching-learning-toolkit/metacognition-and-self-regulation (accessed 20 October 2023).

Flavell, J. H. (1979). Metacognition and cognitive monitoring: A new area of cognitive–developmental inquiry. *American Psychologist, 34*(10), 906–911.

Let's Think in English (n.d.). [Website]. Available at: www.letsthinkinenglish.org

Vygotsky, L. (1962). *Thought and language.* (Edited by E. Hanfmann & G. Vakar). Cambridge, MA: MIT Press.

Williams, W. C. (1938). The Red Wheelbarrow. In W. C. Williams, *The collected poems of William Carlos Williams, Volume 1, 1909–1939.* (Ed. by C. MacGowan). New York: New Directions Publishing.

11

Learner Identity and its Contribution to Successful Outcomes for Students

Genevieve Bent

An Educational Issue

As a science teacher, I have spent a great deal of my time exploring barriers to (my) students pursuing science at higher education and beyond. As a head of department, one of my most important priorities is to raise the profile of my subject, not just academically but in ways that students can engage with and relate to. Over the last 20–30 years, there has been more research and initiatives focused on increasing the participation of underrepresented groups in science, to improve diversity in the sector. Not just here in the UK, but similar in the USA, where there continues to be a visible lack of progression for certain groups in the sciences, such as women (UNESCO, 2019). With many teachers adopting the notion that science is free from identity, biases or culture (Gholston Key, 2000), the 'nature of science' historically has not provided an environment which some of our students can identify with or relate to.

This being said, the research heavily suggests that there is an issue with identity, or rather the lack of identity, not only in science education but in educational contexts generally. This chapter looks at how self and social identity can play a part in improving student engagement, and teaching and learning more generally.

More recently, the idea of learner identity has been introduced to teachers as a key part of metacognition and promoting metacognitive strategies in students. A 'learner identity' can be defined as how someone feels about themselves as a learner and the extent to which they describe themselves as a 'learner'. Kolb and Kolb (2012) described a learner identity as students having the metacognitive knowledge to understand how they learn, particularly their views about their ability to learn. When students have a learner identity, they can see themselves as learners and take on opportunities to extend their learning in the classroom, and in life. Where students do not have a positive learner identity, they will not see themselves as a learner. A learner identity develops over time and students' learner identities sit on a spectrum. Therefore, as teachers, we have a big role to play in helping students adopt and build their own learner identities.

When students are in the early phases of the educational career, they often have conversations about what/who they aspire to be when they grow up. These questions play a part in shaping their 'self' and 'learner' identity, and their responses change over time. How students adapt and respond to building their learner identities can be a product of the metacognitive processes that students undergo.

In their book *Self and Social Identity in Educational Contexts*, Mavor, Platow and Bizumic (2017) explore how identity can be introduced in the classroom to promote learning and influence the academic attainment of learners. A self-identity is made up of an individual's history, memory and expectations, a person's current state, and how they make meaning of the context, in this case, the educational context (Mavor et al., 2017). Having a social identity in an academic environment is believed to improve students' reading, writing and overall outcomes, due to this, a deeper metacognitive insight ought to be taken.

Your Approach

As a classroom teacher, have you made a point of exploring your students' academic experiences before they arrived in your classroom at the beginning of the year? In what ways have you done so? Has it been in a traditional teacher–student dialogue to gain a better understanding of your students, or maybe you have taken a different approach? Focusing on metacognitive strategies to improve students' development of their learner identity, it is important that students can evaluate their own attitudes and approaches to learning while you, as the teacher, facilitate this process. For example, have you given students opportunities to reflect on their learning, not just in a plenary task, but overall, at the end of a term perhaps? Do you give students opportunities to ask questions in relation to their learning and to suggest strategies that they believe are beneficial for their own learning?

What strategies have you previously used to support your students to become more responsible for their own learning and to be more positive about their learning experience? With what sometimes feels like a never-ending curriculum and targets for outcomes, this can feel like a daunting and time-consuming task, as well as low priority, but promoting metacognition by improving your students' learner identities is becoming a highly valued and important process in securing positive outcomes for students at school and beyond.

The Metacognitive Approach

The purpose of this section is to outline some metacognitive strategies to develop learner identity. It provides some suggestions of what to do, how to do it, and the intended outcome/s.

The learner identity of your students is built on where students see themselves and their role in the educational context. This, in turn, is dependent on whether students see themselves as capable of 'doing' the subject, for example 'doing science', as well as communicating this capability to others. The more positively students recognise their ability to learn, the stronger their learner identity will be.

Self-evaluating their learning

How do you move students from being passive learners to becoming learners who actively take responsibility for their learning and develop a positive learning identity? One approach is by designating your students tasks which allow them to evaluate their learning. You can ask them questions about their perception of themselves as learners:

- What are your strengths as a learner (in my classroom)?
- What are your weaknesses as a learner (in my classroom)?
- What learning strategies have you developed that you feel support you in your learning, for example...?
- What have you not tried that could be useful in becoming a more effective learner in my classroom?

All these questions can, and should, be linked to the goals that students set for themselves, whether these are personal, academic or career-oriented goals. This exercise is designed to help students to connect their ideas to the importance of their learning, not just in your classroom but in all their lessons and in their overall learning ambitions. Of course, I would be naïve to think that every student wants to pursue my subject, especially given the access to science education I discussed at the beginning of my chapter. However, the large majority of students do have aspirations, and your classroom is a stepping stone towards them achieving those aspirations; most of your students want to do 'well'. When you direct students to 'think about their thinking', you are assisting them to shape their own perceptions and beliefs about their learning.

In addition, when students are given the opportunity to be reflective about their learning, you are giving them the implicit message that while your voice as the teacher and your authority are important, their voice is valued too. You are also showing them that there isn't just one right approach to learning, but that their approach to thinking and learning is important too, not just them but you as their teacher.

In providing opportunities for students to become reflective in their learning, you are moving them from being not just *aware*, but to being *strategic* and *reflective* in their metacognitive development.

Explicit aims

In terms of promoting metacognition to build learner identity, when teachers set students tasks, whether it is an assignment, a self-reflection task or another goal, they need to be explicit and transparent about the rationale for doing so. To develop learner identity using a metacognitive approach, students should be clear on why they are doing a particular task and what the long-term outcome for learning is. For example, you can say: 'This task is working at a grade 7, but more importantly, it also allows us to develop a deeper understanding of x, y, z' or 'This task allows you to contribute to society in this way due to...'. Students and teachers are then working towards a common goal, with an understanding of shared expectations and a shared value in doing so.

Explicit instruction by teachers consists of sharing the stages of the learning process (related to the learning focus), with pre-planned opportunities for students to build their metacognitive skills at each stage. For example, the planning, monitoring and evaluation stages need to include questions for students to reflect on, while planning, self-monitoring and evaluating their own learning journey. For example, the planning, monitoring and evaluation cycle need to be made explicit to students to develop their understanding. Questions posed to students could include: 'What do you already know about the topic and', 'what gaps in your understanding do you believe that you have'. Naturally, this seems like an easier task to undertake with older, or more advanced learners. However, the Education Endowment Foundation (EEF) describes studies undertaken in primary schools as being more effective than in secondary schools, when carried out for similar periods of time (Education Endowment Foundation, 2018).

Open-ended retrieval opportunities

Retrieval activities are second nature to teachers; embedding opportunities for students to retrieve knowledge from their long-term memory bank is evident in most, if not all, lessons. Adapting what you do from time to time to incorporate metacognitive practices for students is straightforward and may be something you do already. For example:

- What did we do in our lesson yesterday?
- What did we learn in our lesson last week?

These open-ended questions allow students to think back of course, but also allow them to construct their own responses to what they learned during the previous lesson. You will naturally see variation in responses from different learners, but you can overcome some of the initial resistance through modelling and coaching the type of response you would like to see. These responses can be in different forms, whether they are verbal, written in books, or written on mini whiteboards. The most important thing is that students are given the time and space to think and answer. This is unlikely to be achievable in every lesson, but with regular practice, you are prompting students to become more reflective and self-aware and are helping them to shape their learner identity over time.

Self-directed learning opportunities

Allowing students to participate more actively in the design of their learning may sound questionable and unachievable, particularly given Key Stage 4 curriculum constraints, but it is something that can be used flexibly to suit you, your curriculum demands, and/or your learners.

An effective strategy to promote self-directed metacognition is, first, to provide students with an objective or 'big question' on the topic of the lesson and, second, to direct them on the most effective ways to tackle it or answer it, but then, crucially, to give them time to address the task independently. As the teacher, you are facilitating the learning process by telling students what to do and suggesting ways on how to go about it, but then students need to be encouraged to do the task independently. You can scaffold the task to support those whom you know will find it challenging – for example, a planning document, containing columns for knowledge of task, self and strategies, could be used to guide and self-monitor the process.

The EEF's Metacognition and Self-Regulated Learning (2021) describes giving students opportunities to plan, monitor and evaluate as part of promoting metacognition. Something I consistently do with my applied science students is to teach them the principles of whatever concept we are learning that lesson/week. They are then assigned a 'big question' which they need to work through independently, but with my overarching guidance. Then individual students share their work with the rest of the class, in what has become a safe learning environment. Of course, I cannot take this approach in every lesson, but I am consistent in providing my students with opportunities to 'do' my subject, and I am therefore working on building their positive learning identities.

Another strategy to provide self-directed learning opportunities is to use students' self-evaluation feedback and to implement it into future learning time. This has two benefits. First, student feedback is seen to be taken on board, so students know that their thoughts and suggestions are being considered. Second, students can see that the self-evaluation, whenever it is required, is worthwhile and it therefore becomes more powerful over time, for the students and yourself.

Promoting positive dialogue in the classroom

Building a positive learner identity relies heavily on the language that students use to describe themselves in the subject, and how this is monitored. In everyday life, it has long been accepted that people use statements such as 'I was bad at maths' or 'I was always rubbish at science' or something similar. Schools can be a microcosm, where students use sweeping statements to describe their challenges in a subject. This is even reflected by teachers who can also describe themselves in similar ways.

To encourage students to reinforce a positive learning identity, they need to refrain from making negative statements and to be encouraged to use positive ones. A simple way to do this is to disallow students from using negative statements, such as 'I'm not good at...' or 'I'm rubbish at...', in your learning environment, and instead to promote positively framed statements with your students. This requires students to think more reflectively about the way they see themselves as learners in the classroom.

Ideas for the Classroom

It can be difficult to pinpoint where to start when you are provided with a range of strategies, so I will outline my suggestions below.

Reflection on your context is important, as you know your students best. When thinking about your students, where do you see the biggest resistance occurring? Will they be most resistant in talking more positively about themselves or others, for example? Or will they find it more difficult to reflect on their own learning? Reflecting on these things will allow you to plan ways to navigate these challenges.

The easiest place to start is to reframe students' narratives on themselves as being poor learners in your subject. Share with students that you will not allow any of them to talk about themselves negatively in your subject. While this may take some time for students to implement this use of language, it is the most straightforward strategy for you to apply and monitor, and you will see a tangible impact very quickly.

Embedding an evaluation of reflective practices in your classroom will take some time, but the sooner you introduce this to your students, the sooner you can get students to see the benefits of doing so. You can start with a simple feedback form that you ask students to complete. They can produce their feedback via an online submission or as homework, in the first instance. This way you are not taking away from curriculum time or collecting 30 papers to flick through while 30 books are waiting to be marked. Equally, the feedback can take the form of a discussion between a focus group of students across a subject and the Head of Department to capture a range of learners' views of the subject.

Over time, the feedback can incorporate more open-ended questioning about the learning, and not just the subject matter. It can also encourage students to take a more active role in their learning in the plan and monitor stages of the PEM model of metacognition. This will help to build their positive learner identities and promote successful outcomes for your students.

Further Reading

Kolb, A. Y., & Kolb, D. Y. (2012). Learning identity. In N. Seel (Ed.), *Encyclopedia of the sciences of learning*. Boston, MA: Springer. https://doi.org/10.1007/978-1-4419-1428-6_229

This chapter explores what is meant by a learner identity and how it is constructed.

Mavor, K. I., Platow, M. J., & Bizumic, B. (Eds.) (2017). *Self and social identity in educational contexts*. London: Routledge. https://doi.org/10.4324/9781315746913

This book offers a detailed insight on what it means to construct an identity in the education context and how this is achieved through a range of interconnected factors.

Oxford University Press (2022). Why learner identity is key to successful science lessons. *TES Magazine*, 22 June. Oxford: Oxford University Press. Available at: www.tes.com/magazine/sponsored/oxford-university-press/why-learner-identity-key-successful-science-lessons

Along with a colleague from another school, I discuss why learner identity is important to successful (science) lessons and provide approaches for making it happen.

References

Education Endowment Foundation (EEF) (2018). *Metacognition and self-regulation: Education evidence*. Available at: https://educationendowmentfoundation.org.uk/education-evidence/teaching-learning-toolkit/metacognition-and-self-regulation (accessed 19 October 2023).

Education Endowment Foundation (EEF) (2021). *Metacognition and self-regulated learning*. Available at: https://educationendowmentfoundation.org.uk/education-evidence/guidance-reports/metacognition (accessed 19 October 2023).

Gholston Key, S. (2000). *Diversity in science education: Research into practice*. Glenview, IL: Pearson Scott Foresman.

Kolb, A., & Kolb, D. (2012). Learning identity. In N. Seel (Ed.), *Encyclopedia of the sciences of learning*. Boston, MA: Springer.

Mavor, K. I., Platow, M. J., & Bizumic, B. (Eds.) (2017). *Self and social identity in educational contexts*. Abingdon, UK: Routledge.

UNESCO (2019). *Fact sheet No. 55: Women in science*. Paris: UNESCO. Available at: https://uis.unesco.org/sites/default/files/documents/fs55-women-in-science-2019-en.pdf. (accessed 19 October 2023).

12

Connecting the Brain to the Page: The Power of Live Modelling in the Classroom

Kate Allen

An Educational Issue

Why do so many students struggle to get their thoughts onto paper? Most can articulate their ideas but struggle to turn their thoughts into the written word; somehow, the connection gets lost in translation. It's as if there is an overload of information, which prevents our students from even getting started; their brains are their own barriers.

Cognitive load theory

Branded by Dylan Wiliam as 'the single most important thing for teachers to know' (Wiliam, 2017), cognitive load theory is vital in understanding how students learn and, by extension, how best to teach them. Despite only becoming a core component of teacher training programmes in recent years, this theory teaches us vital things about how the human brain works – working/short-term memory, long-term memory, and memory overload. Cognitive load theory also warns teachers about the futility of exposing students to too much information at once (Sweller, 1998), and illustrates the necessity of avoiding cognitive overload.

If we want our students (whatever their ages, whatever the topic) to retain information and learn how to apply it independently, we *have to* have an understanding of the mechanics of the brain.

The more knowledgeable other

Lev Vygotsky's theories centre around the idea that learning and cognitive development are driven by social interaction (McLeod, 2023). In the 1970s, Vygotsky presented his concept of the More Knowledgeable Other (MKO). Children, he argued, learn from adults who have a better understanding of a concept than they do (Vygotsky, 1978). This then links in with his concept of a Zone of Proximal Development (ZPD) where, he states, there needs to be an understanding around what a child can achieve independently, and what they can do if given some support from the MKO (Figure 12.1) (Vygotsky, 1978).

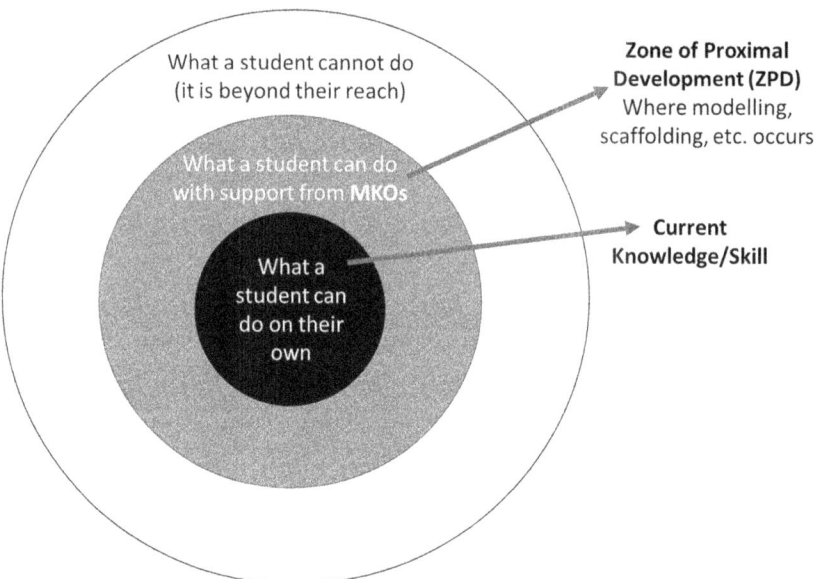

Figure 12.1 Diagram illustrating Vygotsky's ZPD and MKO concepts

As teachers, we all acknowledge the importance of Vygotsky's MKO, and the vital role we play in expanding students' ZPDs; indeed, our very position as teachers places us as the MKO, with the important job of sharing our knowledge with our students. Even when we train to teach, whichever route we take, we rely on observing others teaching before we attempt to teach ourselves. In those moments, our MKOs are the qualified practitioners we observe planning lessons, sequencing the curriculum, and teaching and assessing their students. But, for some reason, we don't seem to put as much emphasis on our primary and secondary students needing to observe learning processes themselves.

It's time to demystify the thinking processes behind constructing well-formed written pieces of work. By illustrating our live thoughts and actions, we can demonstrate how to translate our thoughts into the written word, and remove this mental block which causes our students so much angst.

This chapter will focus on the value of live modelling. We will explore what thinking is, illustrate the connection between thinking and cognitive processing, and explain why live-modelling can be such an effective tool for learning.

Your Approach

We all know that getting ideas onto paper seems to be a huge barrier to a lot of pupils. When it comes to their production of individual responses, how do you currently support your students in translating their thoughts into the written word?

When it comes to independent tasks, how do you ensure that students recognise their own strengths, and understand their own barriers? How do you support pupils in knowing how to overcome these barriers and push themselves forward?

Once you begin to gather verbal or written responses from pupils, how do you support them in developing a depth of complex thoughts and ideas? How do you help them to become critical, evaluative thinkers?

When in front of a class of students, how often do you verbalise your thought process (step by step), rather than presenting students with a pre-constructed model?

How do you model precise mental processes and example answers effectively? How do you ensure that students understand how to follow these processes independently, and do not just copy off the teacher (or one another)? Live modelling is an excellent method of giving tools to students, so they feel more prepared and, therefore, develop a much greater understanding of how to create responses on their own.

The Metacognitive Approach

There is a huge amount of value in sharing, discussing and dissecting modelled answers (WAGOLLs[1]), but how far do students understand the processes by which we created these masterpieces? There is a common assumption among our pupils that teachers 'just know' how to write high-quality responses because we're teachers – it may make you question what came first: the WAGOLL or the teacher?

While creating a pre-prepared exemplar for students to read can be very valuable, there is often a vital component missing which would allow students to understand the process of transferring their thoughts onto paper. In essence, a pre-written model example may illustrate the *results* of the thinking process, but the *process* itself remains hidden.

It would be like giving a video tutorial on how to bake a cake, but turning the camera off whenever you were adding an ingredient or doing anything with the mixture. What did you do with the sugar? What temperature was the oven? Instead, students see the grand reveal of each stage (each delicious layer of cake), but are not guided through the step-by-step process of *how* each layer was actually created (Figure 12.2).

Many of us also utilise WAGOLLs to help to determine whether students understand what each component of the written response should look like, or to illustrate how to structure an answer. In the example in Figure 12.3, the teacher gave students the

---

[1] WAGOLL stands for 'What a Good One Looks Like' and is essentially a good example. You might also come across WABOLLs ('What a Bad One Looks Like'), which are usually used to get students thinking about how to improve a response.

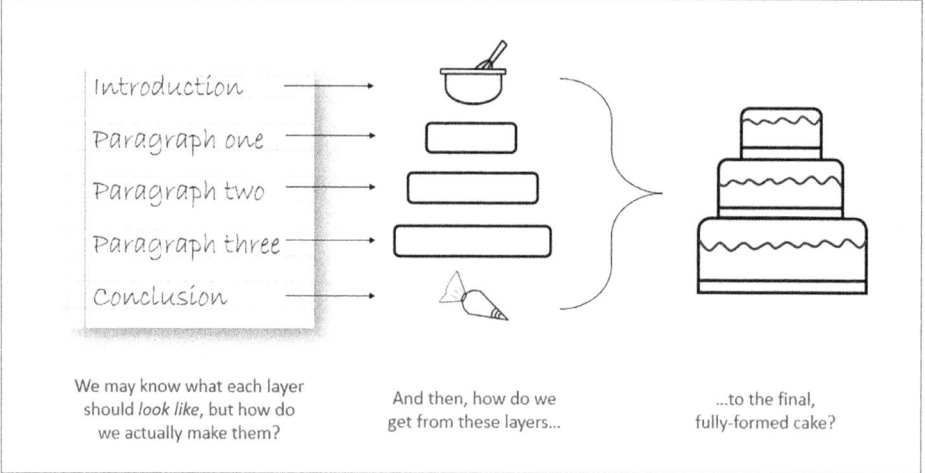

Figure 12.2 A pre-written model example may illustrate the results of the thinking process, but the process itself remains hidden

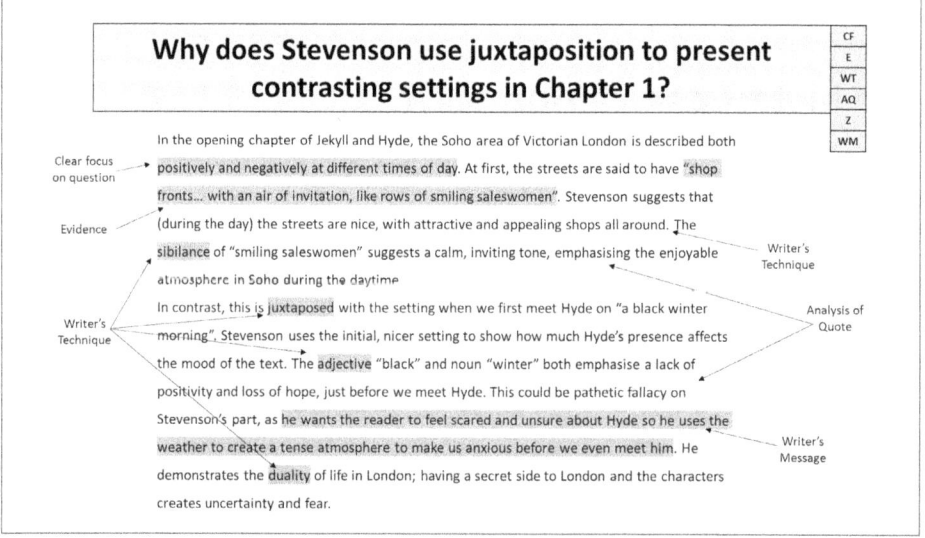

Figure 12.3 An example WAGOLL to determine student understanding of components of a written response

example (unannotated and uncoloured), and asked them to identify each element of the response.

Although the annotation on this example may give the impression that students fully understand what each element of an answer should contain, under these models, students may struggle to recreate each of the component stages themselves: they will know how the cake should look, but not necessarily be able to bake it on their own and get the same quality of result as the example they have seen.

Although there is something to be said for asking students to identify different elements within an example (so we can be sure that they understand what the final product could look like), it should only be used in conjunction with higher-order thinking – in essence, we must include the *meta* for true cognition to occur. Burns (2023) defines the concept of 'metacognition' as combining higher-order ('meta') with thinking ('cognition'). By guiding students through *how* a response is produced, we allow them to understand *how* to enable their own metacognitive thinking.

There is one clear method of facilitating this higher-order thinking: live modelling.

Live Modelling: Demystifying the 'How'

Giving students control

There is now a plethora of research to support the idea that students (of all ages) learn more effectively, and achieve better outcomes, when they have more control over their own learning (Bransford et al., 2000).

The concept of cognitive control suggests that students who gain control over their cognitive processes and learning become more proactive in their own learning, and are more likely to sustain learning and knowledge over a longer period of time (Munakata et al., 2012). But by 'control', we don't necessarily mean that students are dictating *what* they need to learn or whether or not to complete tasks in lessons; rather, they begin to understand *how* they learn, meaning they can take ownership over their own learning and understand *how* to push themselves further. It is cognitive control, but guided.

This links in directly with cognitive load theory: by giving students the tools they need in order for learning to occur without overloading their brains, we facilitate a much higher degree of independent thought and learning (Deleeuw & Mayer, 2008).

For the most effective long-term learning to occur, therefore, we need to reduce students' cognitive load and increase their cognitive control.

To reduce cognitive load, there are a number of steps we can take, which are outlined next.

Thinking time

Give thinking time so students have a chance to process new information and questions before answering them.

- Think – Pair – Share
- Cold calling questioning, with thinking time

Deconstruct the task

Deconstruct the questions/tasks so it's clear what they are being asked to do.

- What are the key instructional words in the question?

Front load vocabulary

Front load new vocabulary – this will help to remove a huge barrier for a lot of students, as well as exposing them to a wider variety of complex language.

- Key definitions and vocabulary lists
- Frayer models
- Translations, where necessary

Avoid the noise

Avoid too much noise within a learning environment – this can cause distractions and overload.

- Refer to behaviour policies within institutions
- Consider SEN/EAL needs

Videos with transcripts

If playing videos in lessons where you want students to refer back to the content for a subsequent activity, provide transcripts as well.

- Key quotes or full transcripts

Logical sequencing

Sequence lessons and schemes of work in a logical way, so students can identify connections.

- Collaboration within departments is key to developing a collective strategy and sequence of learning

Example answers

Regularly use WAGOLLs for written responses.

- Use high-quality example answers for tasks
- Always use top-level responses for examples so students can aspire to higher levels of understanding
- Live-model exemplar answers (illustrated in the next section)

Success criteria

Use clear success criteria for pieces of work.

- Use success criteria alongside WAGOLLs to illustrate what you mean
- Select some key knowledge/skills to focus on for individual pieces of work
- Avoid too many different criteria, avoid cognitive overload

Scaffolding

Provide scaffolding, both verbally and written (before gradually removing it).

- Sentence starters
- Writing frames
- Scaffold strips
- Verbal open questions

Exemplar answers are an excellent way of reducing cognitive load, but to increase cognitive control, we need to teach students *how* to produce them on their own. In his observational learning model, Albert Bandura identified live modelling as a vital component of learning, arguing that children need to be exposed to examples of processes in action in order to understand and learn them (Bandura, 1971). Although he was primarily looking at behaviour and speech, Bandura identified a key link between observing processes before they can be effectively replicated.

Live modelling: Translating thought into writing

Language is 'the parent, and not the child, of thought'. (Oscar Wilde)

For students to be able to produce high-quality written responses, they need to elevate the language of their own thinking processes in order to elevate their critical thinking skills. Several researchers have posed the idea that language is the key to thinking: Ludwig Wittgenstein (1971, p.115) stated that 'the limits of my language mean the limits of my world' and Bertrand Russell (1992, p.92) said that the role of language is 'to make possible thoughts which could not exist without it'. As teachers, we are actively seeking to open up the world for our students, and language is an enormous part of accessing and succeeding in that world.

Lev Vygotsky was the first psychologist to discuss the importance of the inner voice, which he considered to be the unification between language and thought. Vygotsky argued that 'private speech' was an accelerator to thinking and understanding (Diaz & Berk, 1992). But a problem many students face is understanding what those elevated thinking processes *look like*, and so how to replicate them independently.

As Vygotsky said, we need to give students the key to language so that they can formulate their own internal monologues, which are integral to their cognitive development (Vygotsky, 1987). Teachers, therefore, must verbalise their own thinking processes in order to demonstrate what academic thinking looks like, and to expose students to similar language and linguistic framing so that they can mimic it in their own brains.

Spontaneous live modelling

In spontaneous live modelling, the teacher guides students verbally through their thinking process, modelling their thinking processes out loud, while writing on a whiteboard or under a visualiser so that the class can see the resultant translation of thought into the written word.

In the example in Figure 12.4, the teacher was guiding a small group of year 7 students (all very low-level literacy, with various SEN) through a piece of creative writing, based on detective fiction.

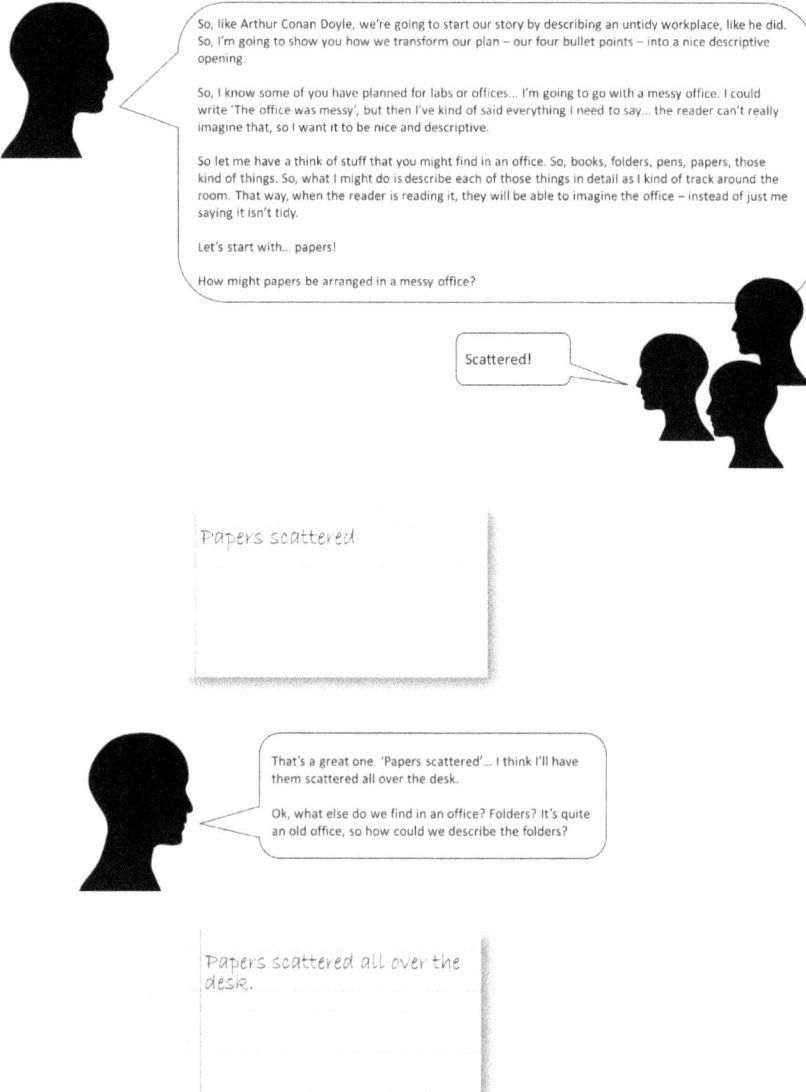

Figure 12.4   Spontaneous live modelling

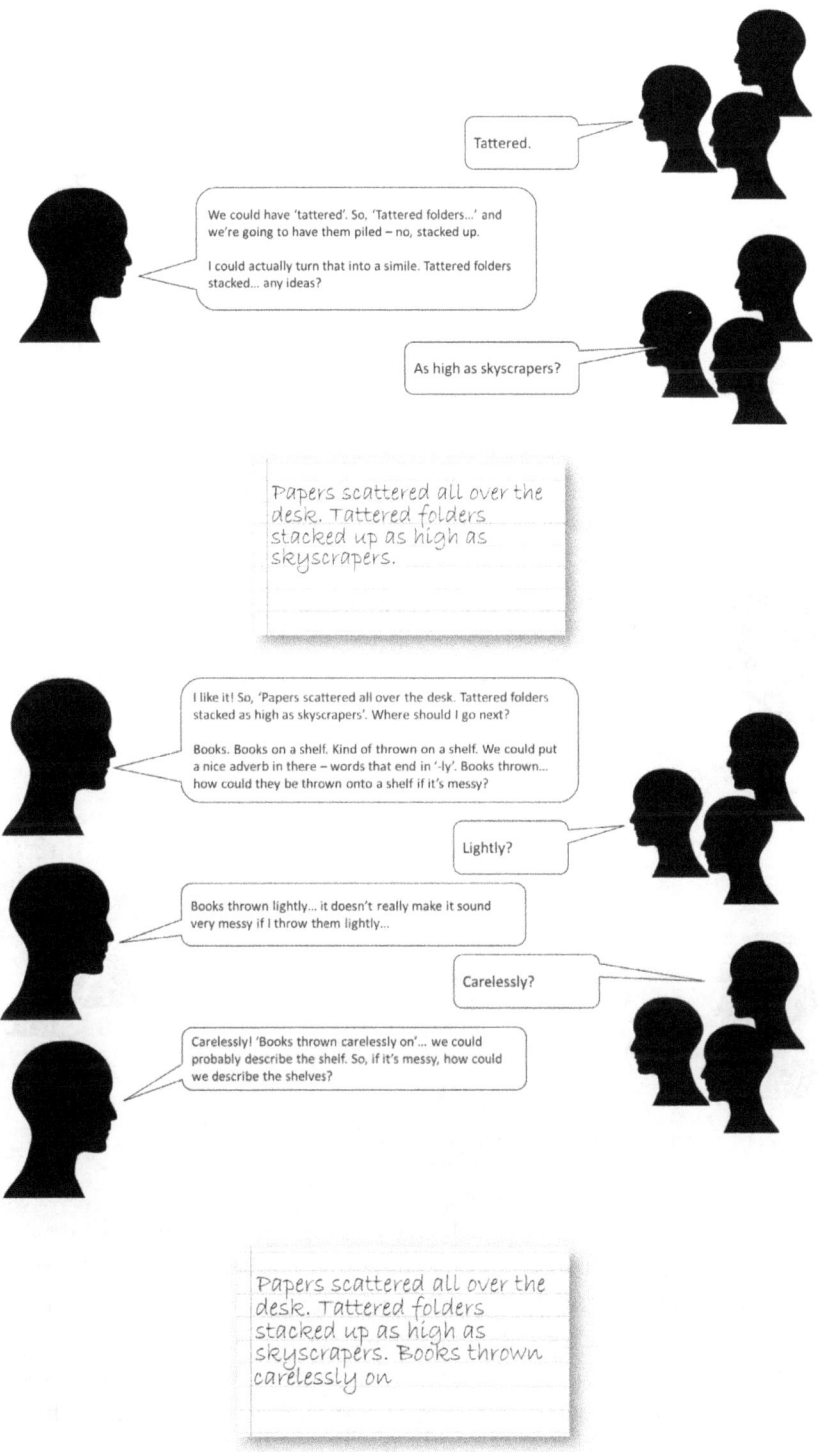

Figure 12.4 Spontaneous live modelling (*Continued*)

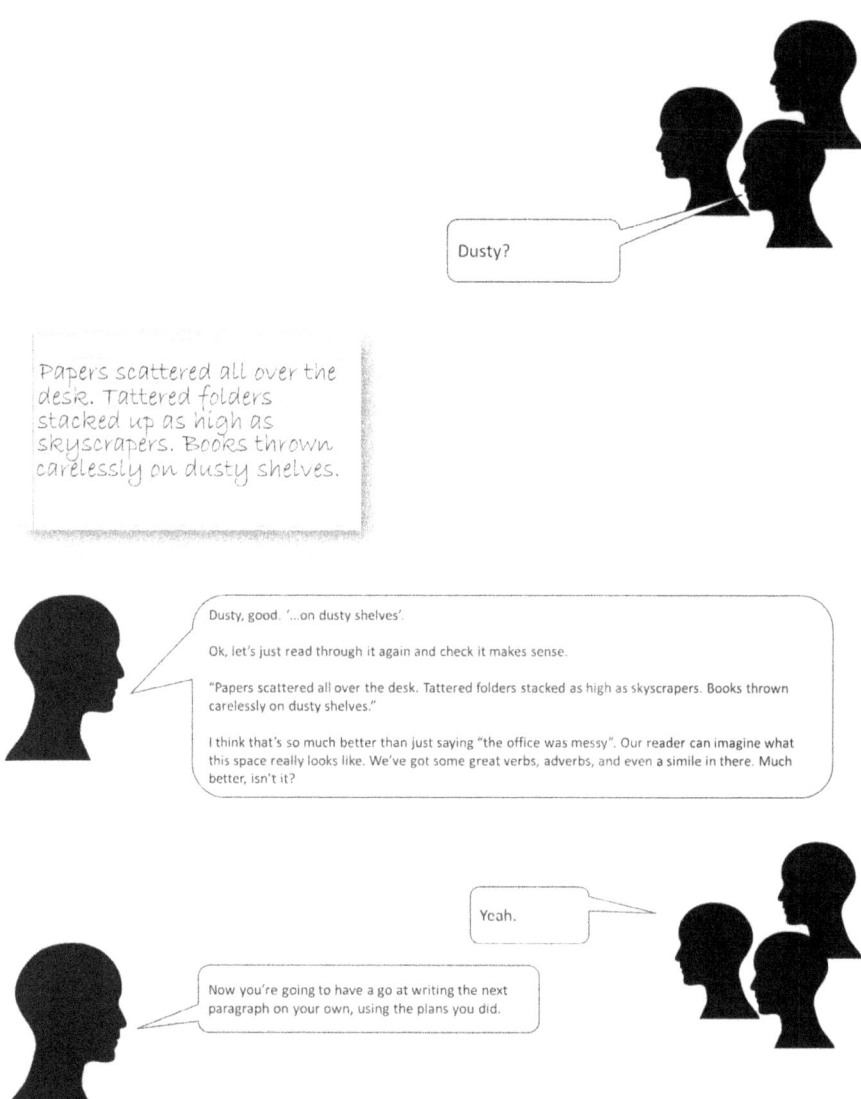

Figure 12.4 Spontaneous live modelling (*Continued*)

In this form of modelling, students do not necessarily write the response down themselves, but they take an active part in helping the teacher to produce it. The final piece should remain visible on the board while students then complete their independent pieces of work, so they can remind themselves of the process.

Spontaneous live modelling is a really valuable method, as it allows students to witness the live thinking and questioning process of the More Knowledgeable Other which, in turn, facilitates their own analytical thinking.

Procedural live modelling

Procedural live modelling is when the teacher talks through their thinking processes, but students are required to make their own notes on what the thinking process actually is. In this method, they are expected to listen carefully to the teacher's justifications for their written choices, determine for themselves which parts of the thought process they think are important, and note them down independently – students are explicitly told *not* to copy down the teacher's notes or example answer. This form of live modelling takes a lot of time and effort, but also fosters a high degree of student independence and active listening.

In the example in Figure 12.5, the year 10 class were writing essays about Romeo. The teacher guided students through her own thought process, showing how she created her own example response.

Thought Process	Teacher Response
I need to highlight the key words	Question: How is Romeo presented throughout the play?
What is my thesis statement? My ultimate point?	In 'Romeo and Juliet', Romeo is immediately positioned as having a different mindset to the other men of Verona, who are more focused on fighting and fleeting romance than long-term love.
I need to say how he is at the start.	In Act One, Romeo is obsessed with the idea of love, but sad that love doesn't make him feel as happy as he thought it would.
I need evidence.	Speaking in oxymorons, Romeo cries "O brawling love, O loving hate".
How does my evidence prove what I'm saying about him?	Romeo laments the love he feels for Rosaline, as it is unrequited. Therefore, although he is convinced that he is in love with Rosaline, this love does not meet Romeo's expectations; instead, it makes him feel upset.
I've mentioned the technique. But why? What effect does it have?	His anger and confusion around the reality of this love are demonstrated through his repeated use of oxymorons, which highlight how far his positive expectations of romantic love have been subverted and destroyed because his love for Rosaline has not been returned.

Figure 12.5 Teacher example response

While listening to the teacher, students noted down what they considered to be important aspects of her thought process, and then used this to later produce their own written responses, as in the example in Figure 12.6.

Highlight key words	How is Romeo presented throughout the play?
Thesis statement	In the play, Romeo is presented as an Elizabethan courtly lover who is conflicted as he is torn between love and violence.
At start - Point	In Act 1, Romeo is depressed because he loves Rosaline and she does not love him back.
Evidence and technique	Romeo uses a series of exclamatory sentences with oxymorons in, crying "O brawling love!"
How does E prove P? Include technique.	Romeo's exclamation here highlights his sadness and frustration about Rosaline not returning his feelings. He feels annoyed that he is having to "brawl" with love, to fight so hard to be loved, only for her to ultimately not love him back. By exclaiming this oxymoron, we get a sense of how betrayed Romeo feels by the whole idea of love: he was led to believe that if he behaved like a courtly lover and wooed Rosaline, she would fall into his arms, but this is clearly not the case. The oxymorons show that his reality is not as easy as he was led to believe it would be.

Figure 12.6 Student response

Another enormous benefit of procedural live modelling is that, by the end of this piece of work, students will have their own structure strip alongside their own model answer, which they can then use again to support them in a similar piece of work.

Modelling mistakes

Certainly, in secondary settings, there is a strange phenomenon where many students are reluctant to write their ideas down – unless they are absolutely certain that what they are writing is correct. There seems to be a fear of making written mistakes when evidence of them cannot be easily erased. As teachers, we recognise the importance of making mistakes as part of the learning process, and so it is vital that we also model making (and correcting) mistakes ourselves.

Some students make mistakes in their writing, but struggle with the concept of proof reading. Indeed, I suspect that if we all had a pound for each student we have told to proof read and, instead, they've just glanced at the page and declared 'yep', then we wouldn't need to beg for glue sticks ever again! Live modelling the thought process behind proof reading is just as important as live modelling the original written response: we need to give students the tools to understand the editing process as *part of* the writing process.

When modelling mistakes, it can be more effective to write under the visualiser. While typing responses is good for clarity (especially if you have tricky handwriting), the ability to completely erase our mistakes from sight on a computer does not necessarily get our point across about risking making mistakes in order to progress learning – we need the errors to be visible so that students see that mistakes are part of learning and writing. On making such errors in our written work, we then need students to hear our thinking processes verbalised and watch us crossing things out, changing words and phrases, and editing spelling and punctuation, etc. (Figure 12.7).

Verbalising thoughts behind the editing process also helps students to understand *why* certain changes have been made – for instance, in the example in Figure 12.7, the teacher guided students through the reasoning, discussing how removing 'the' gave more power to other words.

Removing the model

As with any scaffolding, it is absolutely imperative that we gradually remove any modelling over a period of time. However, our students should reach a point where they no longer need extensive modelling and scaffolding anyway – ideally, before their exams begin!

What the gradual removal looks like will be different for everyone, but if students have been exposed to quality metacognitive thinking processes to support their own cognitive development on a regular basis, over a period of time, they should become less reliant on this form of support anyway during the course of their academic journey.

You may even reach a point with your students where they can position themselves as the More Knowledgeable Other in the classroom – in which case, get them up at the front, live modelling their own thought processes! This approach can be an enormous confidence boost as well.

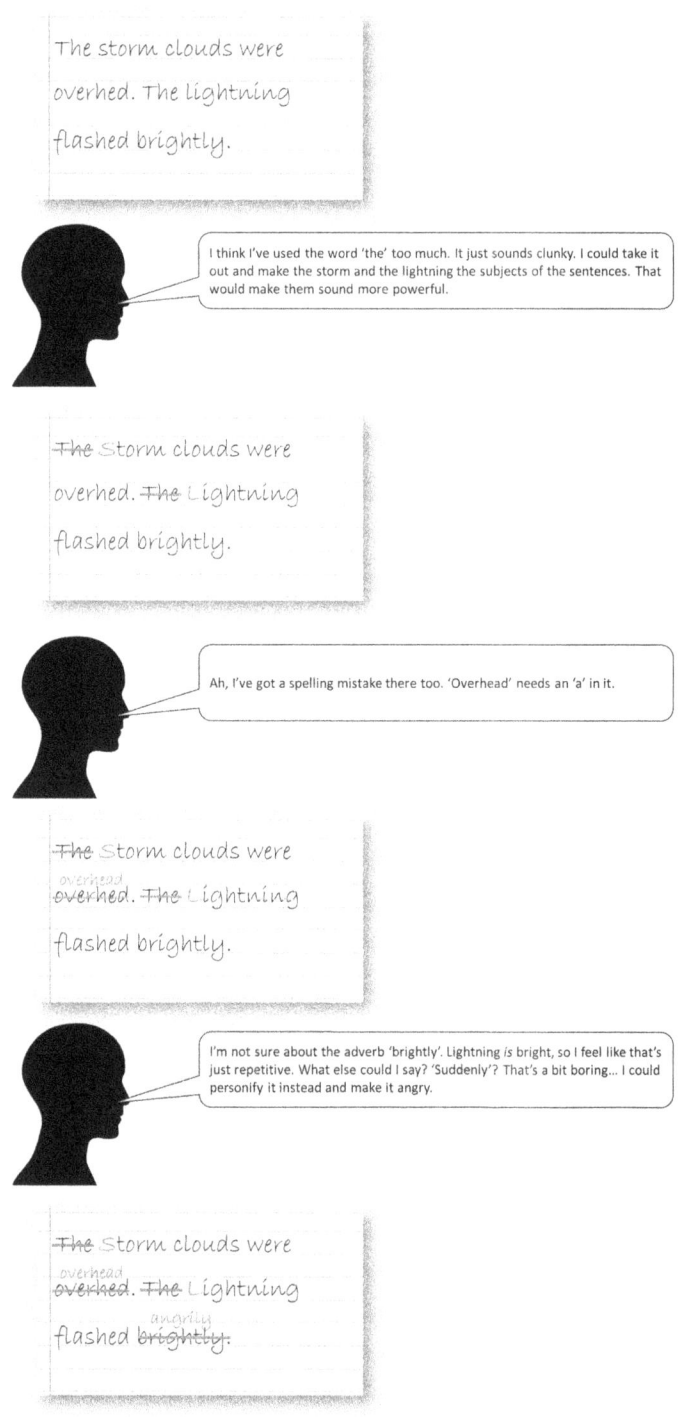

Figure 12.7 Modelling mistakes

Students taking the reins

Neurological research shows that, when a process is repeated, it strengthens connections between the neurons in the brain and stores such processes in our long-term memory (Lynch, 2004). Therefore, repeating spontaneous and/or procedural live modelling, and exposing students to repeated thought processes, causes long-term neurological connections to be forged, which enables our students to utilise such processes again and again and again – independently. In essence, regular live modelling from a More Knowledgeable Other translates teacher modelling into students' independent action.

If we look again at Vygotsky's Zone of Proximal Development, the potential impact of live modelling is enormous. Due to the increased depth of understanding around thinking processes and how to translate thought into action, students expand their repertoire of things they can achieve independently, and the circle of unattainable knowledge decreases (Figure 12.8).

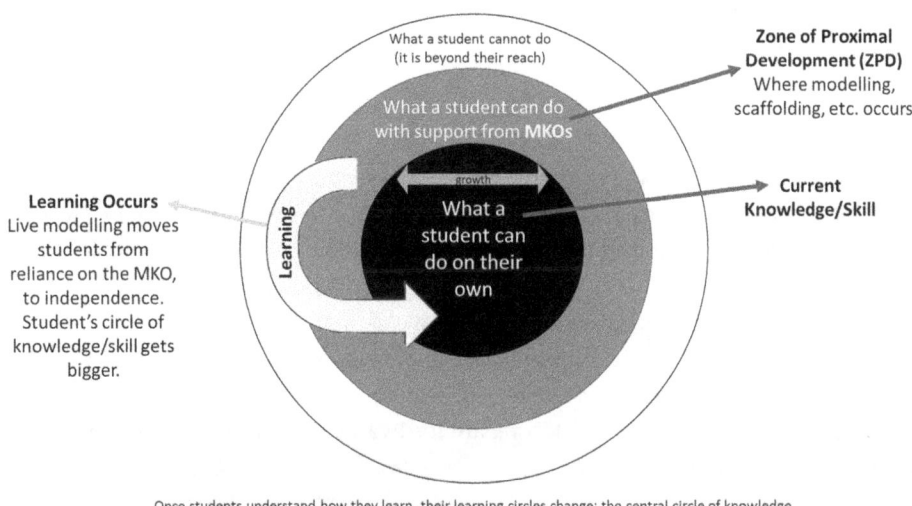

Once students understand how they learn, their learning circles change: the central circle of knowledge enlarges, and the external (previously unattainable) circle shrinks.

Figure 12.8   Vygotsky's Zone of Proximal Development and the potential impact of live modelling

Possible problems

Too much reliance on teachers

There are some concerns about how modelling and live modelling can create too much reliance on the teacher – we all know that some of our students will just copy down the examples we provide (no matter how hard we try to avoid this). Even Vygotsky himself acknowledged that too much reliance on teacher demonstrations can limit the acquisition of certain skills; indeed, he argued, learning does not occur unless children take action themselves (Vygotsky, 1978). This is why a gradual removal of this form of scaffolding is absolutely vital. We need to support students in understanding thinking processes, and then allow them to demonstrate their own understanding so that real learning can occur. For this to happen, we also have to carefully consider our timings.

Time constraints

In a knowledge-heavy curriculum, it can be difficult to find time to dedicate to extensive live modelling, but it is vital. If students don't know how to produce these detailed responses, then the content itself becomes a moot point. The 'how' is the disciplinary knowledge that is vital to their learning.

It is also incredibly important to ensure that enough time is given in lessons for teachers to live model, and just as crucial to allow students to demonstrate these thinking processes themselves by completing their own responses. Students *must* be able to practise the processes they have witnessed/heard in order for the neurological connections to begin to form.

Concerns about quality

Some teachers genuinely worry about being able to produce high-quality responses in a 'live' situation (whether through spontaneous or procedural modelling). There are arguments which focus on the fact that we expect students to do it, so we should be able to do it. However, it is understandable to feel a sense of anxiety in this situation. Unlike our students producing answers, we are incredibly aware that we are trying to guide a class full of students through their education; we are shaping their brains and their thinking processes, and are concerned that we might let them down.

There are some practical ways to prepare for live modelling, even in an apparently spontaneous situation:

- Pre-write a response to begin with, and have it to hand so you know what you're aiming to produce. Over time, you will likely feel less need to do this.
- Practise live modelling with a colleague or a small group of students.
- Accept that you may make mistakes and encourage students to identify how to improve your answers – strangely, they become very enthusiastic about picking us up on our mistakes! In fact, having students explain to you how you could improve your answer actually helps their own cognitive development (whether or not your mistakes were planned).

Ideas for the Classroom

So, if you're interested in trying out some live modelling, how do you get started?

- **Start small**. Rather than diving headfirst into a huge essay, start by breaking down a task or question: live model the thinking process behind how you would begin planning the answer (e.g. examining the key words).
- **Specific focus**. When planning a lesson, focus on one element that you want students to master, and then use live modelling to demonstrate what this looks like and how to achieve it.
- **Cheat sheet**. When you first start live modelling, have a pre-written answer nearby which you can use to guide your 'live' construction. This is often useful when producing higher-level responses. Over time, the teacher, like the students, should remove this element of scaffolding.
- **Embrace the mistakes**. Try not to worry about making mistakes on your live models. Encourage students to spot the errors, and have them explain to you what makes them wrong and how to correct them. If, during live proof reading, students don't spot the errors, but you do, highlight them yourself and talk through your thinking process to demonstrate how you spotted them and the method of correcting them.

Live modelling is one of the best tools for teaching: if we implement it well, regularly, we can rapidly develop our students' cognitive processes, and confidently thrust them into the world of independent learning.

Further Reading

For practical ideas on using strategies to support metacognition in the classroom:

Webb, J. (2021). *The metacognition handbook*. Woodbridge, UK: John Catt.

For more information on cognitive load theory:

Sweller, J. (2011). Cognitive load theory. In J. P. Mestre & B. H. Ross (Eds.), *The psychology of learning and motivation: Cognition in education* (pp. 37–76). Cambridge, MA: Elsevier Academic Press.

For practical information on live modelling in lessons:

Codextrous (2022). Live modelling: Maximising student thinking. *Codextrous* [Blog], 29 May. Available at: https://codexterous.home.blog/2022/05/29/live-modelling-maximising-student-thinking/ (accessed 19 October 2023).

References

Bandura, A. (1971). *Social learning theory*. New York: General Learning Press.

Bransford, J. D. et al. (2000). *How people learn: Brain, mind, experience, and school.* Washington, DC: National Academy of Sciences.

Burns, N. (2023). *Inspiring deep learning with metacognition.* London: Sage/Corwin Press.

Deleeuw, K. E., & Mayer, R. E. (2008). A comparison of three measures of cognitive load: Evidence for separable measures of intrinsic, extraneous and germane load. *Journal of Educational Psychology, 100*(1), 223–234.

Diaz, R. M., & Berk, L. E. (1992). *Private speech: From social interaction to self-regulation.* Hillsdale, NJ: Lawrence Erlbaum.

Lynch, M. A. (2004). Long-term potentiation and memory. *Physiological Reviews, 84*(1), 87–136.

McLeod, S. (2023). Vygotsky's sociocultural theory of cognitive development. *Simply Psychology*, 1 May. Available at: www.simplypsychology.org/vygotsky.html (accessed 19 October 2023).

Munakata, Y., Snyder, H. R., & Chatham C. H. (2012). Developing cognitive control: Three key transitions. *Current Directions in Psychological Science, 21*(2), 71–145.

Russell, B. (1992) *Human Knowledge: Its Scope and Limits.* London: Routledge.

Sweller, J. (1998). Cognitive load during problem solving: Effects on learning. *Cognitive Science, 12*, 257–285.

Vygotsky, L. S. (1962). *Thought and language.* Cambridge, MA: MIT Press.

Vygotsky, L. S. (1978). Interaction between learning and development. In L. S. Vygotsky, *Mind and society* (pp. 79–81). Cambridge, MA: Harvard University Press.

Vygotsky, L. S. (1987). Thinking and speech. In R. W. Rieber & A. S. Carton (Eds.), *The collected works of L. S. Vygotsky, Volume 1: Problems of general psychology* (pp. 39–285). New York: Plenum Press. (Original work published in 1934.)

Wiliam, D. (2017, January 26). *I've come to the conclusion Sweller's Cognitive Load Theory is the single most important thing for teachers to know http://bit.ly/2kouLOq [Tweet].* Twitter. https://twitter.com/dylanwiliam/status/824682504602943489?lang=en

Wittgenstein, L. (1971) *Tractatus Logico-Philosophicus* (2nd ed.) (Original work published 1921). New York: Routledge.

13

Metacognition is a Powerful Tool

Patrice Bain

An Educational Issue

A question I often asked my students on the first day of school: Have you ever studied hard for a test and didn't do well? Year after year, nearly every hand waved in the air. Why is it that students, after spending week after week, year after year in the school system, continue to struggle with learning and exams? In my experience, students have been taught what was in the curriculum but have not, for the most part, been taught how to learn or study. My mission, my mantra became: I'm your teacher and I am going to teach you how to learn.

Although presently, there are many books, articles, and podcasts that focus on learning, this wasn't always the case. In fact, my classroom was the first in the United States where cognitive scientists studied how students learn *in a classroom*. (Up until that time, most research was conducted with college students in laboratories.) Now, teachers and researchers conduct deep dives into the science of learning. In this chapter, I will focus on the powerful principles that researchers studied in my class and the role metacognition plays in successful learning.

Let me begin by sharing my simplified definitions. Learning can be broken down into three steps: encoding, storage, and retrieval. *Encoding* is getting information *into* our heads. *Storage* is where the information goes once it is in our heads. Unfortunately, many of us were taught only these first two steps. In *Powerful Teaching* (Agarwal & Bain, 2019), the question is asked: Too often we focus on getting information into our heads. What if, instead, we focus on pulling information out? This leads us to the third step of learning: *retrieval*. Learning has occurred only if students are able to retrieve, or pull out, the information. We know that learning something initially does not guarantee long-term retrieval. Rather, repeated opportunities to retrieve information, over time, will help to maintain the learning in our memory. These repeated opportunities are called *spaced practice*, or *spacing*. A key principle that students can use to determine whether learning has occurred is *metacognition*. This can be thought of as 'thinking about thinking'. I explained it to my students in this way:

> Metacognition is essential in helping us to discriminate what we know from what we don't. Feedback is crucial and I often say that 'Feedback-driven Metacognition' is a powerful tool.

Too often, students don't have the opportunity to test what they know or don't know until they see the questions on an exam. It is common for students to study what they already know, skipping over the more difficult material. This often leads to an illusion of knowing the material, a form of false metacognition, and results in poor exam scores. I have found that when students spend hours studying for exam after exam and don't do well, feelings of frustration and failure emerge.

Through my work with cognitive scientists, I came to the realisation that incorporating the research findings into my teaching drastically impacted my students' retention of material. Offering no- and low-stakes strategies throughout the course of study enabled students to make that differentiation between knowing and not-knowing material. In this chapter I will focus on the metacognitive strategies I developed that increase grades, knowledge retention, and the confidence of students.

Your Approach

Let me begin by posing some questions. My hope is that you will take a few minutes to reflect upon your answers before reading further. In fact, doing this will begin your own metacognitive path identifying your current practices.

- Do you teach students how to learn *while* you are teaching the curriculum?
- How many opportunities do students have to check for understanding *before* exams?
- In what ways do you provide feedback on student work?
- How can you apply metacognitive strategies into your daily pedagogy?

With these questions in mind, I will discuss the process that allowed me to have a classroom where evidence-informed learning took centre stage.

The Metacognitive Approach

A surprising outcome appeared at the conclusion of the first year of my work with cognitive scientists. The focus, that first year, was on retrieval. Studies confirmed that students scored higher on chapter/unit exams when retrieval had been used throughout the course of study. But how long would students retain the information? Would they still know the information at the end of the school year? After all, learning goes beyond scoring well on exams; the purpose of it is to have the ability to retain and use what was learned. To determine if information had been retained, we decided to conduct an unannounced end-of-the-year exam, thereby seeing what had been retained when further study wasn't an option. The result? Yes! When retrieval and feedback-driven metacognition had been used during the course of study, students were able to get 79% of the questions correct – without any additional study, at the *end* of the school year!

As I looked at the data from this unannounced end-of-year exam, my surprise came when my top student, who had scored 100% on every assignment and test, had retained less than 50% of the material. I spent my summer pondering. I realised, to my surprise, that my students had *mastered* completing homework: read a question, look up the answer, write it down, repeat. 100% accuracy. Yet, I received blank stares when asking questions about the work; classroom discussions were quite dull. Not only was retrieval missing from the homework I assigned, metacognition was as well. How could my students 'think about thinking' when it appeared that homework was more aligned with copying down answers rather than thinking? Developing strategies that encouraged retrieval *and* encouraged thinking became my quest.

When I began creating learning strategies, I thought about examples from my classroom. Let me begin with three scenarios.

1   A question I like to ask: Who was Lady Murasaki Shikibu[1]? Chances are right away you either knew the answer or you didn't. Furthermore, you *knew* if you knew it or not. This is how I explained metacognition to my students and why metacognition is so important. It allows students to distinguish what they know from what they don't.

2   Another question: How many bones are there in the adult human body? What's your answer?[2] Unlike the above scenario, it isn't always as simple as 'I know it or I don't' because sometimes we *think* we know an answer when, actually, we don't. This is called an illusion of learning or, sometimes, false metacognition.

3   Sometimes students got the answers correct because of a lucky guess.

These scenarios helped me to define a path for creating strategies; a crucial step mandated that students had a way to validate the correctness of their answers. The strategies must include feedback-driven metacognition.

In addition, I found differences in the *way* students studied for exams. Students often study by reviewing notes. Yet, we know that just because you *see* something doesn't mean you *know* it. For example, think of a coin you have seen countless times. Can you draw it? Or, without looking at any devices, can you illustrate the Apple logo? Try it!

---

[1]Lady Murasaki Shikibu was a Japanese princess who lived around the year 1000. She is often credited for having written the world's first novel, *The Tale of Genji*.

[2]206

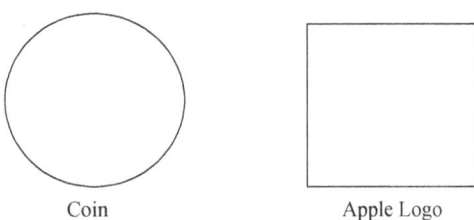

Coin   Apple Logo

Figure 13.1   Can you draw a coin or the Apple logo?

How do these examples relate to studying? Often studying at home and at school include reviewing for exams. In fact, think of the very phrases that are used when we ask our students to 'look over' notes, 're-read' the chapter, or 'see' what was highlighted. These types of strategies lead to ineffective study and habits. From the exercises above (and research) we know that just because we see something doesn't mean we know it. In order to know something, we must be able to retrieve it. Again, feedback-driven meta-cognition is the action that helps us to identify what we know.

Additionally, reviewing notes is a common but ineffective study approach, because students tend to review *what they already know*. Review sheets and notes begin to look familiar, so students *think* they know the material (another illusion of learning). They spend time building up their confidence due to thinking they have that material mastered. I found this to be especially true with struggling students who tend to gloss over unmastered learning and concentrate on what they do know. Let's say we were studying for a test and two of the questions on a review paper asked, 'Who was Maximilien Robespierre? How did the lives of the Third Estate change as a result of the French Revolution?' Although both answers require retrieval, students who haven't been taught to learn would concentrate on the familiarity of the first question rather than the second. What children *don't* know often gets overlooked; it's hard and uncomfortable and gets minimised. It is difficult to study things which haven't yet been mastered! Yet because an exam is over *all* material, students can become disappointed when the test is administered and they don't know the answer. The anticipated success vanishes. Too often, this is where internalised failure begins for students; their effort has no pay-off. This, in turn, often has an impact on motivation. 'If I spend time studying and still fail, why should I study?' Where was the disconnect? Students who score higher grades have often figured out that they must focus their study on the *less familiar* material. It is the students who tend to score in the average to below average range who have not yet learned this. Once again, feedback-driven metacogniton is key.

We know through research that retrieval cannot be a 'one and done' event, but rather, a process where students are given opportunities to retrieve over time (spacing or spaced practice). For this reason, the many opportunities for retrieval require no or low-stakes scores. Of course, high-stakes grades were still used for the end of chapter and unit tests, semester exams, essays and projects, but grading during the *process* of learning was minimal. My students knew that not knowing an answer was not failure; it was simply *not yet* being able to retrieve the answer. Because students had many opportunities to identify and discriminate between what was known versus what wasn't before the high-stakes grades, it allowed them the certainty for learning, high marks and success.

Creating a classroom environment for learning

As previously mentioned, I began every first day of school with: 'I am your teacher and I am going to teach you how to learn.' How did I begin the process? I began with establishing the climate. I discussed my signs, which stated a philosophy I held. The signs were front and centre in my classroom and I referred to them daily (Figure 13.2).

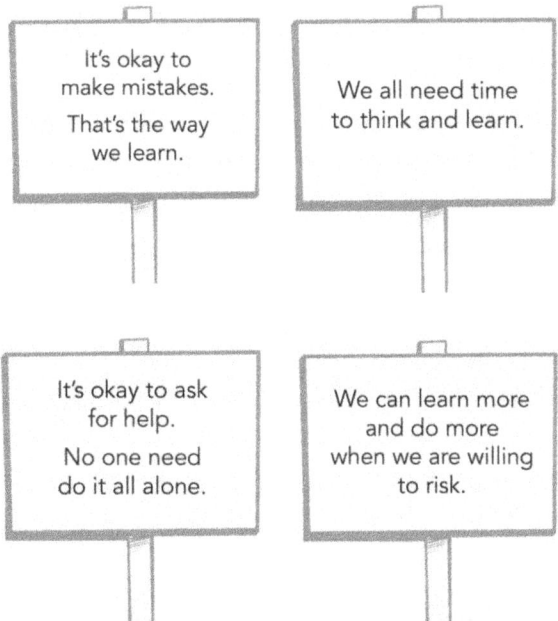

It's okay to make mistakes.

That's the way we learn.

We all need time to think and learn.

It's okay to ask for help.

No one need do it all alone.

We can learn more and do more when we are willing to risk.

Figure 13.2 Classroom signs (reproduced from www.powerfulteaching.org/resources
© 2019 Pooja K. Agarwal, PhD, and Patrice Bain, EdS)

My students understood that my classroom was a safe place. Learning was a *process*. Mistakes are simply the roadmaps that point us in the direction we need to take. Some students will learn at a faster rate. No one will be left behind and asking for assistance is a life-long skill. And, finally, I would encourage my 11-year-old students to attempt new skills whether it was a read aloud, debate, dramatic reading, or defending an opinion.

I knew my students would succeed; I felt it was important to begin where students could not fail. To acquaint them with strategies and processes (such as think, pair, share) I would ask simple questions where no incorrect answer existed.

- What is the latest you ever slept during the holidays?
- What is your least favourite school lunch?

Students wrote answers on a whiteboard, followed by sharing with a neighbour, and ended with a group share led by me. Each day posed two more questions and my students learned that retrieval was simply bringing forth information from memory. By week two, questions asked pertained to the curriculum.

I also used whiteboards as I began teaching the idea of metacognition, but this information was not shared with others. Who was Lady Murasaki Shikibu? (Can *you* retrieve the answer from an earlier page?) After each question asked, I would pause for students to write, followed by me telling them the answer. Boards were erased and new questions were asked. These activities led to the students understanding the role of metacognition and I incorporated more strategies showing how well they were mastering curriculum.

When students know how to learn, they realise that studying for a test does not have to be anxiety-producing. In fact, because they have practised retrieving the material throughout the unit, on quizzes and in class, time spent on test preparation is often cut. Their metacognition has shown them where they need to focus their study for the test. In my school district, 1500 high school students were asked if using researched principles, such as retrieval, made them more or less anxious for unit exams. Here are the results cited in *Powerful Teaching* (Agarwal & Bain, 2019):

- 72% less anxious
- 6% more anxious
- 22% no change

I developed the following strategies based on the research conducted in my classroom and the principles of retrieval, spaced retrieval, and feedback-driven metacognition. My vision for these strategies was that they allowed learning mastery rather than simply completing homework.

Strategy 1: Mini-quiz

My first strategy became the mini-quiz. I called it this because it was quick, short, allowed feedback, and was completed on small, recycled pieces of paper. This daily strategy was low- or no-stakes testing, meaning usually no, or minimal, points were given. Students understood that the purpose was to determine what was learned and what still needed work.

How it works: At the end of each day, I would write questions about important topics we discussed in class on slips of paper and put them in a basket. The following day, students received a small piece of paper on which was a list numbered 1–5 and space at the top for the student's name (Figure 13.3). I randomly chose five questions, reading each one twice, students wrote answers and the papers were collected. I discussed the answers. I reviewed the mini-quizzes at the end of the day, providing information as to correct/incorrect answers. This strategy also gave me feedback as well. If several students missed a similar question, I knew I needed to re-teach the information.

```
Name: _____

1._____

2._____

3._____

4._____

5._____
```

Figure 13.3 A mini-quiz template

Students had daily opportunities to verify what they knew and what still needed work. The mini-quizzes were returned the following day and I gave elaborative feedback answering the questions. This simple activity became a favourite of my students. Rather than seeing *errors*, they saw target areas that required more study. An added bonus was that they began listening more intently in class as their curiosity increased at what might be asked the following day. And, as a result, lively discussions ensued. Time consuming? The entire process took approximately five minutes. It was time well-spent on knowledge retention.

Strategy 2: Four steps of metacognition

I wanted to develop a strategy that took away the guessing of answers, that allowed students to independently check work, and that provided a study tool for exams. I developed an exercise that I called the Four Steps of Metacognition, as set out in Figure 13.4. Below, I demonstrate how this strategy works using retrieval cards.

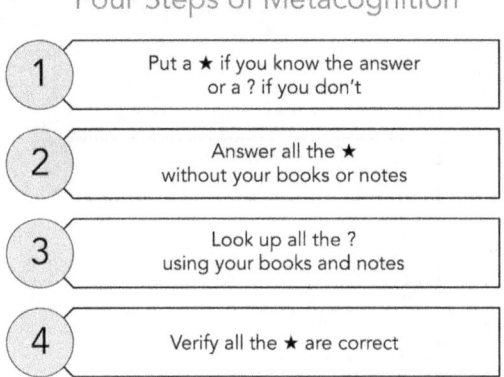

Four Steps of Metacognition

1. Put a ★ if you know the answer or a ? if you don't
2. Answer all the ★ without your books or notes
3. Look up all the ? using your books and notes
4. Verify all the ★ are correct

Figure 13.4 Four Steps of Metacognition (reproduced from www.powerfulteaching.org/resources © 2019 Pooja K. Agarwal, PhD, and Patrice Bain, EdS)

Strategy 3: Retrieval cards

At the end of each lesson, students are assigned retrieval cards. Retrieval cards are similar to flashcards, but with *one key difference*. With traditional flashcards, there's no retrieval or metacognition involved while creating them; students simply look up concepts and write down the answer (Figure 13.5). With retrieval cards, students have the opportunity to retrieve and go through the Four Steps of Metacognition from the beginning, boosting further learning.

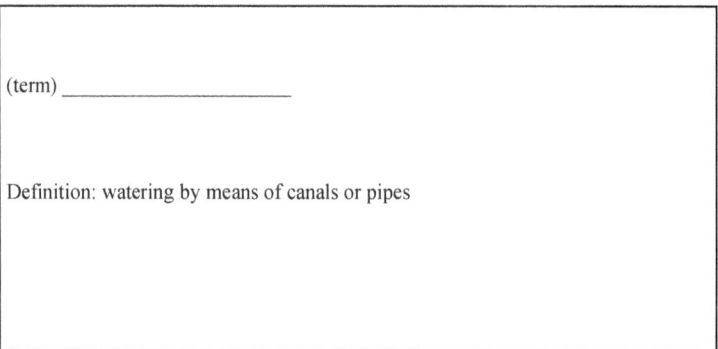

Figure 13.5 A traditional flashcard

Retrieval cards use the researched principles of retrieval, spacing and metacognition. How it works:

- Have the definition on the card leaving the term blank (or vice versa).
- Complete the card using the Four Steps of Metacognition (details follow).
- Learners have the opportunity to retrieve the material *and* get the feedback as to accuracy.

Figure 13.6 is an example.

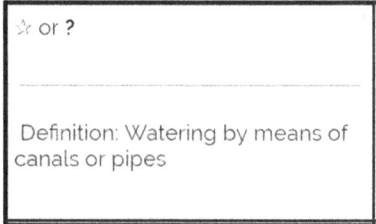

Figure 13.6 A retrieval card

Strategy 4: Applying the four steps of metacognition

- Step 1: Without the use of books or notes, a student makes a judgement of learning: Do I know this or not? A simple star (younger students often prefer a happy face) indicates 'I know it'; a question mark indicates that the answer isn't known.
- Step 2 is answering the questions that are known. This is an important step because sometimes we *think* we know an answer, but we don't.
- Step 3 is the first time the student opens up a book or notes, finds the answer, and writes it down.
- Step 4 is double checking, verifying, that what you thought you knew is correct.

I am sometimes asked, 'Can I change the question mark to a star after I get it correct?' My answer is no. One of the purposes of the Four Steps is for students to make the judgement of learning and to readily identify the areas that require focus. Keeping with the original judgement aids the process. The added benefit is when this process is used, students know where to target study time for exams.

How would you complete the cards in Figure 13.7 using the Four Steps to Metacognition?

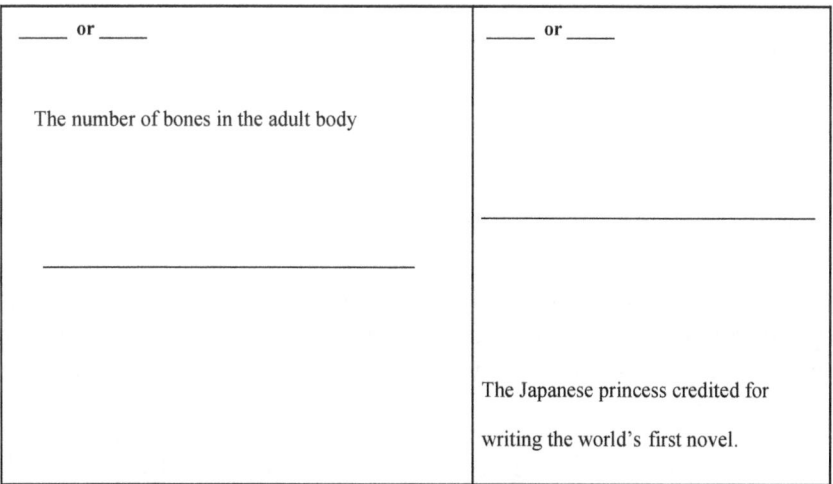

Figure 13.7   Retrieval cards using the Four Steps of Metacognition

Metacognition sheets

Whereas retrieval cards were used at the end of each lesson, metacognition sheets were used prior to exams. Another difference is that while retrieval cards concentrated on terms and definitions, metacognition sheets had the added element of essential questions for essays and critical thinking activities. In addition, my students knew that just because something was listed on a metacognition sheet did not mean it was guaranteed to be on an exam. Rather, I could be spacing out questions for future learning. The same four steps are used in the example in Figure 13.8 from my class.

Metacognition Sheet

★	?	Items to Know	Answer
		Maximilien Robespierre	
		Definition of "revolution"	
		How did each revolution change the lives of working people?	
		How did the social pyramids change as a result of the revolutions?	

Figure 13.8 A metacognition sheet (reproduced from www.powerfulteaching.org/ resources © 2019 Pooja K. Agarwal, PhD, and Patrice Bain, EdS)

Participating in research changed my thinking and pedagogy. Teaching my students how to learn was transformational. The largest gains were found in struggling students. It was as if the act of learning had been a secret code to which, before, they had not been privy. As they mastered the strategies, they soared. We now know *how* we learn. It is our responsibility and duty to impart this knowledge to our students. And, ultimately, our goal should be to demonstrate to students that they succeed when they are in charge of their own learning. Feedback-driven metacognition is paramount. In fact, I found it crucial for student success.

Ideas for the Classroom

- Identify where you are on the 'How do we learn?' spectrum.
  - ○ No matter if you are a novice or a seasoned veteran, there is a wealth of information available, such as introductory articles and books or research-driven deep dives.
  - ○ Curious how to begin? You've already started by reading this book. Connect with the authors and other like-minded educators and researchers via social media.

- Identify where your students are on the 'How do we learn?' spectrum.
  - Chances are your classroom is filled with students of all abilities. Some may excel and receive high grades. Some, perhaps, are the opposite and bring negativity.
  - Explain *how* learning happens. Provide strategies where the students will not fail.
  - Encourage your students to use research-informed terminology such as encoding, retrieval, metacognition and spacing, to name a few.
  - Commit to having a research-informed classroom.
  - This doesn't mean becoming an immediate expert. Start small.
  - Provide activities for students to identify what they know from what they don't while learning.
  - Take advantage of the strategies available to you; tweak them to fit your pedagogy and students.
  - Use low and no-stakes grading during the *process* of learning. Save the high-stakes grades for tests, projects and exams.
  - Boost students' knowledge and creativity by encouraging them to develop metacognitive strategies.

Further Reading

My journey into the discovery of learning, which is frequently cited in this chapter, is chronicled in:

Agarwal, P. K., & Bain, P. M. (2019). *Powerful teaching: Unleash the science of learning*. San Francisco, CA: Jossey Bass.

I coined the term 'Teaching Triangle' to promote the all-important collaboration between student, parent/carer, and teacher. A guide that can be instrumental in incorporating the teaching triangle can be found in:

Bain, P. M. (2020). *A parent guide to powerful teaching*. Woodbridge, UK: John Catt.

My strategies can be downloaded at: www.powerfulteaching.org/resources

I've been very fortunate to have been invited onto podcasts and to write articles about learning. These can be found at: https://tinyurl.com/yahj7er4

My co-author of *Powerful Teaching*, Dr Pooja Agarwal, has a wonderful site filled with tips, research and newsletters. It can be found at: www.retrievalpractice.org

Powerful Teaching Book Club is a website that links teachers around the globe. It can be found at: www.facebook.com/groups/powerfulteaching. Please feel free to join us!

And, finally, my educational connections on Twitter inspire me! You can reach me at: www.twitter.com/patricebain1

Reference

Agarwal, P. K., & Bain, P. M. (2019). *Powerful teaching: Unleash the science of learning*. San Francisco, CA: Jossey Bass.

14

Integrating Metacognition into the Curriculum

Daniel Muijs

Introduction

In this chapter I will discuss the relationship between metacognition and curriculum. It can seem hard to incorporate metacognition, but in this chapter, I will look at a number of examples of how we can build in activities that enhance metacognitive thinking across a sequence of lessons. To do so, we will look at lessons from Key Stage 2, Key Stage 3 and Key Stage 4, in both humanities and STEM subjects. We will also look at the ways curricula themselves can be deliberately designed to incorporate the development of metacognition.

Developing Metacognition

There is by now plenty of evidence that metacognition can help to improve pupil attainment (Hacker et al., 2009; Pressley & Harris, 2006). More importantly, developing metacognition is an important life skill, which will help young people to become lifelong learners and thrive in their chosen area of work or life. It is therefore not surprising that more and more schools have been looking to incorporate metacognition into teaching, and that the Education Endowment Foundation (EEF) guidance on metacognition is one of their most downloaded items (Education Endowment Foundation, 2021).

A lot of research has been done on metacognition (Christian Bokhove and I found over 1500 articles published in a 10-year period when we reviewed the evidence), and we do know quite a bit on how to develop metacognition in children and young people (Muijs & Bokhove, 2020). The core principles are:

1 Teach pupils about what metacognition is and why it matters.
2 Teach pupils cognitive strategies, like retrieval practice or spaced learning.
3 Teach pupils metacognitive strategies, like planning, monitoring and evaluating their work.
4 Model your own use of metacognitive strategies.

5 Provide scaffolds to help pupils use those strategies during independent or group learning tasks.

6 Gradually reduce scaffold use.

7 Integrate metacognition into classroom teaching rather than use standalone 'learning-to-learn' lessons.

There are, however, some problems with this advice. First, it is not necessarily the case that the evidence is equally strong across subjects or phases. As with much educational research, most studies have been done in English and maths, so there is a lot less evidence in other subjects. This matters, as one of the key findings from research is that developing metacognition should be done in a way that is integrated with the subject, and not as a context-free skill. So this makes the fact that there is little research in some subjects problematic. That doesn't mean we cannot use metacognition in those subjects (such as RE or history), but it does mean that we need to be careful to think about context and the subject-specific learning strategies and approaches that may be required. The general principle of metacognition is important to all subjects, however.

There is significant research on developing metacognition in most age groups, and in particular among primary- and secondary-age pupils. There is less research on early years, although we do know that children start to develop metacognition at an early age as they interact with parents and their environment. Children don't, however, develop metacognition to a sufficient level in and of themselves, and certainly don't all do so at the same rate, which is why we need to teach it.

One thing to remember is that if we are starting the process of integrating metacognition into our teaching, we should assume that pupils have relatively little prior knowledge of learning strategies. Therefore, we will need to explicitly teach them strategies such as interleaving (when interleaving pupils switch between topics when they study rather than study the topic in one block) or self-testing.

Another challenge we frequently encounter is that pupils forget to use the metacognitive strategies they have been taught, to plan, to review, or to evaluate. Repetition is necessary, and it can therefore be useful to provide pupils with prompts. There are a number of ways of doing this, such as with worksheets during class tasks and during homework, and the use of prompting apps has also been found to be helpful (Breitwieser, 2023).

An issue with incorporating metacognition into teaching is that a lot of the suggested methods and activities can take a significant amount of time. Teachers and schools may therefore struggle to integrate the teaching of metacognition into a crowded curriculum. At times, schools attempt to solve this problem by mandating particular activities as part of lesson structures across the school, but this is not particularly helpful, for a number of reasons. First, it is clear that such an approach does not take into account the context-specificity of metacognition. As the evidence suggests, it's not a one-size-fits-all approach, so (just like most teaching!) the approach will need to be adapted to pupils, topic, etc. Second, not every lesson will lend itself to the use of methods to develop metacognition, and this again should be at the discretion of the expert teacher. Finally, mandated approaches can lead to a tick-box attitude among both the teacher and the pupils, while the essence of metacognition should be to take a thoughtful approach to learning, and to actively engage with the learning process. So we need to think carefully about how we can address issues of time and fit when developing our pupils' metacognitive knowledge and skills.

In practice, when we think in a curricular way, we need to understand the teaching as a sequence of lessons about a particular topic. This means that it makes no sense to try to ensure that every lesson follows the same structure, or contains the same activities, as this will lead to a mismatch between curricular aims and activities. The lesson is not the right unit of analysis. Metacognition, too, is not something we can simply teach through knowledge or activities, but is something that needs to be developed over time. Metacognition is fundamentally about changing the way pupils think about and reflect on learning, which in turn will allow them to more carefully and effectively select learning strategies. This development needs to be built iteratively into the curriculum.

In this chapter I will describe some examples of how we can successfully integrate metacognition into the curriculum. Before we do that, we do have to discuss a little bit what we mean by curriculum, as there are a range of different definitions in the literature.

What Do We Mean By Curriculum?

Basically, definitions of curriculum range on a continuum from broad to very broad indeed. On the very broad indeed end, curriculum is described as 'everything that happens in a school'. This includes pedagogy as well as content of teaching, and also what happens outside the classroom, including, for example, how behaviour is managed in the corridors, or what the culture of the school is. These things are often defined as the 'hidden curriculum'. This does make sense in terms of pupil learning, as of course we learn a lot about how we should behave and interact with each other in the broader school community. This hidden curriculum also matters for developing metacognition, as interaction and talk are key to this, especially among younger pupils.

The problem with this definition of curriculum, though, is that it does not distinguish between different elements and so doesn't give us a way to talk more specifically about the content of what we teach. Content matters, and we have rightly seen increasing interest in curriculum (albeit in many cases driven by Ofsted's inspection framework), following a long period in which the emphasis was firmly on pedagogy. Learning and teaching are not just about the how (pedagogy), but also about the what. We can, for example, teach unchallenging and low-level content well, or teach pupils the wrong thing. We can even teach harmful content in a pedagogically valid way. So content counts!

That's why, in this chapter we will use a more limited definition of curriculum, developed by Ofsted:

> 'The curriculum is a framework for setting out the aims of a programme of education, including the knowledge and understanding to be gained at each stage (intent); for translating that framework over time into a structure and narrative, within an institutional context (implementation) and for evaluating what knowledge and understanding pupils have gained against expectations (impact/achievement)'. (Ofsted, 2019, p.4–5)

Of course, this definition is now pretty well known across education in England, and has led to a lot of activity around the development of things like curriculum maps, knowledge organisers, etc. This emphasis on content may seem a little at odds with an emphasis on metacognition, which is about developing dispositions and skills in our pupils. However, this view is misguided. Of course we need pupils to learn subject content, but we also want them to develop transferable skills for lifelong learning. Both matter and strengthen each other.

So how do we build metacognition into the curriculum? There is no fixed way of doing that, but, using the principles mentioned above, we can look at building up metacognitive strategies within the curriculum. The key is to incorporate the sequence of planning, reflecting and evaluating into the sequence of lessons.

Here are some examples of how this can be done for both primary and secondary.

Example 1: Integrating Metacognition into a KS2 History Topic – Exploring Viking Invasions of England Through Metacognition and Learning-to-Learn Activities

Objective: Pupils will learn about the Viking invasions of England while developing metacognition and learning-to-learn skills.

Materials:

1   Visual aids (maps, images of Vikings, England, and Viking ships).
2   Age-appropriate books, articles, or online resources on the Viking invasions.
3   Writing materials (notebooks, pencils, coloured markers).
4   Metacognition tools (metacognitive prompts, self-assessment forms).
5   Art supplies for creative activities.
6   Optional: Historical fiction books or Viking-related stories.

Lesson 1: Introduction to Vikings and England

Opening Activity (15 minutes):

1   Start with a short video clip or a story about Vikings and their invasions to introduce the topic and get pupils' attention.

Main Lesson (25 minutes):

2   Use direct instruction and visual aids to show pupils where the Vikings came from and where they invaded in England. Discuss the reasons for the Viking invasions.
3   Read a simple text or story about a Viking invasion, emphasising key points.

Metacognition Activity (10 minutes):

4   Introduce the concept of metacognition. Ask pupils what they think they already know about the Vikings and what they want to learn. Write their thoughts on the board.
5   Provide metacognitive prompts like: 'What do you think you will find most interesting about the Vikings? What do you think will be challenging to understand?'

Day 2: Learning about Viking life and the invasions

Main Lesson (20 minutes):

6   Start with retrieval practice questions to retrieve knowledge from the previous lesson.
7   Explore Viking life, their ships, clothing, and daily activities through direct instruction, visuals and discussion.
8   Show a map with the Viking invasion routes in England, explaining their major attacks and settlements.

Metacognition Activity (20 minutes):

9   Divide pupils into small groups and provide each group with a different source of information about the Vikings (e.g., a book, an article, or an online resource).
10 Ask pupils to read the source, take notes, and give each pupil a role within the group, such as summariser. One pupil could be tasked with noting down what they found hard to understand, and what they have learnt from the activity. Encourage them to ask questions and express their thoughts.
11 Afterward, ask each group to share one interesting fact they've discovered.

Day 3: Creative expression and reflection

Creative Activity (20 minutes):

12 Engage pupils in a creative activity such as drawing, writing, or acting to help them express what they've learned about the Vikings.

Metacognition and Reflection (15 minutes):

13 Bring the class back together and have a discussion about what they've learned. Use metacognitive prompts like: 'What surprised you the most? What strategies did you use to learn about the Vikings?'

14 Have each pupil complete a self-assessment form where they reflect on what they've learned and what they want to know more about.

Homework (Optional):

15 Encourage pupils to read a historical fiction book or a story related to the Vikings for fun.

Assessment (Optional):

16 You can assess pupils based on their participation in group discussions, the creative activities, and their self-assessment forms.

Closure (5 minutes):

17 Summarise the key points about the Viking invasions, emphasising the importance of metacognition.

This lesson plan integrates the study of Viking invasions with metacognition, promoting critical thinking and self-awareness among primary school pupils. Of course, not all metacognitive development needs to happen across a sequence of lessons. In the following example we will look at developing metacognition in a KS2 maths lesson.

Example 2: Integrating Metacognitive Development into a KS2 Maths Lesson – Solving Multiplication Word Problems

1 Set a clear learning objective, for example, 'Today, we will learn how to solve multiplication word problems.'

2 Activate prior knowledge: Ask pupils to recall and share their prior knowledge related to the topic. This helps them to make connections and activate their existing understanding. For example, ask them to share any strategies they have previously used to solve word problems.

3 Model metacognitive thinking: Demonstrate metacognitive thinking by thinking aloud as you solve a word problem. Explain the strategies you are using, why you are using them, and how you are monitoring your progress. For example, say, 'I am going to read the problem carefully, underline the important information, and then decide which operation to use.'

4 Provide guided practice: Give pupils a series of multiplication word problems to solve in pairs or small groups. Encourage them to use the metacognitive strategies

you modelled and discuss their thinking with their peers. Circulate the room to provide support and ask probing questions to deepen their understanding.

5   Reflect on learning: After pupils have solved the word problems, bring the class back together for a reflection discussion. Ask pupils to share their strategies, challenges they faced, and what they learned about their thinking process. This encourages metacognitive reflection and helps pupils to become aware of their own learning process.

6   Provide feedback and next steps: Give specific feedback to pupils about their problem-solving strategies and metacognitive thinking. Highlight areas of strength and suggest areas for improvement. Encourage pupils to continue practising metacognitive thinking in future math lessons.

By integrating metacognitive development into the lesson, pupils will not only improve their problem-solving skills, but also develop a deeper understanding of their own thinking processes and become more independent learners.

Example 3: Integrating Metacognitive Development into a KS3 Geography Topic – Plate Tectonics

Lesson 1: Introduction to Plate Tectonics

Objective: Introduce the concept of plate tectonics and lay the foundation for further exploration.

Day 1: Introduction and metacognition activity

Engage (10 minutes):

Show images and videos of natural disasters like earthquakes and volcanic eruptions.

Ask pupils to share what they know and what questions they have about these events.

Instruction (20 minutes):

Present a brief overview of plate tectonics using visual aids.

Discuss Earth's structure and the role of the lithosphere.

Activity – Think–Pair–Share (15 minutes):

Ask pupils to reflect on what they've learned so far.

In pairs, have them share their thoughts and questions.

Then, as a class, discuss their findings and questions.

Homework (5 minutes):

Repeat the principle of plan – monitor – evaluate.

Get pupils to develop a plan for studying a text on plate tectonics assigned to them.

Lesson 2: Plate boundaries

Objective: Explore different types of plate boundaries.

Day 2: Plate boundaries and metacognition activity

Retrieval practice (10 minutes):

Check for understanding from previous lesson.

Discuss what pupils learned from the previous lesson.

Explore (20 minutes):

Introduce the different types of plate boundaries (divergent, convergent, and transform).

Explain the movements and geological features associated with each type.

Activity – Metacognition Journal (15 minutes):

Provide pupils with a metacognition journal.

In their journals, ask them to write down what they find most interesting or challenging about plate boundaries.

Encourage them to reflect on their learning process and what they can do to improve their understanding.

Group Activity – Plate Boundary Simulation (30 minutes):

Divide pupils into groups.

Provide materials to simulate plate boundary interactions (e.g., cardboard for plates, markers for boundaries).
Have each group create a model to demonstrate one type of plate boundary.

Lesson 3: Plate tectonics and earth's features

Objective: Explore the impact of plate tectonics on Earth's surface features.

Day 3: Features and metacognition activity

Recap (10 minutes):

Review the different types of plate boundaries using retrieval practice activities.

Explore (20 minutes):

Discuss how plate tectonics influence the formation of mountains, ocean basins, and volcanic islands.

Activity – Concept Map (15 minutes):

Ask pupils to create a concept map illustrating the relationship between plate tectonics and Earth's surface features.

Hands-On Activity – Modelling Mountain Formation (30 minutes):

Provide materials for a hands-on activity in which pupils model mountain formation due to convergent boundaries.

Get pupils to plan the activity, thinking about the materials needed, knowledge required, and where to search for additional knowledge.

Provide sheets for reflection on how the activity is going half-way through.
Provide an evaluation sheet with questions on what they would have done differently, what knowledge and skills were required to complete the activity, and what they have learnt from it.

Lesson 4: Historical perspectives and metacognition reflection

Objective: Explore the history of plate tectonics and encourage metacognition reflection.

Day 4: History and metacognition reflection

Recap (10 minutes):

Review the concepts covered in the previous lessons.

Explore (20 minutes):

Present the history of plate tectonics, including the contributions of scientists like Alfred Wegener and the evidence that supports the theory.

Activity – Socratic Seminar (30 minutes):

Conduct a Socratic seminar where pupils discuss the historical development of plate tectonics.

Encourage them to reflect on how scientific knowledge evolves over time and the role of critical thinking.

Metacognition Reflection (15 minutes):

Have pupils reflect on how their understanding of plate tectonics has evolved.

Ask them to identify areas of strength and areas they still find challenging.

Lesson 5: Assessment and application

Objective: Assess pupils' understanding and apply their knowledge.

Day 5: Assessment and application

Quiz (30 minutes):

Administer a quiz to assess pupils' knowledge of plate tectonics, plate boundaries, and Earth's surface features.

Application Project (60 minutes):

Assign a project where pupils can choose an aspect of plate tectonics and create a presentation, report, or model to demonstrate their understanding.

Metacognition Discussion (15 minutes):

Lead a class discussion where pupils share how they applied metacognitive strategies to improve their learning during the unit.

Conclusion and Reflection (10 minutes):

Conclude the unit by discussing the importance of plate tectonics in understanding the Earth's dynamic processes.

Throughout these lessons, encourage metacognitive strategies such as think–pair–share, journaling, concept mapping, and reflection. This will help pupils develop a deeper understanding of plate tectonics while also becoming more aware of their own learning processes.

Example 4: Integrating Metacognitive Development into a KS4 Computing Lesson – Online Safety

Lesson 1: Introduction to online safety and metacognition

Objective: Understand the importance of online safety and introduce metacognitive strategies for learning.

Day 1: Introduction and metacognition activity

Starter (15 minutes):

Start with a discussion about the positive aspects of technology, followed by potential risks and challenges.

Ask pupils to share their experiences and concerns regarding online safety.

Instruction (20 minutes):

Introduce the concept of online safety, including privacy and identity protection.

Explain the importance of being aware of one's digital footprint.

Activity – Online Safety Brainstorm (15 minutes):

In pairs or small groups, have pupils brainstorm potential online safety concerns and their consequences.

Discuss their findings as a class.

Metacognition Activity – Think-Aloud (10 minutes):

Introduce the 'think-aloud' strategy where pupils verbally express their thought processes while learning.

Apply this strategy to reflect on what they've learned about online safety.

Lesson 2: Online privacy and identity protection

Objective: Explore strategies for protecting online privacy and identity.

Day 2: Online privacy and identity protection

Recap (10 minutes):

Review the key concepts from the previous lesson.

Instruction (20 minutes):

Discuss strategies for protecting online privacy, such as strong passwords, two-factor authentication, and privacy settings.

Explain the importance of thinking before sharing personal information online.

Activity – Create a Strong Password (15 minutes):

Guide pupils in creating strong, unique passwords.

Discuss the importance of changing passwords regularly.

Metacognition Reflection (15 minutes):

Ask pupils to reflect on their online behaviours and discuss the changes they plan to make to enhance their online privacy and security.

Lesson 3: Recognising and reporting concerns

Objective: Learn how to identify and report various online concerns.

Day 3: Recognising and reporting concerns

Recap (10 minutes):

Use retrieval practice to review the importance of online safety and privacy.

Instruction (20 minutes):

Introduce common online concerns, such as cyberbullying, online harassment, scams, and inappropriate content.

Discuss the importance of identifying and reporting these concerns.

Activity – Scenarios (20 minutes):

Present real-life scenarios related to online concerns.

In small groups, have pupils discuss how they would respond and report the issues.

Metacognition Discussion (15 minutes):

Lead a class discussion about the challenges of recognising online concerns and the importance of seeking help when needed.

Lesson 4: Reporting mechanisms and digital citizenship

Objective: Understand the reporting mechanisms and practise responsible digital citizenship.

Day 4: Reporting mechanisms and digital citizenship

Recap (10 minutes):

Review the key online concerns and the importance of reporting them.

Instruction (20 minutes):

Discuss different reporting mechanisms, including how to report concerns to school authorities, social media platforms, and law enforcement.

Activity – Digital Citizenship Pledge (20 minutes):

Ask pupils to create a digital citizenship pledge outlining their commitment to responsible online behaviour.

Metacognition Reflection (15 minutes):

Have pupils reflect on how the development of the pledge has or has not improved their knowledge and understanding of online safety, and what activities they might do to enhance this further.

Lesson 5: Final assessment and application

Objective: Assess pupils' understanding and encourage responsible online behaviour.

Day 5: Final assessment and application

Quiz (30 minutes):

Administer a quiz to assess pupils' knowledge of online safety, privacy, and reporting concerns.

Digital Citizenship Project (60 minutes):

Assign a project where pupils can create an informative poster, presentation, or video on online safety and responsible digital citizenship.

Get pupils to plan an activity, thinking about the materials needed, knowledge required, and where to search for additional knowledge.

Provide sheets for reflection on how the activity is going half-way through.

Provide an evaluation sheet with questions on what they would have done differently, what knowledge and skills were required to complete the activity, and what they have learnt from it.

Metacognition Discussion (15 minutes):

Lead a class discussion where pupils share how they applied metacognitive strategies to improve their understanding of online safety and digital citizenship.

Conclusion and Future Planning (10 minutes):

Discuss the importance of continued vigilance and responsible online behaviour.

You will see that each of these examples has a somewhat different structure. This is to illustrate that there is no one way to do this, but that metacognition can be incorporated into the form of curriculum planning you and your school use.

Classroom Talk

A key aspect of developing metacognition is classroom talk. An approach that has been found to be effective at increasing metacognitive skills in pupils is dialogic teaching (Alexander, 2018). Dialogic teaching is a teaching approach that emphasises the importance of dialogue and discussion in the learning process. It involves encouraging pupils to engage in meaningful conversations, ask questions, and reflect on their own thinking. Key elements of dialogic teaching are discussion and interaction, Socratic questioning, collaborative learning, reflection and feedback, and active listening.

Dialogic teaching can help develop metacognition in several ways:

1 **Reflection**: Through dialogue and discussion, pupils have the opportunity to reflect on their own thinking processes. They can examine their own thoughts, ideas, and reasoning, and evaluate the effectiveness of their approaches. This reflection promotes metacognitive awareness and helps pupils to become more conscious of their own thinking.

2 **Questioning**: Dialogic teaching encourages pupils to ask questions and engage in critical thinking. By asking and answering open-ended questions, pupils are prompted to think deeply about a topic, consider different perspectives, and evaluate their own understanding. This process of questioning and self-assessment fosters metacognitive skills.

3 **Self-regulation**: Dialogic teaching helps pupils to develop self-regulation skills, which are essential for metacognition. Through dialogue and discussion, pupils learn to monitor and control their own learning processes. They become more aware of their strengths and weaknesses, set goals, and make adjustments to improve their learning outcomes.

4 **Collaboration**: Dialogic teaching often involves collaborative learning, where pupils work together in groups or pairs. Through this collaboration, pupils have the opportunity to share their thoughts, listen to others' ideas, and engage in constructive discussions. This collaborative learning environment enhances metacognition by allowing pupils to compare and contrast different viewpoints, reflect on their own understanding, and adapt their thinking based on peer feedback.

Overall, dialogic teaching provides a supportive and interactive learning environment that promotes metacognitive development. It encourages pupils to think about their own thinking, engage in reflective practices, and take ownership of their learning processes.

Conclusion

If we want to develop metacognitive skills in our pupils, we need to incorporate them into our subject teaching. Separate 'learn-to-learn' lessons don't work, as pupils don't transfer the knowledge into their subjects. With an often overly full curriculum, this may sound a bit daunting. But as the examples above hopefully show, incorporating metacognition does not involve major changes to what teachers already do, and activities and techniques can be incorporated into a sequence of lessons relatively straightforwardly.

Of course, such activities do take up some lesson time, but in light of the demonstrated advantages of metacognitive development for pupils, I would say that effort is worth it.

References

Alexander, R. (2018). Developing dialogic teaching: Genesis, process, trial. *Research Papers in Education, 33*(5), 561–598.

Breitwieser, J. (2023). *Promoting self-regulated learning in children's daily lives: The effects of a mobile intervention.* Paper presented at the Bi-annual Conference of the European Association for Research in Learning and Instruction, Thessaloniki, Greece, 23 August 2023.

Education Endowment Foundation (2021). *Metacognition and self-regulated learning. Guidance report.* https://d2tic4wvo1iusb.cloudfront.net/production/eef-guidance-reports/metacognition/EEF_Metacognition_and_self-regulated_learning.pdf?v=1704684474

Hacker, D. J., Dunlosky, J., & Graesser, A. C. (2009). *Handbook of metacognition in education.* New York/London: Routledge.

Muijs, D., & Bokhove, C. (2020). *Metacognition and self-regulation: Evidence review.* London: Education Endowment Foundation (EEF). Available at: https://d2tic4wvo1iusb.cloudfront.net/production/documents/guidance/Metacognition_and_self-regulation_review.pdf?v=1697174914

Ofsted (2019). *Education Inspection Framework, Overview of Research.* https://assets.publishing.service.gov.uk/media/6034be17d3bf7f265dbbe2ef/Research_for_EIF_framework_updated_references_22_Feb_2021.pdf

Pressley, M., & Harris, K. R. (2006). Cognitive strategy instruction: From basic research to classroom instruction. In P. A. Alexander & P. Winne (Eds.), *Handbook of educational psychology* (2nd ed., pp. 265–286). Mahwah, NJ: Erlbaum.

Index

Printed in the USA
CPSIA information can be obtained
at www.ICGtesting.com
JSHW062123250924
70274JS00007B/219

9 781529 627916